Windows Azure Programming Patterns for Start-ups

A step-by-step guide to create easy solutions to build your business using Windows Azure services

Riccardo Becker

PACKT PUBLISHING enterprise
professional expertise distilled

BIRMINGHAM - MUMBAI

Windows Azure Programming Patterns for Start-ups

First published: October 2012

Production Reference: 1161012

Published by Packt Publishing Ltd.
Livery Place
35 Livery Street
Birmingham B3 2PB, UK.

ISBN 978-1-84968-560-3

www.packtpub.com

Cover Image by Sandeep Babu (sandyjb@gmail.com)

Credits

Author
Riccardo Becker

Reviewers
Michael Collier
Neil Mackenzie

Acquisition Editor
Dilip Venkatesh

Lead Technical Editor
Unnati Shah

Technical Editors
Devdutt Kulkarni
Arun Nadar
Rohit Rajgor
Azharuddin Sheikh

Copy Editor
Brandt D'Mello

Project Coordinator
Sai Gamare
Anugya Khurana

Proofreader
Maria Gould

Indexer
Rekha Nair

Graphics
Valentina D'Silva

Production Coordinator
Nitesh Thakur

Cover Work
Nitesh Thakur

About the Author

Riccardo Becker works full-time as a Principal IT Architect for Logica, in the Netherlands. He holds several certifications, and his background in computing goes way back to 1998, when he started working with good old' Visual Basic 5.0 (or was it 6.0?). Ever since, he fulfilled several roles, such as Developer, Lead Developer, Architect, Project Leader, Practice Manager, and recently, he decided to accept the role of Principal IT Architect, in which he focuses on innovation, cutting-edge technology, and specifically on Windows Azure and cloud computing in general.

In 2007, he joined the Microsoft LEAP program, where he got a peek at the move Microsoft was about to make on their road to the cloud. Pat Helland gave him that insight, and since the first release of Windows Azure on PDC 2008, he started to focus on it, keeping track of the progress and the maturity of the platform. In the past few years, he has also done a lot of work on incubation with his employer, raising awareness on cloud computing in general and Windows Azure.

I would like to thank all my colleagues who were counterparts with me on various subjects in the world of Azure. Special thanks to my dear colleague and friend, Raymond Binnendijk en Rémon ter Haar, who helped me out throughout the whole project.

I also would like to thank the folks from Packt Publishing, especially Sai Gamare, who helped me keep on track and on schedule, despite some obstacles and some changes that I made to the original outline.

Special thanks to my employer Logica for all the opportunities that have helped me in realizing this book. It is thanks to the daily job and to getting the opportunity to focus on these subjects that I have come to this point of having enough substance to write this book.

About the Reviewers

Michael Collier is a Windows Azure MVP and serves as a National Architect for a Microsoft SI partner that specializes in Windows Azure. He has nearly 11 years of experience building Microsoft-based applications for a wide range of clients. Michael spends his days serving as a developer or architect, helping clients succeed with the Microsoft development platform. He also enjoys speaking about Windows Azure at local user groups as well as at regional and national conferences. Michael is also the founder of CloudDevelop as well as of the Central Ohio Cloud Computing User Group in Columbus, OH. You can follow Michael on Twitter at www.twitter.com/MichaelCollier and on his blog at www.MichaelSCollier.com.

Neil Mackenzie has been kicking the tires of Windows Azure since PDC 2008. He works for Satory Global, helping companies use the Windows Azure platform. Neil wrote the *Microsoft Windows Azure Development Cookbook* for Packt Publishing. He is a Microsoft MVP for Windows Azure. Neil tweets occasionally on @mknz.

www.PacktPub.com

Support files, eBooks, discount offers and more

You might want to visit www.PacktPub.com for support files and downloads related to your book.

Did you know that Packt offers eBook versions of every book published, with PDF and ePub files available? You can upgrade to the eBook version at www.PacktPub.com and as a print book customer, you are entitled to a discount on the eBook copy. Get in touch with us at service@packtpub.com for more details.

At www.PacktPub.com, you can also read a collection of free technical articles, sign up for a range of free newsletters and receive exclusive discounts and offers on Packt books and eBooks.

http://PacktLib.PacktPub.com

Do you need instant solutions to your IT questions? PacktLib is Packt's online digital book library. Here, you can access, read and search across Packt's entire library of books.

Why Subscribe?
- Fully searchable across every book published by Packt
- Copy and paste, print and bookmark content
- On demand and accessible via web browser

Free Access for Packt account holders

If you have an account with Packt at www.PacktPub.com, you can use this to access PacktLib today and view nine entirely free books. Simply use your login credentials for immediate access.

Instant Updates on New Packt Books

Get notified! Find out when new books are published by following @PacktEnterprise on Twitter, or the *Packt Enterprise* Facebook page.

Table of Contents

Preface

Windows Azure was officially announced at PDC 2008, but looking back, I had a quick look in the kitchen of Windows Azure in 2007 while I was visiting Redmond during the Lead Enterprise Architect Program (LEAP) sessions. Pat Helland, a senior architect at Microsoft, gave a talk on *The irresistible forces meet the movable objects*.

Pat described the nature of the forces where he pitted big servers and fast CPUs against commodity hardware (ordinary machines you can buy everywhere). *Moore's Law*, (The number of transistors on circuits doubles every year) is applicable to many hardware components. Though still accurate, it is getting more and more expensive to double CPU speed. Increasing CPU speed is still possible, but at a price. The costs for scaling out a single server are generally higher than scaling up to multiple processors or servers. If we look solely at the speed of the CPU, we can conclude that the growth is flattening. Parallel computing is cheaper than scaling out single servers.

Looking back at the history of Windows Azure, Pat Helland actually stated that there should be something like low-cost, highly-available, high-bandwidth, high-storage, and high computing power-based datacenters, all around the world, that can run both existing and new applications.

Guess what? The concept envisioned was officially announced at PDC 2008! Windows Azure was born, and this very first release of the platform actually contained everything that was envisioned during this talk on LEAP 2007. Lots of cheap hardware runs in datacenters all around the globe that offer massive computing power, storage, and bandwidth. All these components are available like electricity; you start paying from the moment you start using it. Operational expenses (OpEx) instead of capital expenses (CapEx) enable you to experiment more easily, since you do not need to buy hardware but just take it from Windows Azure. When your experiment is successful and you need more computing power or storage to serve all your customers, you can easily scale up.

This book elaborates on different features from the Windows Azure platform. The central theme of the book is a fictitious company, Geotopia. This company decided to build its own social network by leveraging the abilities of the Windows Azure platform.

What this book covers

Chapter 1, The Concepts of Windows Azure, introduces Windows Azure, the cloud offering from Microsoft. It describes the author's first contact with the "cloud" in general and how Microsoft decided to put a great amount of effort into realizing Windows Azure.

Chapter 2, A Startup Scenario, shows how a brand new, ambitious company just opened its doors. Geotopia consists of enthusiastic developers and architects who jointly created a new view on social networking. It is not a basic user interface where plain text dominates but a compelling map interface, offering users the ability to treat it as their social canvas and drop video and images, and create messages based on their location or on the location of their interest. Users can recommend locations, shops, or other points of interest by adding comments or multimedia and tell their friends about it. This chapter describes the requirements for Geotopia.

Chapter 3, Create Your Solution, teaches us how to create an organized Windows Azure solution with Visual Studio 2010. Both a web and a worker role are created together, with a Silverlight client acting as the Geotopia canvas, based on Bing Maps technology. We will also learn to run cloud projects locally on our own machine and debug them. As the last step, the initial solution is actually deployed to Windows Azure.

Chapter 4, Storing Your Data, is a deep dive into the storage fundamentals of Windows Azure. It outlines the architecture of Windows Azure Storage and its underlying architecture. You will also learn how to operate the different Storage offerings, such as blobs, queues, and tables.

Chapter 5, SQL Database, digs deeper into the scalable cloud database service that Microsoft offers and is a part of the Windows Azure platform. The chapter shows how to set up a SQL database and outlines best practices and guidelines. You will also learn how to fully leverage the power of Data Sync.

Chapter 6, Key Features Explained, outlines different features from the platform (previously known as AppFabric). You will learn how to make use of Service Bus and how to enable messaging between your applications. Also, key features such as Caching, Windows Azure Connect, Access Control Service, and Windows Azure Traffic Manager are explained in detail, as is how you can benefit from them.

Chapter 7, The Billing Aspects of Windows Azure, describes in great detail all the different billing aspects of Windows Azure. You will learn how the different components of the platform are charged and how you can get a good grip on the Windows Azure costs.

Chapter 8, Windows Azure Patterns, provides a step-by-step walkthrough on how to make use of the Enterprise Library Integration Pack in your cloud services. It not only provides great detail on autoscaling and how to achieve this, but also drills down on transient fault handling and how to implement a gatekeeper pattern to enhance security in your cloud service.

Chapter 9, Application Lifecycle Management, briefly explains Application Lifecycle Management in general and some specifics with respect to ALM on the Windows Azure Platform.

Chapter 10, Windows Azure Security, explains how the Security Development Lifecycle (SDL) is applicable for Windows Azure projects. The chapter also depicts some typical security features on the platform.

Chapter 11, What's New in Windows Azure, contains a brief overview of new features of Windows Azure, released in June 2012.

What you need for this book

In order to run the code snippets given in the book, you will need:

- Visual Studio 2010.
- Windows Azure SDK, the latest version.
- Access to Bing Maps and a valid account key. This can be retrieved from http://www.bingmapsportal.com.

Who this book is for

This book is for developers and architects who are experienced with Microsoft .NET technology and web technology in general, but may or may not be experienced with the latest version(s) of the .NET framework. Some general knowledge on cloud computing is preferred, but not mandatory.

Conventions

In this book, you will find a number of styles of text that distinguish between different kinds of information. Here are some examples of these styles, and an explanation of their meaning.

Code words in text are shown as follows: "you need to run the following command: `set-executionpolicy remotesigned`"

A block of code is set as follows:

```
While(true)
    {
        CloudQueueMessage message = queue.GetMessage();
        if(message != null)
        {
            //process it
            Process(message);
            Queue.DeleteMessage(message);
        }
    }
```

New terms and **important words** are shown in bold. Words that you see on the screen, in menus or dialog boxes for example, appear in the text like this: "By selecting a geotopic and clicking on **Play this story**, consecutive topics that are related to the selected ones will also be played chronologically."

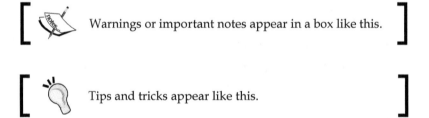

> Warnings or important notes appear in a box like this.

> Tips and tricks appear like this.

Reader feedback

Feedback from our readers is always welcome. Let us know what you think about this book—what you liked or may have disliked. Reader feedback is important for us to develop titles that you really get the most out of.

To send us general feedback, simply send an e-mail to `feedback@packtpub.com`, and mention the book title through the subject of your message.

If there is a topic that you have expertise in and you are interested in either writing or contributing to a book, see our author guide on www.packtpub.com/authors.

Customer support

Now that you are the proud owner of a Packt book, we have a number of things to help you to get the most from your purchase.

Errata

Although we have taken every care to ensure the accuracy of our content, mistakes do happen. If you find a mistake in one of our books—maybe a mistake in the text or the code—we would be grateful if you would report this to us. By doing so, you can save other readers from frustration and help us improve subsequent versions of this book. If you find any errata, please report them by visiting http://www.packtpub. com/support, selecting your book, clicking on the **errata submission form** link, and entering the details of your errata. Once your errata are verified, your submission will be accepted and the errata will be uploaded to our website, or added to any list of existing errata, under the Errata section of that title.

Piracy

Piracy of copyright material on the Internet is an ongoing problem across all media. At Packt, we take the protection of our copyright and licenses very seriously. If you come across any illegal copies of our works, in any form, on the Internet, please provide us with the location address or website name immediately so that we can pursue a remedy.

Please contact us at copyright@packtpub.com with a link to the suspected pirated material.

We appreciate your help in protecting our authors, and our ability to bring you valuable content.

Questions

You can contact us at questions@packtpub.com if you are having a problem with any aspect of the book, and we will do our best to address it.

1
The Concepts of Windows Azure

"The irresistible forces meet the movable objects."

– Pat Helland

In this chapter, we will provide an overview of Windows Azure and also briefly explain the history of the platform, why it was created, and why it is interesting and applicable for startup companies. We will also explore the evolution of Windows Azure from its early days back in 2008 right to where it is today. The internals of Windows Azure and the way Microsoft **datacenters** work will also be explained from a user experience perspective. It describes exactly what happens under the hood of Windows Azure after a developer deploys an application to the platform. The last sections of the chapter contain brief overviews of key features of the platform.

Red Dog

Ray Ozzie arrived at Microsoft in 2005 and stated that survival of the company hinged on a shift to cloud computing. He wrote a manifesto called *The Internet Services Disruption* in which he stated that there are three tenets that dramatically shift the whole landscape around computing. From his point of view, it was essential to embrace those tenets in Microsoft's products and services. These tenets are as follows:

- Advertisement-supported economic models
- New delivery and adoption model
- Demand for user experience that "just works"

The essence of this manifesto is that he emphasized that the world was changing, the demands of customers were changing, and technology was changing. It was the beginning of a process that finally resulted in the Windows Azure platform.

 Cloud computing enabled a move from packaged solutions with fixed license-based models to resilient services with flexible payment options.

After the release of Vista and the new Office suite, a project group was formed with top engineers, and Ray Ozzie asked Amitabh Srivastava to lead the project. Also, David Cutler (writer of VMS and leader of the Windows NT team) was involved with this revolutionary initiative. The codename of Windows Azure used to be Red Dog. Virtual machines on Windows Azure are still named with the prefix **Red Dog (RD)**.

Windows Azure announcement

On October 27, 2008, at the Professional Developers Conference, Ray Ozzie announced Windows Azure and highlighted its capability in delivering services. The first commercially available release in 2010 of the platform contained:

- The Cloud OS (confusingly also called Windows Azure) that offers service management and provisioning, storage, computing power, and networking capabilities
- SQL Azure, offering a Database-as-a-Service (currently known as SQL Database)
- Microsoft .NET Services, containing features such as workflow and access control (currently known as Windows Azure Service Bus, formerly known as AppFabric)

It was the start of a new era that brought us all into the world of services, agility, faster time to market, new ways of monetizing IT assets, operational expenses versus capital expenses and more. Ever since, Windows Azure has evolved into the mature, enterprise-ready platform it is right now, offering more services, with time.

A quick start on Windows Azure

Windows Azure is about **cloud computing**. Cloud computing, though, is a vague description of different aspects. Windows Azure is actually a platform that is offered to you as a service (**PaaS**, meaning Platform as a Service). PaaS enables us to fully concentrate on the application itself and leave all the plumbing to the cloud provider, in this case Microsoft. PaaS offers the management of networking, storage, servers, virtualization, OS, databases, and runtimes. The only thing that's left is the actual application, and that is most important for us since the application is our added value.

How it works internally

Windows Azure runs in large datacenters all around the world. A datacenter is filled with containers, and containers have a lot of servers inside (around 2,000).

Windows Azure offers abstraction to the developer by offering computing power (CPU and memory), storage (disk), and bandwidth (networking hardware). This enables us to treat Windows Azure as a black box without bothering about the internals, although we are curious about the way it works! Well, at least I was.

The best way to describe how a cloud application is created and finally deployed onto a machine in the datacenter is to use an example. Back in the early days, when you wanted to deploy an application, you needed to order hardware, be patient, and install operating systems, database servers, runtimes, and other bits. In the new world of cloud computing, you only need a credit card and a Live ID.

First steps

From a developer's perspective, the main entrance to Windows Azure is through the Windows Azure portal (or through the Service Management API, but I'll cover that later in this book). Operators can look at Windows Azure from the Microsoft System Center.

When you go to http://windowsazure.com, you are able to sign up to the Windows Azure Platform. After creating a billing relationship with Microsoft by using your credit card or the invoicing option, you are able to access Windows Azure. The Windows Azure platform portal is your main entrance to massive-scale computing and storage. The following screenshot shows what the portal looks like and how you can access the different features of Windows Azure.

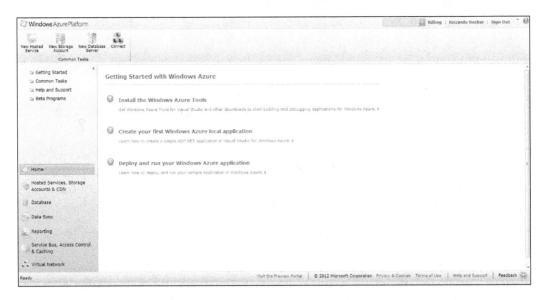

From this portal, you can create applications (hosted services, as per June 2012, called cloud services), enable storage, create databases, and access other offerings from the Windows Azure platform. Let's have a close look at the **New Hosted Service** option and actually create your first Windows Azure application. Let's prepare the next step by creating a logical area on Windows Azure for your first application.

Click on **New Hosted Service**, and fill out the **Create a New Hosted Service** screen, as shown in the following screenshot:

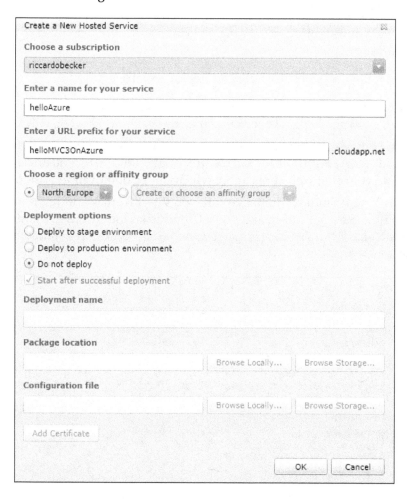

You need to pick another name, since the URL prefix needs to be globally unique, and of course, your subscription will be a different one. After clicking on **OK**, the environment is created for you, and the DNS name entered in the URL textbox is reserved. If you choose the **Do not deploy** option, only the DNS name will be reserved and you will not get a bill yet, but you can also decide to create the hosted service together with deployment, if you have your binaries and configuration files ready. Hosted services that you create can easily be deleted, and the DNS name will be available again for others.

Creating and deploying a website on Windows Azure

In order to get your application running on Windows Azure, you need to follow a few initial steps.

Perform the following steps to create and deploy a website:

1. Install the prerequisites on your machine (you can find them at `http://www.microsoft.com/download/en/details.aspx?id=15658`).

2. After downloading and installing both the Windows Azure SDK and Windows Azure Tools for Microsoft Visual Studio 2010, you are able to create your first web application, which can be deployed to Windows Azure.

3. Start Visual Studio 2010 (make sure you select **Run as administrator**), go to **File | New | Project**, and select **Cloud** from the **Installed Templates** tab. Name it `MyFirstAzureProject` and click on **OK**. The following screen appears:

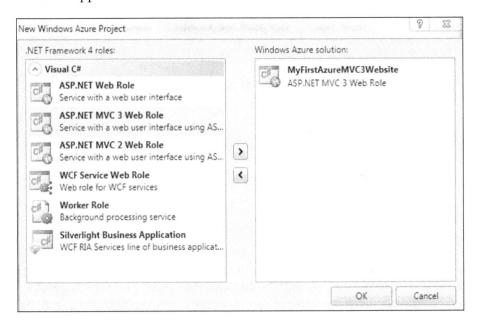

As you can see, creating a Windows Azure service does not mean that you need to learn new skills or new tools; you can leverage your existing .NET skills.

4. Select **ASP.NET MVC3 Web Role** and name it **MyFirstAzureMVC3Website**. A **Web Role** is in fact a Windows 2008 virtual machine with Internet Information Services enabled. This enables the Web Role to be accessible through the Internet. By picking the MVC3 Web Role, we can again benefit from the already available knowledge on MVC3.

5. After clicking on **OK**, you need to pick what project template is used to create the MVC3 Website. For now, it's ok to select the **Internet Application** and leave the rest of the options at their default values.

6. Now click on **OK**, and the solution is created for you:

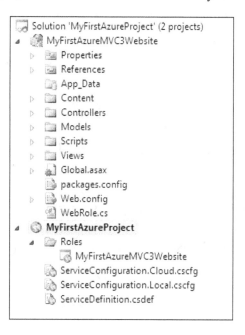

Your solution looks like an ordinary Visual Studio 2010 solution, but with a few additions to it. As it is a cloud project, not only is the MVC3 project created, but also a cloud project. In the MVC3 project, you will see a class file named **WebRole.cs**. This standard MVC3 website is ready to be deployed to Windows Azure. The website will run, but some default settings point to local development storage; these will cause the application to crash if somebody tries to reach the deployed website. We will get back to that later on.

7. To demonstrate upgrade and fault domains, change the **ServiceConfiguration.Cloud.cscfg** file, and change the **Instances** count to 2:

```
<Instances count="2" />
```

8. This causes two instances of your web role to be deployed on Windows Azure. They are identical, with the same binaries, but having two instances of the same web role running increases availability and enables the website to handle more traffic.

This configuration spins up two servers, has your application deployed onto them, and also creates a load balancer on top of them. Try to imagine how much work this is in a traditional datacenter.

First deployment

This section will guide you through the deployment of your Windows Azure project.

1. Right-click on the MyFirstAzureProject node in your solution and select **Package**.

2. A new popup window appears, but for now it is sufficient to click on the **Package** button.

3. Windows Azure Tools will now build your project, zip the binaries, and create the service configuration file.

4. A Windows Explorer window is opened, and you will see the result of the "packaging" action—a large binary package (.cspkg) and the configuration file. Copy the location of this folder.

5. Go back to the Windows Azure portal and select the recently created hosted service.

6. Right-click on the **Hosted Service** entry and select **New Production Deployment**.

7. Name your deployment, select the recently created files in the **Package location** and **Configuration file** textboxes, and click on **OK**.

 A warning appears, telling you that you need to create at least two instances to guarantee the 99.95 percent uptime the Windows Azure Compute service-level agreement (**SLA**) offers.

An SLA is a service contract in which the level of service is formally defined. Please go to http://www.windowsazure.com/en-us/support/legal/sla/ to get details about the SLA.

When two or more instances of a role are running in different fault and upgrade domains, Microsoft can offer at least a 99.95 percent (of the time) Internet connectivity of the designated roles. An availability of 99.95 percent means that your service is guaranteed less than 5 minutes down per week, inside the Fabric.

In the previous section, we deployed our Windows Azure project by using the Windows Azure portal and the **Package** option in Visual Studio. But what actually happened after uploading the package?

Upgrade domains

Upgrade domains are groups of nodes that are updated consecutively when there is a new Windows Azure OS version available or when you update your role. As stated before, the Windows Azure SLA is based on having two instances of each distinctive role run in at least two upgrade domains. You can choose to have only one instance of your role running, but this means that on every upgrade (OS, patch, security fix, or role upgrade) that causes a reboot your service will be unreachable.

Organizing your roles in more than one upgrade domain prevents your service from being offline because when one instance is down because of the update, the other one is still running, since it's in a different upgrade domain. The number of upgrade domains your role instances are put in is configurable in the service definition file (**ServiceDefinition.csdef**) in your solution. By default, the number is **five**, but you can change this at any time. After redeploying your service, your roles will be distributed among the number of upgrade domains you defined using the Fabric Controller. The capacity of your service during an OS upgrade is one, divided by the number of update domains. So, when you have five role instances running in five upgrade domains, your service capacity will be reduced by 20 percent during the whole upgrade process.

 Upgrade domains enable availability of your services during a Windows Azure OS update.

Fault domains

A fault domain is a physical unit of failure and can be mapped to physical infrastructure. A fault domain can be a complete rack or a single computer depending on the organization of the datacenter. Fault domains are meant to enhance fault tolerance of services. Keep your service running at all times, even during a hardware failure in the datacenter. Deploying your services into more than one fault domain will keep your service running, even when, for example, a top rack switch breaks down. Fault domains are physically grouped hardware areas inside the datacenter.

> The purpose of fault domains is to avoid single point of failure for your services and to maintain availability.

Fabric Controller

The **Fabric Controller (FC)** acts like the "kernel" for the datacenters. It has two major tasks:

- Resource allocation and provisioning of described hardware and network resources (datacenter hardware)
- Service lifecycle and health management based on applied service model and binaries (Windows Azure services)

The FC itself is an application running across different fault domains (just like your services) to ensure its availability. The FC runs on several nodes, and only one instance is the primary FC. All other instances are running in sync with the primary one.

Internals of a node

The FC is in charge of all the hardware inside the datacenter.

> Servers are placed in racks, racks are organized in clusters, and all the clusters together form the datacenter. A cluster contains approximately 1,000 servers.

Before being able to deploy your service on a single (or several) node(s), the FC actually turns on a node. After that the following process takes place:

1. The node boots from the network using Preboot Execution Environment (PEX). A maintenance OS image is downloaded to the node and boots into it. The maintenance OS contains a fabric agent, and the FC communicates directly with this host agent.

2. The maintenance OS downloads a VHD with the operating system for the host partition. This OS contains an FC host agent. The maintenance OS then restarts the node and boots onto the operating system for the host partition.

3. The FC tells the FC host agent how many partitions need to be set up, depending on the "deployment" request. If a user wants to deploy a multicore VM size, this automatically means that the node can contain fewer instances, since fewer CPUs are available. On the partition, there is a base VHD and a differencing disk. This works in a similar way with Hyper-V technology, since the OS is a version of Hyper-V, written for Windows Azure. The guest VHD contains a modified Windows 2008 Server version, so that it can integrate with the Windows Azure hypervisor.

The following figure presents what a node looks like after the partitioning and provisioning of the guest OSs, including the agents that are needed to enable communication between the FC and the guest OSs.

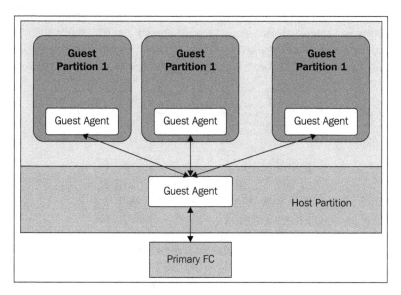

After these steps, the FC can deploy the MVC3 website we created in previous sections.

Deployment steps

The FC processes the service model you provided during the deployment step. In this case, we told the FC to deploy two instances of our **MyFirstAzureMVC3Website** node. The VM size is **Small**, by default. This means 1 CPU core, 1.75 GB of memory, about 230 GB of local storage, and reserved bandwidth of 100 Mbps.

 For more information on the characteristics of VM sizes, please visit http://msdn.microsoft.com/en-us/ library/windowsazure/ee814754.aspx.

The FCs create two guest partitions, as described in the previous sections, located in two different upgrade and fault domains. The FC then pushes the package (containing the binaries and the configuration file) to the target host agents. The host agents both create a guest partition that fulfills the service model we provided and starts the guest partitions. The guest agents both start the web role we created and call the role entry point, which is located in WebRole.cs. From this point, the role reports the heartbeats back to the host agent, so that the FC can monitor and maintain the health of roles. A role without a heartbeat for a period of time is considered unhealthy and is restarted.

The final step is that the FC programs a **load balancer (LB)** that routes the traffic to our website and divides it to the two role instances. Windows Azure equally spreads traffic across web role instances that are part of the same deployment. Having multiple instances of the same web role enables your website to handle more user traffic. The following figure shows where the instances are copied and run inside the datacenter, bearing in mind the upgrade and fault domains.

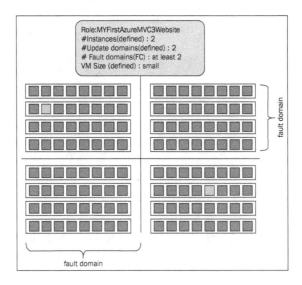

Our website is running now, has an uptime of 99.95 percent, and remains available, even in case of hardware failure or OS updates initiated by Windows Azure.

Core components of Windows Azure

Windows Azure is often referred to as a platform, but what is actually inside that platform? As you have seen in the previous sections, Windows Azure offers a place where you can run your website, but during the evolution of the platform, more and more features were added. Beside running a client-facing Internet application, it also offers a place where you can run your application code that has no user interface at all (long-running computations or asynchronous tasks), It even offers the possibility of deploying a Windows Server 2008 R2 image to migrate your legacy applications to the cloud and offer the same level of scalability and availability. The underlying infrastructure of every type of role (web, worker, or VM) is a virtual machine that is handled by Windows Azure and that takes care of load balancing and failover. The pricing for every role type is similar and is based on the size of the underlying virtual machine. The details of the pricing models are described in *Chapter 7, The Billing Aspect of Windows Azure*.

Compute

The Windows Azure platform offers three different types of roles:

- Web roles
- Worker roles
- VM roles

This section explains the differences between these different role types.

Web roles

Web roles run an Internet Information Services web server that can be used to host your frontend web application. It is easy to deploy a web role, and load balancing is included in the offering. You can use both the HTTP and HTTPS protocols.

Worker roles

A worker role is typically used for long-running or asynchronous tasks that require no user input. A common application scenario is a configuration that consists of both web and worker roles, where the web roles are as thin as possible, only handling traffic and being highly responsive to the user. The worker roles take care of the actual work (placing an order, performing a workflow). Queuing mechanisms enable loose coupling and offer you the ability to achieve fine-grained scaling (for example, only scale up your web roles to enhance).

Virtual machine roles

Virtual Machine (VM) roles allow you to deploy your own Windows Server 2008 R2 image to Windows Azure and host it in a hosted service, just like you do with a web or worker role. Applicable scenarios are applications that require OS customizations or native applications running in a standalone fashion. The VM role allows full control of the application environment (for example, registry settings or the old-fashioned .ini files) and enables you to migrate existing applications quickly to Windows Azure and benefit from the PaaS abilities the platform offers. Applications that take a long time to install or that require user input, or applications that are stateless, are suitable candidates to deploy as a VM role. A VM role gives you control over the virtual machine and allows you to build a suitable image from scratch, upload it to Windows Azure, and get it running. You can install software on the VM image and then upload it.

Just like web and worker roles, VM roles benefit from the automation Windows Azure offers, such as load balancing and failover. Full administrator privileges allow you to connect to the VM role and perform OS tweaking and troubleshooting. The cost structure for a VM role is the same as that of web and worker roles, in that you pay by the hour and based on the actual instance size.

 Keep in mind that Windows Server licensing costs are included in the charges, but any additional license costs of third-party components remain the same. Putting things on the cloud doesn't automatically transform license-based fees to pay-as-you-go fees.

Database

Windows Azure offers both a relational Database-as-a-Service feature and a way to synchronize traditional SQL Server databases with SQL Azure databases and vice versa.

 The Database-as-a-Service offering used to be called SQL Azure, but in the June 2012 release of Windows Azure, Microsoft decided to rename it to SQL Database.

SQL Database

Windows Azure offers a relational Database-as-a-Service. Windows SQL Database (formerly known as SQL Azure) is a scalable and highly available database service and can be available in just seconds. It is built on top of SQL Server technology and offers (mostly) comparable functionality. The main difference from a developer perspective is that you do not connect to a SQL Server but directly to a database (it is Database-as-a-Service after all). Using SQL Database keeps you from installing, configuring and managing any servers or databases, including mirroring and implementing failover procedures.

SQL Database is still what you expect it to be—a fully relational database system that can be queried by SQL statements (or Linq, of course). After creating a SQL Database, you are able to reach it not only from your cloud application, but also from your on-premises environment. It fits perfectly into a hybrid or distributed scenario where tiers are spread all over on-premises and cloud systems.

Using SQL Database offers the following:

- **Use the same tools and knowledge you already have, such as the Management Studio and T-SQL**: There is no need to learn new technologies or API to use the full power of SQL Database
- **The ability to grow in size up to 150 GB**: SQL Database is getting more and more enterprise-ready both in size of the offered SLAs and high availability
- **Scale out easily**: Using SQL Database Federations drastically simplifies the scaling out to multiple databases to grow beyond the 150 GB limit and to support multi-tenant solutions
- **Fast creation of databases**: Getting a database online is just a click and a few seconds away

Data Sync

Data Sync is a mechanism that provides easy synchronization between SQL Database and SQL Server database premises. Setting up Data Sync is just a matter of configuration and releases you from writing complex database scripts to synchronize and export/import data. Data Sync offers a fine-grained control on what tables or columns to synchronize, or even a subset of rows and columns. Combining Data Sync together with, for example, Traffic Manager, enables you to create geographically wide applications where both application and data are as close as possible to your customers.

Storage

Besides SQL Database, Windows Azure also offers other storage capabilities that are secure, highly scalable, and available.

All data in the Windows Azure storage is replicated at least three times in the same datacenter to offer high availability and prevent the loss of data. Window Azure storage offers:

- **Blobs**: A storage service that enables storing any arbitrary data, such as video or other binaries
- **Tables**: A storage service that enables storing information in a tabular fashion with rows and columns
- **Queue**: A storage service that enables messaging between applications or parts of your application
- **Windows Azure Drive**: A storage service that enables users to mount a Blob as a drive

Binary Large Object

Binary Large Object (blob) storage is a storage service that allows you to store massive data such as video and audio into the cloud in a logical structure and offers you the same advantages as Windows Azure does with its other services, such as availability, scalability, and redundancy.

Table Storage

Table Storage has the ability to store data in a tabular way, with rows and columns. It is possible to store different entities in the same table. It is not possible to create foreign keys between Table Storage tables (a NoSQL database).

Queue

Queues provide a way to enable messaging between your services in a reliable way. It can help you build scalable, loosely-coupled applications by implementing message-based communication between parts of your application.

Windows Azure drive

Windows Azure drive allows you to mount a blob as an NTFS VHD, and a drive letter is assigned to it. You can use traditional IO API (`System.IO` namespace) to manipulate Windows Azure drive.

We will go into much more detail and provide different code examples on how to use Windows Azure Storage in *Chapter 4, Storing Your Data*.

Business analytics

SQL Azure reporting allows you to enrich your Windows Azure application with reporting capabilities in a way you did before, by using SQL server reporting 2008 R2. This removes the need for on-premises installations of reporting servers but still enables you to create rich reports with tables, charts, and other compelling visualizations, and to additionally scale your reports and benefit from the underlying Windows Azure Platform-as-a-Service capabilities.

SQL Database reporting offers you the ability to:

- Quickly set up a reporting infrastructure
- Benefit from the pay-per-use philosophy that Windows Azure offers
- Take advantage of the scalability and high availability the platform offers
- Generate reports in multiple file formats, such as Excel, Word, and PDF
- Make use of the same tools as Business Intelligence Design Studio
- Provide access to reports and data in a secure, authenticated, and authorized manner

Service Bus

The Windows Azure platform offers a powerful mechanism to build secure messaging and relay capabilities for your distributed and loosely coupled applications. Applications may be on-premises, in the cloud or hybrid.

Integrate your enterprise application, running in your own datacenters, with applications running on Windows Azure. Use the **Service Bus** to build applications that can scale out more easily and reduce dependencies between components within your distributed applications.

Service Bus offers brokered messaging, meaning a scalable way to store messages, and the ability to implement a publish/subscribe pattern by using topics and subscriptions, allowing you to publish messages to hundreds of subscribers. Beside messaging, Service Bus also offers relayed messaging, enabling your applications running on Windows Azure to call back to applications running inside your datacenter. It lowers the burden on maintaining NATs and firewalls, keeping you focused on the actual business value of your applications.

Content delivery network

Content delivery networks (CDNs) enable you to move your data close to your clients. There are multiple CDN nodes all over the world, and the CDN caches your data at locations as close to your customers as possible, to enhance performance. CDN can cache static content like pictures, movies, and software, as well as streaming media. CDN can be turned on, both on hosted services and storage accounts. Enabling CDN on your data is just a click away in the Windows Azure portal; see the following screenshot:

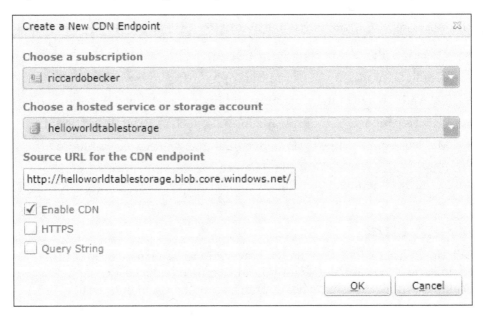

CDN relies on the same network infrastructure as high-available services, such as Windows Update and Bing Maps, from Microsoft itself.

Caching

Windows Azure offers a caching mechanism that is distributed and in-memory. It is distributed, because the physical memory of different servers can be used as a single entity. It is in memory, because the cached items are stored in physical memory only and will not be swapped to disk or whatsoever, to keep up the high performance.

Using caching can speed up your application and minimize the round trips needed to your database or other stores. Typical candidates for caching are frequently used, read-only data (such as lookup tables), user session data (such as a shopping cart), and typical application data that requires a "singleton" approach.

Virtual network

Virtual network offers networking capabilities that help you migrate and integrate applications and release you from the plumbing burden of low-level networking issues.

Virtual network consists of two major concepts:

- Windows Azure Connect
- Traffic Manager

New features were added in June 2012 and are mentioned in *Chapter 11, What's New in Windows Azure*.

Windows Azure Connect

Windows Azure Connect (WAC) enables you to create network connectivity between applications running on Windows Azure and resources in your own datacenter. Setting up a "secure" connection based on IPSec between Windows Azure roles (web, worker, or VM) requires an agent to be installed on your local, on-premises machine that needs to be reached from the cloud. This mechanism does not require any changes to your network topology. Consider WAC as being a VPN, not on a gateway level but on a machine level.

Windows Azure Traffic Manager

Windows Azure Traffic Manager (WATM) enables fine-grained control on load balancing incoming traffic to multiple hosted services. By default, Windows Azure load balances all incoming web requests equally over the role instances. WATM enables load balancing across different hosted services with different DNS names. This can enhance performance (reducing network latency, but increasing the necessary hops) and availability by setting up "standby" hosted services that handle incoming requests if your primary hosted service is completely down.

By managing the traffic to your services, it is possible to ensure high performance, availability, and robustness of your services. WATM can provide a failover mechanism when it detects that one of your services is down. WATM detects some when a service is down and immediately reroutes traffic to the next closest (configured) service.

WATM policies can be set up on the Windows Azure portal very quickly and offer you three types of load balancing methods:

- **Based on performance**: WATM directs traffic to the hosted service with the least internet latency. Remember that this is only applicable if your hosted service is deployed in multiple Windows Azure regions.

- **Based on failover**: Traffic is directed to one single hosted service, but when the WATM is unable to detect a "heartbeat", it changes the DNS records and redirects all the traffic to the hosted service next in line. When this phenomenon occurs, your application will be unavailable for a few minutes, since the WATM needs to detect the heartbeat failure and update the DNS records.

- **Based on round robin**: The WATM uses a round-robin algorithm to equally spread traffic among every hosted service configured in the policy, as defined in the Windows Azure portal. When a listed hosted service is unavailable (no heartbeat), it is automatically removed from the round-robin list.

Windows Azure Active Directory

Windows Azure Active Directory (WAAD) is a cloud service that offer identity and access functionality to both Windows Azure applications, on-premise applications, applications in a hybrid scenario, and even to Microsoft Office 365, the online SaaS equivalent to Microsoft Office. WAAD relies on the proven technology and capabilities of Active Directory, so that migrating your application to the cloud can be made easier.

Access Control Services (ACS) can offer end users a single sign-on experience across all cloud and hybrid applications. You can move your authentication and authorization logic away from your core applications and make it highly configurable by moving it to ACS. ACS is built on open industry standards, such as WS-Trust and WS-Federation, and SAML 2.0 and Simple Web Token, allowing non-Microsoft programming languages to access the WAAD capabilities as well. An internet portal is available, allowing you to set up authentication and authorization rules outside the boundaries of your application.

ACS offers you:

- Single sign-on capabilities: Moving away from custom identity stores and authorization logic enables you to focus on the core functionality of your application.

- Interoperability with your corporate Active Directory via ADFS: Allowing you to deploy, for example, your intranet applications to cloud and still maintain the single sign-on experience.

- Incorporation of identity providers: Enabling you to make use of popular social media such as Facebook and identity, such as Google, Yahoo!, and Windows Live ID. A detailed example of using Facebook as an identity provider is given in *Chapter 6, Key Features Explained*.

Marketplace

Windows Azure Marketplace allows you to access SaaS applications and datasets comparable with an app store. You can also offer your applications on the marketplace and open up a global market for your product and/or datasets. Windows Azure Marketplace allows you to:

- Access datasets and services from third parties: Security, audit trails (who accessed what resource at which time), billing, and authentication are handled by the Marketplace and let you focus on your application. Open standards such as OAuth and OData allow you to reach beyond platform borders.

- Quickly monetize your SaaS solution or datasets and enable financial transactions all over the world in different currencies: Create trial offers and terms of use, and report on usage, traffic, and sales.

- Search for data or services that suit your needs.

Summary

This chapter introduced Windows Azure, the cloud offering from Microsoft. It described the author's first contact with "cloud" in general and the history of the platform, and how Microsoft decided to put a great amount of effort in realizing Windows Azure.

A first deployment of a MVC3 website to Windows Azure was demonstrated. After the first deployment, we took a deep dive in the internals of Windows Azure and we saw in great detail how the platform actually works and how availability and fault-tolerance is maintained.

The next section is about the core concepts of Windows Azure. It provides an overview of the different features, providing a high-level description of the offerings.

The next chapter describes a fictitious startup company with a new idea for social networking. Throughout this book, this scenario of the next-gen social network will be used for code snippets and how to use different Windows Azure features related to this scenario.

2
A Startup Scenario

"If there's something you want to build, but the tech isn't there yet, just find the closest possible way to make it happen."

– Dennis Crowley, Co-founder of Foursquare

This chapter describes a fictitious company named Geotopia. Geotopia has a totally new idea on how a social network should work. The introduction will describe core user features in detail and the must-have requirements that the final solution should meet. Geotopia plans to launch the new social network as soon as possible and is looking for an online platform that meets its demands. A small survey around different cloud offerings is made.

The chapter also contains a high-level architectural overview of the proposed solution. It maps different Windows Azure concepts to key user features, explaining why they are a good fit. The outlined architecture is the starting point for the rest of the chapters, and every code example will point back to the features described in this chapter.

Introduction

Geotopia is a brand new company that was founded at the end of 2011. It is a small company with only a few developers, who are also in charge of the company. The company is innovative and agile and is therefore willing to explore new technologies and opportunities that are made possible by cloud technologies. All developers and architects are skilled in Microsoft technologies, and by applying Windows Azure technologies they can leverage their current knowledge and only need to learn new concepts offered by the platform. By applying Windows Azure, it enables them to learn these new concepts and gain experience. Geotopia strongly believes in its concept and wishes to launch the next-generation social network as soon as possible. The team has a perfect mix of skills to quickly start realizing the next-gen social network.

BizSpark

As Geotopia is a startup company that just opened their doors, they are looking for low-cost initiatives to support them and help them start their business quickly. Microsoft offers a program called **BizSpark** that helps startup companies succeed and offers them all the resources they need.

BizSpark is a global program that supports startups by offering them access to critical resources, such as software development tools, a network of industry experts to connect to, and marketing support to enhance visibility.

The reason why Microsoft offers this program is that it believes that accelerating startups helps them to build partnerships with future successful companies.

In order to file for a BizSpark position, a company needs to be:

- In business for less than three years
- Making less than one million dollars in annual revenue
- Privately held
- Engaged in developing software-based products a the core business of the startup

The program is renewed annually and lasts for a maximum of three years (if the requirements are still met).

The BizSpark program offers several advantages for members to help startups succeed:

- **Software**: Gain access to Microsoft development tools and licenses. Also included are free Windows Azure resources that are very helpful in this case.
- **Support**: Get access to both technical and business training at very competitive rates or even for free.
- **Two technical incidents per startup**: Microsoft will manage each incident until it is resolved.
- Gain access to MSDN Ultimate newsgroups, online library, and more.

- **Connect to BizSpark Network Partners around the world**: This includes investors, incubators, and mentors.
- **Visibility**: Become visible to an audience of potential customers, investors, partners, and so on, and become part of this global ring.

Program roles

BizSpark offers four distinguished roles:

- **Champ**: For Microsoft employees who work with Partners, Startups, and Hosting parties. Champs approve requests for joining BizSpark and are able to recruit candidates.
- **Network Partner**: A member of the local software business (non-Microsoft employees) who is involved with guiding startups and partners, offering mentoring, coaching, advice, and possible financial help.
- **Startup**: A new company offering software-based products or services (the actual candidate for the program).
- **Hosting Partner**: A Network Partner that offers hosting services for Startups.

In our case, we are the Startup that wants to enroll into the program. The next paragraph shows how to enroll.

Enrolling into the program

In order to take advantage of the BizSpark Startup program, you need to fill out a form on the `https://www.microsoft.com/BizSpark/Startup/Signup.aspx` website. After accepting both the BizSpark Start Agreement and the BizSpark Program End User License Agreement (EULA), you are directed to the online registration form.

This is similar to the one in the following screenshot:

After filling out the registration form, you are taken to the **Build your BizSpark Profile** page. Fill out this page, describe your Startup profile, and enter your visibility level (for now, private will do).

After this, the Startup profile process has started and you will receive an e-mail stating that it will take around five working days to complete the process. After successful completion, you have access to lots of resources and help, to accelerate your freshly started business.

Geotopia's goals

After several brown-bag lunch sessions, the people from Geotopia identified several key features, from both a user's perspective and from nonfunctional requirements, that must be implemented in the first release of Geotopia. Time to market is very important and will make or break the success of Geotopia.

Geotopia concluded that the unique concept for their social network is based on location. The standard environment for users will be a map, focused on their current or preset location, that offers them an overview of interesting events, messages, and multimedia localized around their current whereabouts.

The main canvas of Geotopia is a map based on Microsoft's Bing Maps technology and offers the user a central overview of his or her activities and interests, around a specific location.

In order to make Geotopia easy to access and make use of existing identity providers, it will enable users to sign up using their existing credentials (besides signing in with a dedicated Geotopia account).

People can choose to subscribe to Geotopia with their current Facebook credentials or make use of a new Geotopia account.

For mobile users of Geotopia, the position (if allowed) can be determined by the application itself. People running Geotopia on their desktop or laptop can specifically set their current location on **Geotopia canvas**.

Users can set their current location by using the Geotopia canvas or by making use of the GPS functionality in their device.

People can add their photos, videos, and other multimedia to their Geotopia environment by simply clicking on the map, in the most obvious location (for example, where the photo was taken), selecting the designated file, adding comments, and posting it to their Geotopia canvas. The user can decide to what kind of audience this multimedia is visible (private, friends, friends of friends, or public).

Users can point and click on the Geotopia canvas to upload the multimedia they want to share with the world. Visibility is managed by the user and can be set at any time.

Users can award posts or uploaded multimedia or messages of any kind with a system that is based on recommendations. The more recommendations a "geotopic" receives, the more prominent it will be on the canvas. A network of lines appears around the geotopic to be able to link back to users who actually awarded the geotopic. People can also see a list of the most popular geotopics at any time for any specific location or area. An area can be drawn on the Geotopia canvas and will appear in an elliptical shape.

Geotopia offers users the ability to recommend geotopics by a simple click system. Geotopics will become more prominent on the canvas if they are getting more popular. Users are able to see the most popular geotopics at their location or in a specific, custom-drawn, geographical area.

Speed, performance, and a top-notch user experience are key features of Geotopia. Geotopia wants to offer the lowest network latency possible to avoid hiccups or delays in its daily use.

Geotopia is built as a geo-wide application that is capable of servicing thousands or millions of users by using the scalability that the Windows Azure platform offers and by placing data as close to users as possible.

Windows Azure offers a standard **service-level agreement** (**SLA**) to its consumers. Check the SLA online at `http://www.windowsazure.com/en-us/support/sla/` to know about the service-level agreements offered by Windows Azure in detail. Generally, the compute SLA is 99.95 percent and the storage SLA is 99.9 percent.

By applying Windows Azure technologies, such as the Windows Azure Traffic Manager, and setting up different hosted services in different datacenters, Geotopia wants to create the highest availability possible and mitigate risks of services being unavailable.

Social media networks are available on different devices. Geotopia wants to penetrate the mobile market as well by offering a full service Geotopia client to popular mobile platforms such as iPhone, Android, and Windows Phone.

The mobile versions of Geotopia offer additional location-aware services and notifications.

People need to be able to replay conversations on the Geotopia canvas, a map-based user interface where users can point and click. By selecting a geotopic and clicking on **Play this story**, consecutive topics that are related to the selected ones will also be played chronologically. Geotopics with multimedia in their body will automatically be played to offer the user the ability to quickly catch up on existing conversations.

Geotopics can be selected as a starting point, and after that, the Geotopia canvas is able to show and play geotopics chronologically, to offer users a multimedia experience.

Users can sign up free of charge and make use of the full service Geotopia offers. The platform offers special features to companies who want to advertise and become visible on the Geotopia canvas. Users can recommend companies to their friends, and these will show up in a semi transparent way on their Geotopia canvas.

Companies can sign up to Geotopia and offer advertising to potential customers. People won't be bothered by advertising but will only be signaled if something interesting appears, based on the user's preferences, and if it appears in their immediate geographical surrounding.

The staff of Geotopia want to be able to run reports on analytical data. It is important for the company to get insight into the use of Geotopia, so that it is able to predict how many Windows Azure resources its solution will consume. This allows it to predict future costs but also to see how many users, videos, data, images, and so on are roaming around Geotopia.

 The solution needs to deliver aggregated data around users and their actions into clear reports that can be run and printed by the administrators of Geotopia.

Geotopia prototype

After a few sessions on the brand new concept of Geotopia, a developer built a Geotopia prototype by using Microsoft Expression Blend. This development tool can help you to create Silverlight or Windows Presentation Foundation (WPF) applications quickly and helps you prototype or demonstrate initial versions of your product.

See the following screenshot to get an impression of the very first prototype of the Geotopia canvas:

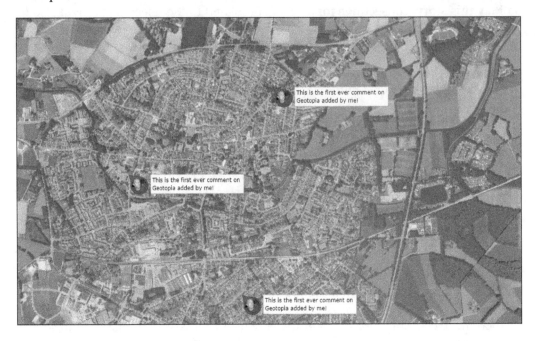

As you can see on the canvas, messages are decorated with a so-called pushpin. In order to be able to filter messages and comments, layering will be added to the solution. Users need to be able to turn layers on and off, grouped by friends, by region, or by interests. The next prototype will contain these concepts. Ideally, only pushpins are shown on the map to get a plain canvas. Hovering over a pushpin will display the comments, photo, video, or other content.

TFS in the cloud

Now that we have all the minimum features spelled out, we want to administer them and keep track of progress and changes in the features. A first step on Application Lifecycle Management is made. Geotopia decided to use Visual Studio Team Foundation Service Preview. Basically, it is Team Foundation Server offered as a service and hosted in Microsoft datacenters. **Community Technology Preview (CTP)**, is free of charge and helps with the setting up of source control, builds, and work-item management, quickly. Geotopia wants to apply a proper development process, keep track of bugs, user stories, test cases, and set up a daily or nightly build. Since Geotopia is built from scratch, the team needs to have the ability to be flexible and chooses to follow an Agile development process. You can set up your own preview account by going to `http://tfspreview.com/`. You can watch a short how-to video and see how you can connect from Visual Studio to the online **Team Foundation Service (TFS)** and start doing your work. After signing up with your Live ID and getting the invitation code, you can create a team project from the Team Foundation Service Preview portal. Since the people at Geotopia are used to working on Agile projects, and the way they approach the Geotopia project needs to be flexible and deliver in short iteration, pick the MSF for Agile Software Development 6.0 - Preview 2 process template and click on **Create Project**. After this step, you are ready for true Application Lifecycle Management in the Cloud!

See the following screenshot:

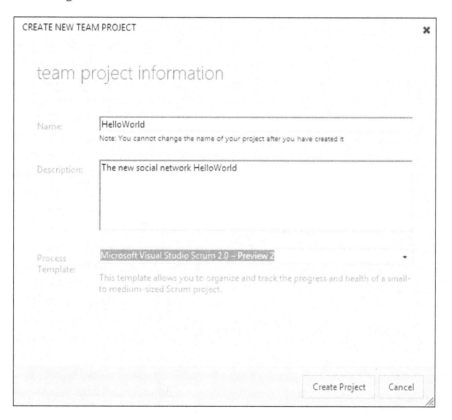

A new team project is created, and after creation, you can navigate to the main page of the project you just created. In the following screenshot, you can see what this portal looks like:

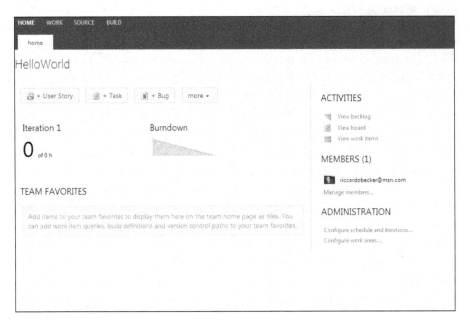

The portal lets you add user stories, tasks, bugs, issues, and test cases. We will explain Application Lifecycle Management specifically for Windows Azure in *Chapter 9, Application Lifecycle Management*.

Connecting to TFS Preview

Besides managing your TFS instance from the portal, it is also possible and very convenient to connect from your IDE directly to your Team Foundation Service instance. Connecting works in a similar manner as connecting to on-premise TFS. Verify that you have Team Explorer installed and available. In your **Team Explorer** window, click on the **Connect to Team Project** button to connect your IDE with your TFS environment.

A dialog appears that enables you to select the appropriate Team Foundation Server option. In our case, this drop-down item contains no servers yet. We need to add the one we just created online. Click on the **Servers...** button and click on **Add...**, in the next screen. At this time, you can add a specific TFS server to your **Team Explorer** window.

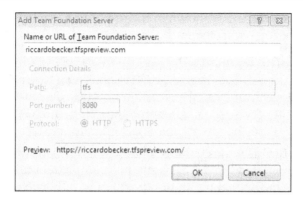

In the previous screenshot, my configuration is entered, and after clicking on **OK**, we need to sign in with our Live ID. After signing in successfully, the online instance of TFS is added to Team Explorer!

After adding the new Team Foundation Server to Team Explorer, we pick the project we want to connect to. We added our first prototype, and since the project is set up as being an agile project, the following structure appears in my IDE.

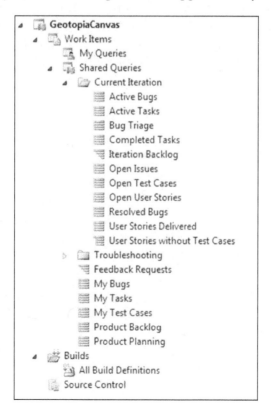

The Geotopia canvas structure is shown in the previous screenshot. A typical team project contains three top-level elements:

- **Work Items**: This node shows typical queries you can execute against the Team Foundation Server repository. It enables you to see Bugs, Tasks, Test Cases, Issues, and all other work item types. Out-of-the-box, it also contains — for every single user — some typical, frequently used queries with a "My" prefix. These show work items assigned to the currently signed in user.

- **Builds**: The **Builds** node contains all builds definitions (if any), and queued as well as completed builds. Clicking on a completed build displays the output of the individual build. Builds can now fully run on the Microsoft infrastructure, and you can set up continuous integration. (Previously, you needed to have local Build Controllers to create a build.)

- **Source Control**: Contains all the sources available in the repository, including history, audit trail, and so on. In the next chapter, we will demonstrate how your solution can be added to Source Control.

Querying Tasks

To get a quick overview of the tasks assigned to you, double-click on the **My Tasks** in the **Work Items** section of the Team Explorer. The screen presented shows all the tasks that are assigned to the logged-in user. In the **My Queries** node, you can define your own queries in an easy way by assigning values to fields and selecting the result set you need.

Summary

A brand new, ambitious company just opened its doors. Geotopia consists of enthusiastic developers and architects who have jointly created a new view on social networking. This is not a basic user interface where plain text dominates, but a compelling map interface, offering users to treat it as their social canvas and drop video and images and create messages based on their location or on the location of their interest. Users can recommend locations, shops, or other points of interest by adding comments or multimedia and telling their friends about it.

Opening up their solution for mobile users will increase the number of users for Geotopia in an unpredictable way. As the solution evolves, the Windows Azure platform usage will also evolve and necessitate the need for a detailed look inside in the use of Geotopia.

By entering the Microsoft BizSpark program, the company can make use of Windows Azure resources and get in contact with experts and get some marketing power and visibility.

The Team Foundation Service that is available for free enables the company to quickly set up an Agile project to deliver its first prototype of Geotopia as soon as possible.

Different requirements for Geotopia were described, and these will be the basis for the rest of this book.

The next chapter focuses on creating a typical Windows Azure solution structure with Visual Studio 2010. It not only describes how to organize your own solution, but also shows how to connect to a different online service Microsoft offers; Team Foundation Services preview. The first prototype of Geotopia is also created and highlights some applied technologies, such as Bing Maps.

3
Create Your Solution

"In software, we rarely have meaningful requirements. Even if we do, the only measure of success that matters is whether our solution solves the customer's shifting idea of what their problem is."

— Jeff Atwood, writer of the blog, Coding Horror

This chapter focuses on the structure of a typical Windows Azure solution in Visual Studio, and specifically on the proposed solution structure of our fictional company, Geotopia. It not only helps you to organize your own solution structure inside the IDE, but also demonstrates how to use the online version of Team Foundation Server in conjunction with the development environment.

Since Geotopia also relies on Bing Maps, this chapter also describes how to use Bing Maps in combination with Windows Azure.

The last part of the chapter demonstrates the second prototype of Geotopia. At the end of this chapter, we will have a fully operational solution that can be deployed on Windows Azure, has Silverlight parts in it, and has a connection to the online TFS preview environment that supports a SCRUM approach and a source repository, all together set up with a build environment.

Solution structure

This section shows, in detail, how to create a typical Windows Azure solution and set up the Azure environment to support our scenario. This includes creating a storage account and Service Bus settings.

Organizing a solution in VS 2010

One major advantage of developing for Windows Azure is that you don't need to learn a completely new platform or development environment.

Before you can start developing Windows Azure services, you need to install the Windows Azure SDK and appropriate tools (if needed). You can find the downloads at http://www.windowsazure.com/en-us/develop/downloads/.

To create a **Cloud Service**, start up your Visual Studio 2010, click on the **File** menu, and choose **New | Project** to bring up the New Project wizard. On the left-hand side, you see all the installed templates you can choose from. Select the cloud template and give an appropriate name to your project—in our case, it will be **GeotopiaPrototype2**—and then click on **OK**.

The **New Windows Azure Project** screen appears, and for now, we just add an **ASP.NET MVC 3 Web Role** (ASP.NET MVC3 project) for our user interface and a **Worker Role** named **Geotopia.Processor** is created, and a **Worker Role** for background processing that will be at the heart of Geotopia.

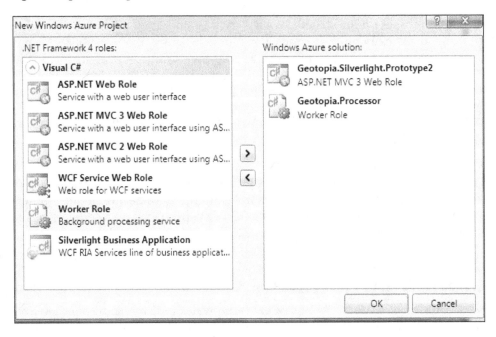

After clicking on **OK**, a dialog regarding the ASP.NET MVC3 project appears. Just leave the initial settings as is and click on **OK**.

The solution is created and three projects show up in the solution, as shown in the following screenshot:

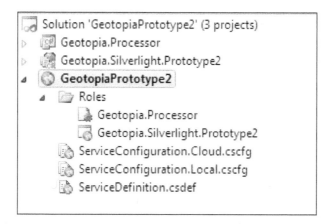

Geotopia.Processor is a project that contains a worker role that will do background processing for the Geotopia solution.

Geotpia.Silverlight.Prototype2 is an MVC3 solution that will also host the Silverlight part of the Geotopia solution. The project remains an ASP.NET website but enables us to embed some Silverlight parts in it, such as the Geotopia canvas. Other features and screens of Geotopia will be ordinary ASP.NET screens with code-behind.

The Cloud project specifies both the service model and configuration. This means that for every web or worker role in the project, a role will be specified in the Cloud project. For every role in the Cloud project, you can define the service model and configuration. There are two variants of the configuration files:

- **Local variant**: This is used when you run your Windows Azure project on the emulators

- **Cloud variant**: This is used when you deploy your project to Windows Azure

You can manually change the configuration settings by double-clicking the `.cscfg` file. The Visual Studio IDE opens the configuration file and it can be edited since it is marked up as an XML document.

Visual Studio provides tools to support modifying the configuration. Double-clicking the designated role brings up the **Properties** tab, as follows:

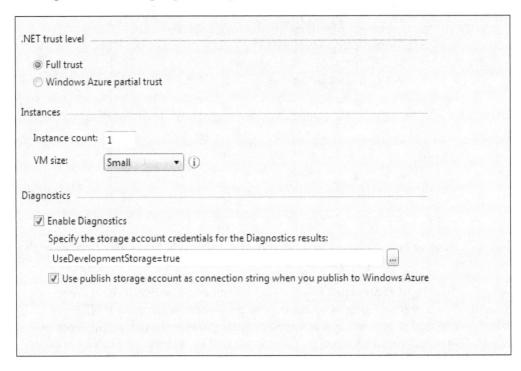

The .NET trust level allows you to set the trust level to **Full trust** or to **Windows Azure partial trust**.

The difference between the options **Full trust** and **Windows Azure partial trust** is that explicitly setting the **.NET trust level** to partial trust restricts any code except for .NET from running. Also, .NET assemblies that require full trust will not run. From a security point of view, it is always wise to set the trust level as low as possible. The **Instances** part enables you to set the initial number of instances of the role that are started. It also enables you to select the VM size for this role. Remember that both options influence the cost of your deployment.

The **Diagnostics** option allows you to enable the collection of diagnostics data for your application. This data can not only be used for debugging your application, but also for gathering metrics on performance and other metrics that are interesting for your application. All this information is stored in the storage account that is configured here.

Compute and storage emulators

The compute and storage emulators (formerly known as development fabric) are installed on your machine as part of Windows Azure Tools. These emulators enable you to develop, run, and debug your Cloud solutions without deploying them to Windows Azure. Deploying to Azure is time-consuming and increases your debugging time drastically. Running your solution initially in the emulators avoids this lengthy operation of deployment. The emulators run your web and worker roles locally and emulate the storage capabilities by using a SQL Express instance. Storage tables, queues, and BLOB storage are persisted in a database on this SQL Express instance.

You also have the ability to specifically set the service configurations for either **Local** or **Cloud**, as shown in the following figure. This means that, in our case, the local variant uses development storage, and the Cloud variant will use the actual storage account inside our Windows Azure subscription, but you can use it to differentiate in any setting that will be used in either **Cloud** or **Local** deployment. This makes you very flexible with running and debugging locally, while deployment and setting the right connection strings to storage and possible SQL Database instances is just a matter of configuration.

Let us set our **Local** configuration for both roles and have the emulators run two instances of our worker role and three instances of our web role. The frontend needs to be highly reactive, and therefore, the number of instances of our web role needs to be sufficient to handle all the expected web requests. The processing of the workload is done by the worker roles that are running in the background.

After setting the instance counts of both roles, press *F5* to run the initial solution. The configuration will cause five instances to run. After deployment, it will cause five VMs to be created by Windows Azure.

What happens next is that the emulators are initialized and started, and your project actually runs locally, while providing the same experience as if it was running in the cloud. There are some differences between the emulated and the cloud environment.

[Please go to `http://msdn.microsoft.com/en-us/library/`
`windowsazure/gg433135.aspx` to read about the exact differences.]

An icon appears in the tray on the right-hand side of your screen, and by right-clicking it and selecting **Show Compute Emulator UI**, you bring up the emulator screen.

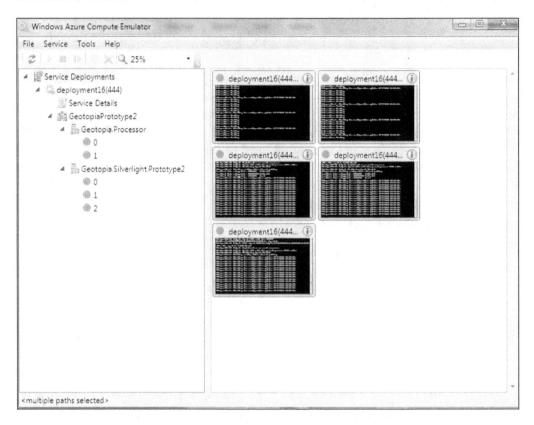

As you can see in the previous screenshot, there are two instances of the **Geotopia. Processor** worker role and three instances of the **Geotopia.Silverlight.Prototype2** web role. The web role is up and running and just shows the default MVC3 website.

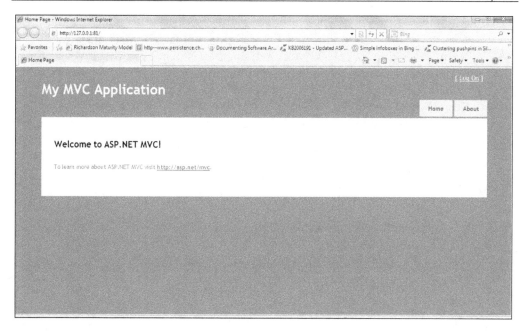

Bing Maps

Since Bing Maps is at the core of Geotopia, we need to sign up to use Bing Maps. Go to www.bingmapsportal.com and use your Live ID to sign in. Next, create a new account by filling out some information and agreeing with the Bing Maps API terms of use. After creating a new account, we will have the key at our disposal that we need to authenticate our Bing Maps application. We will need this key later in this chapter.

Download the Bing Map Silverlight Control SDK from http://www.microsoft.com/download/en/details.aspx?id=2949 and install the SDK. Two important assemblies are installed in the designated folder, namely, Microsoft.Maps.MapControl.Common.dll and Microsoft.Maps.MapControl.dll. You need to reference these assemblies from the Silverlight project.

Adding Silverlight to cloud

The next step in creating the second version of the prototype of Geotopia is to create a Silverlight application that is part of the MVC3. As we are using MVC, we need to create a view that encapsulates the Silverlight application. The steps to create and add a Silverlight application are described as follows:

1. Add a new Silverlight application by right-clicking the solution file and selecting **Add | New Project | Silverlight** from **Installed Templates**. Name it GeotopiaCanvas. Next, a dialog box is displayed that gives us the opportunity to have the Silverlight application hosted in a new web project or in an existing web application. In our case, we can pick the **Geotopia. Silverlight.Prototype2** project, which is the MVC3 ASP.NET application. Leave the rest of the configuration as default.

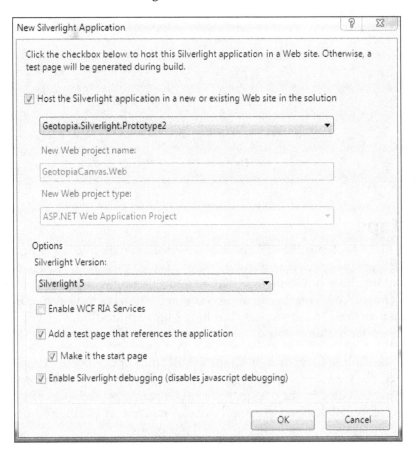

2. The Silverlight project is created and added to the solution. Additional .html and .aspx files are added to the existing MVC3 web application and tagged as the startup page. This means that when you run the Cloud project, both the worker role and web role are started, but the web role isn't displaying the initial MVC3 screen anymore. Instead, the empty Silverlight application is displayed.

3. We want some parts of the application to be Silverlight and some to be plain HTML/ASP.NET. For now, only the Geotopia canvas is based on Silverlight technology. A new folder appears in the MVC3 project called `ClientBin`. This folder is created by the IDE and contains the binary of the Silverlight project and makes it available in the web application.

4. Remove the `.html` and `.aspx` files from the MVC3 ASP.NET project. In the project properties of the MVC3 project, set **Start Action** to **Current Page** instead of `GeotopiaCanvasTestpage.aspx`. See the following figure:

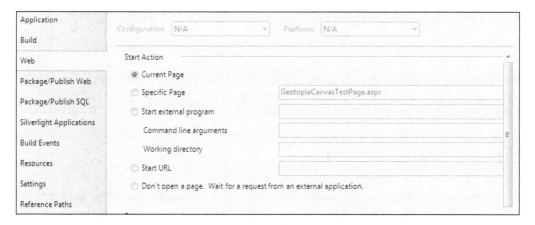

5. Go to **View** that will show the Silverlight part. In our case, it is the `index.cshtml` file in the `Views\Home` folder. The code of the `index.cshtml` file looks similar to the code in the following fragment:

```
@{
    ViewBag.Title = "Home Page";
}


<h2>@ViewBag.Message</h2>
<p>
    To learn more about ASP.NET MVC visit <a href="http://asp.net/
mvc" title="ASP.NET MVC Website">http://asp.net/mvc</a>.
</p>
```

6. Replace the code inside the `index.cshtml` file with the following code, to embed the newly created Silverlight application:

```
@{
    ViewBag.Title = "Displaying Silverlight in MVC3 view";
}
```

```
<h1>@ViewBag.Message</h2>
<object data="data:application/x-silverlight-2,"
type="application/x-silverlight-2" width="400" height="300">
  <param name="source" value="ClientBin/GeotopiaCanvas.xap"/>
  <param name="background" value="red" />
  <param name="minRuntimeVersion" value="4.0.60129.0" />
  <param name="autoUpgrade" value="true" />
  <a href="http://www.microsoft.com/getsilverlight/get-started/
install/" style="text-decoration:none">
  <img src="http://go.microsoft.com/fwlink/?LinkId=161376"
alt="Get Microsoft Silverlight" style="border-style:none"/>
  </a>
</object>
```

At this point, the solution is capable of combining Silverlight parts with general ASP.
NET parts. From here, we take the solution to the next step and create the Geotopia
canvas as being at the heart of our solution.

Embedding Bing Maps

In order to show the Geotopia Canvas, based on Bing Maps technology, replace the
XAML code in `MainPage.xaml` with the following code fragment. Make sure you
add references to the two Bing Maps assemblies, `Microsoft.Maps.MapControl.`
`Common.dll` and `Microsoft.Maps.MapControl.dll`. Replace `<your key here>`
with your own private Bing Map key, which you can find on the Bing Maps portal.

```
<UserControl x:Class="GeotopiaCanvas.MainPage"
    xmlns="http://schemas.microsoft.com/winfx/2006/xaml/
presentation"
xmlns:x="http://schemas.microsoft.com/winfx/2006/xaml"
xmlns:d="http://schemas.microsoft.com/expression/blend/2008"
xmlns:mc="http://schemas.openxmlformats.org/markup-
compatibility/2006"
xmlns:Microsoft_Maps_MapControl="clr-namespace:Microsoft.Maps.
MapControl;assembly=Microsoft.Maps.MapControl"
  mc:Ignorable="d"
  d:DesignHeight="300" d:DesignWidth="400">

  <Grid x:Name="LayoutRoot" Background="White">
<Microsoft_Maps_MapControl:Map x:Name="GeotopiaCanvas"
CopyrightVisibility="Collapsed" ScaleVisibility="Collapsed" Na
vigationVisibility="Collapsed" LogoVisibility="Collapsed"
Mode="Aerial" CredentialsProvider="<your key here>"
ZoomLevel="15" Center="51.9266891479,6.5928997993" Height="Auto"
Width="Auto">
```

```
            <Microsoft_Maps_MapControl:MapLayer
    x:Name="mapLayer"/>
            </Microsoft_Maps_MapControl:Map>
        </Grid>
</UserControl>
```

When you hit *F5* to start debugging the application, both the web and worker roles will start running in the compute emulator. Your default web browser will start and show the first version of Geotopia!

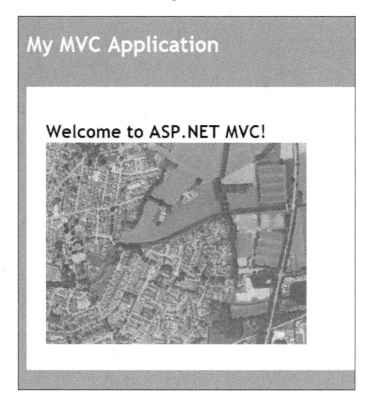

The Bing Maps Silverlight control is fully functional and initially shows my hometown! This is caused by the Center property of the Bing Maps to be set with latitude and longitude information in `MainPage.xaml`. You can drag the map and use your mouse scroll to zoom in and out.

Setting up TFS preview

The final step to set up our development environment with the initial projects that we need for the realization of Geotopia is to connect the solution with the TFS preview account we created in *Chapter 2, A Startup Scenario*.

Connecting with TFS Preview

This section contains a step-by-step approach on how to connect your Visual Studio IDE with the TFS Preview environment.

Right-click on the solution item and pick **Add Solution to Source Control**. The next dialogue appears as follows:

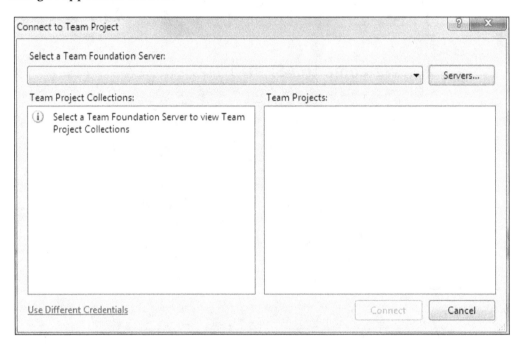

As we did not add any servers yet, click on the **Servers...** button and add our TFS preview URL, select **HTTPS** as the protocol, and click on **OK**. The TFS preview URL was provided when signing up to the preview. Next, we need to log in with our Live ID. Enter your Live ID credentials and close the dialog. Add a new project in your TFS preview environment by selecting the **Create a team project** option, and provide the name for the project, an optional description, and the process template that you want to use. The selected process template determines which methodology is used for this project.

Right-click on your solution and choose **Add Solution to Source Control**. The following dialog box appears:

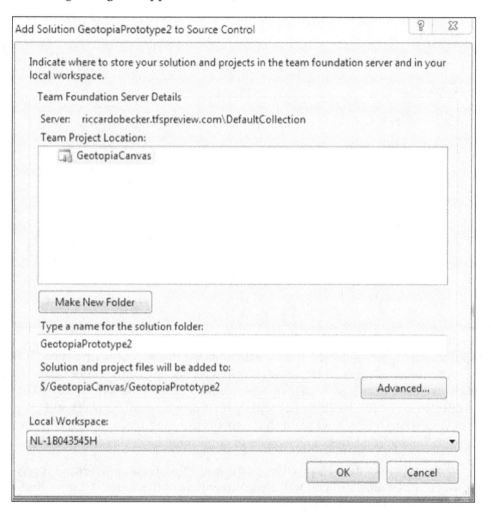

Select the appropriate **Team Project Location** (in this case, **GeotopiaCanvas**) and click on **OK**. You can see that your complete solution is associated with the team project. Now, you need to **Check In** to add all the files from the solution to **Source Control**. Right-click on the solution item and click on **Check In**.

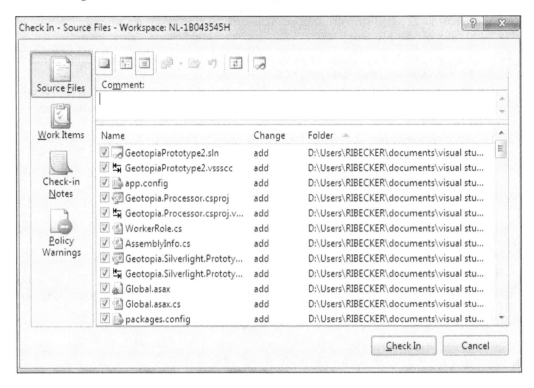

In this dialog, you can see all the files that are affected by the "check in" action. In this case (since nothing is checked in yet), all our files will be added to Source Control after we click on **Check In**. After clicking on **Check In**, every file is added to Source Control. From this point, you can work on Geotopia with multiple team members and keep track of your source code. Your team then benefits from the Team Foundation Server features, including build and other aspects of application lifecycle management.

When you navigate to the TFS preview portal and select **Geotopia Team Project** and click on the **Source** tab, you will see an overview of the Source Control tree, as shown in the following screenshot:

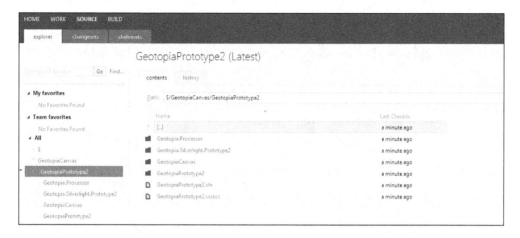

In the next chapter, we will also set up a build for Geotopia and set up a fictional team that will work on the solution.

Publishing to Windows Azure

Now that we have our initial solution containing an MVC3 project containing a Silverlight component, a worker role, and a web role, we need to configure the publishing to Windows Azure. This will allow us to build, package, and upload our solution to Windows Azure.

Right-click on the Cloud Service project, in our case **GeotopiaPrototype2**, and click on **Publish**. A wizard is displayed, as shown in the following screenshot:

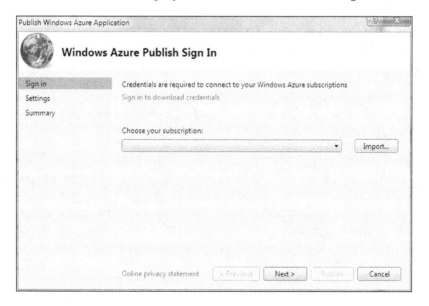

Since we don't have anything configured yet, we need to set up the publishing process from scratch. It is possible to download the .publishsettings file by clicking the **Sign in to download settings** option. A file is downloaded to your machine, and the next step would be to **Import...** this file and get the previous screen prepopulated. Right now, we follow the complete process to clarify the different steps. Select the dropdown and choose **Manage...**, and then select **New**. A dialog is displayed, as shown in the following screenshot:

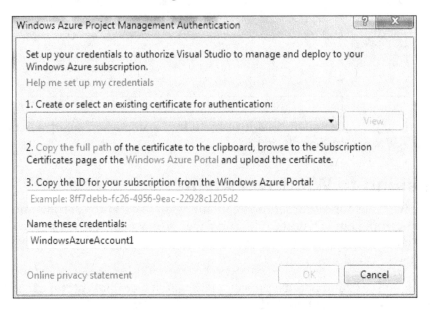

In this dialog, you need to associate a certificate with your subscription ID. Besides manual deployment on the Window Azure portal using the Live ID for authentication, it is also possible to deploy your solution in a different way. This can be accomplished by using the Service Management API of Windows Azure (refer to http://msdn.microsoft.com/en-us/library/windowsazure/ee460799.aspx to dig into the details of this Service Management API). In order to be able to use the Service Management API, you need to authenticate it with a so-called management certificate.

The subscription ID can be found at your http://windows.azure.com portal. Copy and paste your ID in the appropriate field. Next, select the dropdown and click on **<Create...>**. You need to enter a friendly name for the certificate next, and in our case we choose **GeotopiaCertificate**. A certificate is created in your local store. Copy the full path by clicking on the associated hyperlink in the dialogue. Next, go to the Windows Azure portal and upload the newly created certificate.

You can do this by selecting the **Hosted Services, Storage Accounts & CDN** tab, and next, the **Management Certificates** and the **Add Certificate** actions from the ribbon.

The **Add Certificate** action displays a dialog that enables you to browse to the certificate to be uploaded. In our case, we copied the location to the clipboard. Click on **Browse**, paste the location in the dialogue, and click on **OK**. The certificate we created in Step 1 is uploaded to your Windows Azure environment and is then available for use in conjunction with the three ways of deploying to Azure:

- The easiest way is to do it directly from Visual Studio, as we are doing here.

- You can manually upload your binaries (after you've packaged them) on the portal. In that case, you won't need a certificate to authenticate yourself but just your Live ID.

- Use the Service Management API to build your own deployment mechanism (for example, embedded in a nightly build script). Usage of the Service Management API also needs a certificate.

 Please go to `http://msdn.microsoft.com/en-us/library/windowsazure/ee460799.aspx` to find an extensive reference on the REST-based service management API.

After executing all the steps from the previous sections containing the web and worker roles, both configured by the accompanying configuration file, the following situation exists:

- There are five virtual machines created by Windows Azure, because of the number of instances we have set in the configuration file.

- During deployment, you can choose to deploy to production or staging. Both environments are identical; only the URL to get to them differs. The staging environment is useful for testing purposes. After approval of the "test version", a deployment can easily be swapped from Staging to Production and we can get the appropriate DNS name (URL) for your application.

- Your application is up and running and is reachable to the whole world.

- The billing starts, and accessing your application and using Windows Azure resources will cost you money from now on.

Summary

In this chapter, we saw how to create a Visual Studio 2010 solution with a typical Cloud Service component. We set up a web role and a worker role, an MVC3 ASP. NET project based on the Razor rendering engine, as well as a Silverlight application that embeds the Geotopia canvas. Bing Maps was added to the solution and enabled us to create a working canvas based on a geographical view that we will develop further into a rich user experience.

We created the initial solution and had it run in the compute emulator. We then configured the preview of Team Foundation Server online and added our solution to Source Control to keep it safe, tracked, and make it available for multiple developers and architects to work on Geotopia as a team.

Finally, we published our initial version of Geotopia to Windows Azure, setting up the configuration and enabling easy, one-click deployment to Azure from within Visual Studio 2010.

The foundation of our solution is ready, and all constraints are met to take the prototype to the next level.

The next chapter will dig into the details of the Window Azure Storage services and its capabilities.

4
Storing Your Data

"The desktop metaphor was invented because one, you were a standalone device, and two, you had to manage your own storage. That's a very big thing in a desktop world. And that may go away. You may not have to manage your own storage. You may not store much before too long."

— Steve Jobs

This chapter describes the different storage services Windows Azure offers. It describes typical scenarios that touch the Geotopia case. It is possible to store geographical information for the location-based messaging capabilities in Geotopia. It can also save user profile information, in addition to standard Facebook and Twitter profile information. Geotopia can also store media such as video and graphics that can be part of the geotopics users can post.

In this chapter, we will describe and demonstrate how to use table storage, blobs, queues, the content delivery network, and SQL Azure and its different services, for example synchronization.

Storage

Here, we shall describe in detail the different storage types and their typical uses. The Windows Azure storage services provide secure and scalable storage capabilities that offer the same high-class availability as you are used to on the platform. It offers a 99.9 percent **service-level agreement (SLA)**. This means that Microsoft guarantees that at least 99.9 percent of the time, valid requests to the storage system are processed correctly. Blobs, tables, and queues are stored on the Windows Azure platform and are replicated at least twice in the same datacenter to offer maximum availability. When a hard disk crashes or some other failure occurs, the platform will still be able to offer the storage service. Blobs and tables are replicated to another datacenter on the same continent. For example, large images stored in blob storage in the Amsterdam datacenter are also replicated to the Dublin datacenter. The platform is therefore able to offer maximum availability of your data, even in the case of an earthquake or some other major event that brings down a datacenter.

What is Windows Azure storage?

Windows Azure offers different forms of persistency on its platform. These features vary from storing large amounts of unstructured data up to relational data. The Windows Azure portal provides a quick overview of all the storage services.

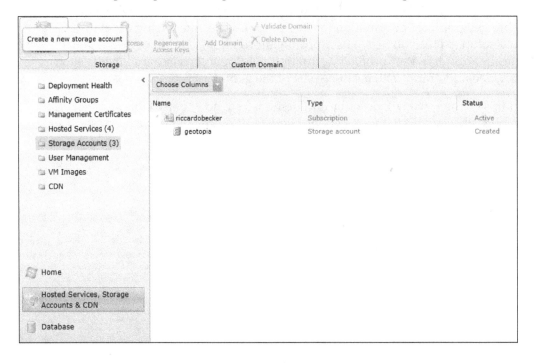

In the preceding screenshot you can see the **Storage Accounts** (in this case, **geotopia**) and the **SQL Database** offering under the **Database** tab.

There are four types of storage understood to be part of **Windows Azure Storage (WAS)**, as follows:

- **Blobs**: They offer the ability to store large binary objects and metadata, for example multimedia files, in a filesystem-like fashion.

- **Queues**: They offer capabilities of storing messages in a best-effort, **First In, First Out (FIFO)** queue, enabling developers to build large-scale, loosely-coupled, and asynchronous solutions. Typically, queues are used to separate work between the web and worker roles, where web roles commonly enter a workload in the queue and worker roles do the actual processing work.

- **Table storage**: This is a NoSQL, row- and column-based entity store where you can perform CRUD operations on nonrelational data. Storage offers the ability to store large amounts of schemaless (different entity types in a single table) data.

- **Windows Azure drive**: This is a **virtual hard disk (VHD)** and is an abstraction layer on top of Azure blobs and can be mounted as an NTFS drive from a web or worker role. After mounting the Azure drive, it can be manipulated with the file handling functionality the `System.IO` namespace offers. Windows Azure drives can help you migrate a solution quicker to the cloud while upholding the persistency mechanisms already built in the on-premise application. It can also help to provide a persistent store for otherwise stateless web and worker roles. When either one of these roles is restarted you are still able to recover data that is stored on a Windows Azure drive.

In general, storage operations are authenticated using a mechanism using the account name and a strong key. Blobs can be configured to be publicly accessible. Imagine all the resources, such as images and videos, from a website to be placed in blob storage, and therefore be publicly accessible.

Windows Azure offers a cloud version of Microsoft SQL Server called SQL Database. SQL Database (formerly known as SQL Azure) offers similar functionality as the non-cloud SQL Server databases (using the same TDS protocol) but with a few restrictions. We will discuss these later in this chapter.

Besides the storage types briefly described in the preceding section, the platform also offers some volatile storage capabilities. These types are not persistent and will be lost when the fabric controller restarts your instance(s). This can happen in the following circumstances:

- When an instance of your role crashes
- When the guest virtual machine crashes and the Fabric Controller misses heartbeats
- When the agent crashes and the FC misses heartbeats
- When some hardware issue occurs

Depending on the type of failure, the FC might decide to restart your role, to restart the underlying virtual machine, or to migrate your role to a different node (in the case of hardware failure).

Local storage provides the ability to write to disk in an old-fashioned way, for example, `C:`. Windows Azure Caching, the cloud variant of the Windows Server AppFabric Caching service, offers a caching mechanism that can speed up your application and reduce the amount of roundtrips to a database, for example.

First of all, we will create a storage account on the Windows Azure portal. The diagram just after the following screenshot depicts how this can be done. For the geotopia solution, obviously we need a **geotopia** storage account! We will create the storage account in the same region as our hosted services to have high bandwidth and the lowest latency. Also, the bandwidth is not charged when your roles and your storage accounts are in the same region. You can find more information on the bandwidth costs at `http://msdn.microsoft.com/en-us/library/windowsazure/jj136829.aspx`.

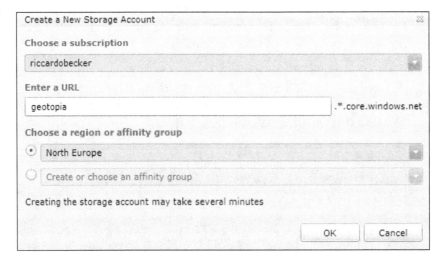

To visualize the concepts of the Windows Azure Storage service, have a look at the following diagram:

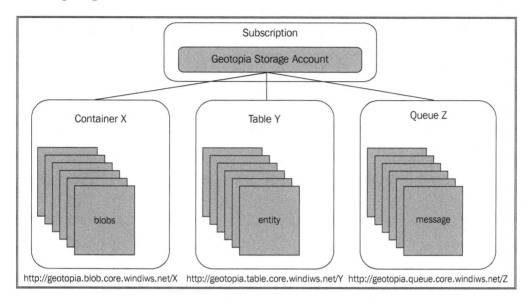

The central entry point to WAS is an account (being a part of your subscription), where the name of the account uniquely distinguishes the URI endpoints to blob, queue, and table storage. A single subscription can contain up to five different storage accounts, enabling us to logically separate storage needs. The number of different storage accounts can be increased on request.

In this case, we have defined a storage account named **geotopia**. This name is uniquely defined throughout the platform and the name is now claimed.

Blob storage is organized by using containers. You can add containers to your storage account, but they cannot be nested. Containers can contain multiple blobs. Blobs can be addressed individually, like the one at `http://geotopia.blob.core.windows.net/cntr1/image1.jpeg`. Blobs are organized in containers and have the following form:

```
http://<account>.blob.core.windows.net/<container>/<blob>
```

Keep in mind that a container must be unique within a storage account and a blob must be unique within a container. Table storage is organized by tables. A single table can contain multiple entities in any schema. This means that the table can contain rows that are not equal and have different columns. A table can be addressed in a similar way as a blob by using the storage account name and the table name. A table can be addressed, as follows:

```
http://<account>.table.core.windows.net/<tablename>
```

Queues are organized similarly and a single storage account can contain multiple queues, each of them uniquely identified by the queue name. A queue can hold multiple messages. A queue can be addressed as follows:

```
http://<account>.queue.core.windows.net/<queuename>
```

Blobs

The following table lists and describes all the characteristics of blobs:

Characteristic	Description
Container	This is a way of grouping blobs. Containers can be publicly accessible (for example, videos and images), or privately as well. To access blobs in a private container use one of the storage keys. If you want to make private blobs accessible, you can use shared access signatures.
Blob	This is stored in a container and can hold up to 8 KB of metadata including the name and value.
Storage account	This is the namespace for accessing blobs. It can have multiple containers.
Block blobs	This is a blob type suitable for streaming workloads and consisting of a sequence of blocks. The maximum size for a block blob is 200 GB.
	Updates to a block blob are committed in a two-phase fashion (uploading blocks first and then committing the blocks, both being one transaction all together). First, a set of blocks is uploaded. When the uploading is finished, the block list is committed and the blob then consists of the uploaded blocks.
Page blobs	This is suitable for random read/write actions. The primary use case is to contain VHDs. The maximum size is 1 TB.
	Updates are committed immediately.

Table storage

The following table provides the description of the characteristics of table storage:

Characteristic	Description
Storage account	This is the namespace for accessing tables. It can have multiple tables.
Table	This can contain entities that have different schemas.
Entity	This is a row in a table where data is stored in a column-like fashion. Properties can be added while different rows can have different properties. This means that the rows can have different schemas.
	A maximum of 255 properties are allowed.
	The maximum size of an entity is 1 MB.
PartitionKey	This is mandatory. It is an important property of an entity, as it is used to distribute the entities over many servers. All entities with the same PartitionKey property comprise a partition. These entities are stored closely together and the table service can move the partitions around to improve performance and scalability.
RowKey	This is mandatory. It is a unique identifier of the entity within a partition. The PartitionKey and RowKey properties together uniquely identify an entity in a table.
Timestamp	The platform handles the timestamp of an entity and can be useful for optimistic concurrency.
Sorting and querying	Tables are sorted by PartitionKey and RowKey. Querying tables by using these keys is the most efficient way of querying. Therefore, carefully consider which PartitionKey and RowKey properties you use in any scenario.
Allowed types	Properties can be of the following types—string, int64, int, GUID, double, DateTime, bool, and byte[] (up to 64 KB).

Queues

The following table provides information on the characteristics of queues:

Characteristic	Description
Storage account	This is the namespace for accessing queues. It can have multiple queues.
Queue	This can contain multiple messages. The maximum queue size is limited by the limit on the storage account. Nevertheless, don't use queues as a persistent storage mechanism.
	As with blobs, queues can have metadata.
Messages	These have a lifespan of one week. The maximum message size is 64 KB.

Inside storage

This section provides an in-depth overview of the Windows Azure Storage architecture and gives you a peek under the hood of the distributed storage offering of the Windows Azure platform.

Storage architecture

The storage architecture consists of three layers, as depicted in the following diagram:

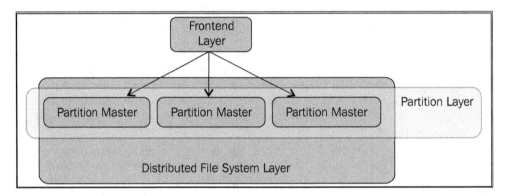

All storage transactions and interactions start at the **frontend (FE)** layer. This layer accepts the requests and, if needed, it also authenticates and authorizes the requests. The FE layer looks up the right partition master in a partition map (an index, stored on every FE) and routes the requests to the right partition master. The partition map contains information about partitions and the server on which the partitions reside.

The partition layer handles the partitioning of all storage objects available on the platform. Every storage object (blob, table, entity, or queue) contains a partition key, which implies that the object belongs to a single partition and therefore resides on exactly one partition server. Furthermore, the partition layer takes care of where to store which partition on which server and load balances the requests across the servers.

The **Distributed File System (DFS)** layer at the bottom of the stack takes care of the actual storing of data on disks and is responsible for upholding the promised SLA. It distributes and replicates data across the server and takes into consideration the fault and upgrade domains.

This can be summarized into a step-by-step overview, as follows:

1. A storage request is sent to the right FE by doing a DNS lookup to redirect the request to the appropriate datacenter.
2. The FE takes the incoming request.
3. The FE processes the incoming request (authenticate and authorize).
4. The FE takes the partition key from the request.
5. The FE looks up the right partition server in the partition map by using the The partition key.
6. The FE reroutes the request to the correct partition server.
7. The partition server checks if the data is cached in the partition server (only for a HTTP GET request, obviously) and returns it. If not in the cache, the request is sent to one of the DFS servers where a replica of the data resides. A non-read action is directly sent to the DFS server that holds the original data (not from one of the replicated servers).
8. The DFS server involved executes the requests (read/write) directly at the underlying disks and returns the status. A PUT, POST, or DELETE request is successful only if the data involved is also replicated successfully. In the case of a GET request, the data is also returned.
9. The FE gets the response from the partition server.
10. The FE sends it back to the client.

Storage availability

This section describes how the storage service maintains its availability, the precautions it takes, and how it makes sure it can meet the SLA. This means that, in 99.9 percent of the cases, valid requests for adding, editing, reading, and deleting information will be processed correctly. Additionally, the SLA is also about your accounts being connected to the internet gateway of the datacenter.

Fault domains

How does the storage service maintain its availability? All the servers from the three different layers are divided across different fault domains. When a hardware failure occurs, the service still remains available while the platform brings up a new server and starts replicating again.

When one of the FE servers becomes unavailable, the load balancer detects this and takes the affected FE server out of the list of available servers. This means that any request is sent to the FE servers that are available.

When one of the partition servers becomes unavailable, the storage system reassigns partitions to the other servers that are available. To notify other FE servers of this change in partitioning, the partition map is updated as well. Reassigning a partition does not mean that data is actually moved from one disk to another, as this is the job of the DFS layer.

What happens when a DFS server goes down? The partition layer stops using the DFS server as long as it is unavailable. Instead, the partition layer uses one of the replicas. When the DFS server is down for too long, other replicas of the data are created to make sure the storage SLA can be upheld.

Upgrade domains

As with other services and servers on the Azure platform, the servers in the storage architecture are divided across upgrade domains. When services are upgraded, Microsoft uses so-called "rolling upgrades" to maintain the highest level of availability so that only $1/X$ of the servers are down during an upgrade (X is the number of fault domains). For example, when a service is spread across five upgrade domains, only 20 percent of the capacity is down for a certain amount of time. In the storage architecture, all services in each layer are divided across upgrade domains.

When a domain is about to be upgraded, the platform marks the affected DFS servers as being part of an upgrade. This means that the DFS servers are not used during the actual upgrade. After the upgrade, the server is marked as being available again. Proper working of the server is validated before the platform goes on to the next upgrade domain.

Replication

Data inside WAS is replicated several times and spread out to the different fault and upgrade domains. All replicas of data are accessible from all of the partition servers and DFS servers.

Data from blobs, tables, or queues is persisted in extents. An **extent** is a unit of storage on disk and replication. Every extent is part of the replication process, and an extent as a whole is replicated. All data is broken into these extents and spread across different DFS servers. When you upload a video of 100 GB to blob storage, the system breaks this file down into extents, for example, of 1 GB (the system decides). In this case, there will be 100 extents of 1 GB each, which are replicated thrice. 300 extents are spread around the system, potentially on 300 different DFS servers. This will allow for high I/O throughput, as a request is not throttled only onto one server. Every extent of a single storage unit (blob, table, or queue) is spread across different fault domains as well as upgrade domains.

The storage service keeps a checksum of all data written to the DFS servers. Data is regularly read, and the checksum is verified. On every read request, the checksum is validated. When a checksum validation happens to fail, the replica is removed and another replica is created by using either one of the other valid replicas. This process is an important responsibility for the storage system to maintain healthy data and replicas and thus meet the SLA.

Microsoft also offers a geo-replication capability of the storage system. This means that data is not only replicated in a single datacenter but also across other datacenters. This will protect your data from incidents that affect a single datacenter, although it brings up questions regarding data privacy and regulations.

Partitioning

We have talked about partitioning before and introduced the abstract "partition key" in the table storage area, but how does this concept work inside the storage service?

In the queue service, every queue is its own partition. All the messages are kept closely together. In the table service, all entities with the same `PartitionKey` property are a partition. In the blob service, every single blob is its own partition.

Storage metrics

The storage service meets certain metrics regarding scalability. The maximum capacity for a storage account (defined on the subscription level) is 100 TB. The scalability target for throughput is 5,000 operations per second for a storage account. The maximum bandwidth is 3 Gigabits per second. If you need to go above these metrics, you need to find other ways to allocate your data, for example, by using different storage accounts.

Messages in a queue are served from a single partition (queue name) and can handle up to 500 messages per second. If you need a bigger throughput, consider using multiple queues.

Tables can be served from different partitions, depending on what `PartitionKey` is provided. A table named "customers" with entities having a unique `CustomerID` as `PartitionKey` will lead to a partition per customer. In this case, all the data belonging to a certain customer will be placed on a single partition.

> Choosing the right partitioning approach is important, as it affects the way the entities are distributed across partitions. When you use the same `PartitionKey` property for entities that belong together, for instance, every purchase order for a customer contains `CustomerID` as `PartitionKey`.

The grouping depends on the way the table is going to be accessed. If the entity you are storing in the table contains a single key property (for example `CustomerID`), use it as the `PartitionKey` property. If the entity has two different key properties, use one of them as `PartitionKey` and the other as `RowKey`. If the entity contains even more key properties, compile a composite key of concatenated properties.

Blobs are partitioned by their names and container names. This means that a container cannot hold blobs with the same name. In other words, blobs are always kept in a unique partition.

Table storage usage

This section focuses on the table storage facility of the storage service. As described previously in this chapter, tables can contain millions and millions of entities up to the maximum of 100 TB per storage account. Partitioning your data the right way has a large impact on performance.

A closer look at tables

Tables store entities, and entities may be of any shape. This means that entities of, say, the customer and product types can be persisted in the same table.

Tables and properties do have some characteristics, which are listed in the following table:

Characteristic	Description
Names are case-insensitive.	Using upper or lowercase characters does not affect operations on tables, though the case is preserved by the storage service.
Names are at least three and at most 63 characters long.	
Names can only contain alphanumeric characters.	
Names cannot start with a numeric character.	
Names can be described by a regular expression.	`^[A-Za-z][A-Za-z0-9]{2,62}$`
Property names are case-sensitive.	Names need to follow the rules for C# identifiers and can be up to 255 characters long.

Characteristic	Description
An entity can have a maximum of 255 properties.	This actually means 252 custom properties and three fixed ones (`PartitionKey`, `RowKey`, and `TimeStamp`).
All data in one entity cannot be larger than 1 MB.	
The user is responsible for the value of the `PartitionKey` and `RowKey` properties, while the system takes care of `TimeStamp`.	
The `PartitionKey` and `RowKey` properties cannot contain some special characters.	The forward and backward slashes (/ and \), the hash sign (#), and the question mark.
Supporting datatypes.	`byte[]`, `bool`, `DateTime`, `double`, `GUID`, `int`, `long`, and `string`.

The `PartitionKey` property is important in the way load balancing takes place on the storage platform. Every entity with the same `PartitionKey` property is stored on the same partition server. The `RowKey` property is a unique identifier for an entity within the partition. The `PartitionKey` and `RowKey` properties together are the primary key, and both must be included in any write operation on the table (insert, update, or delete). The `TimeStamp` property is a `DateTime` property that is controlled by the table service. It contains the last modified date and time of the entity. The property is used by the storage system to provide optimistic concurrency. An update or deletion of an entity can only be done when the timestamp matches the one on the storage system. Every change to an entity updates the timestamp as well.

Choose the right key

In the old-fashioned **relational database management systems (RDBMS)**, there are ways to select the right key(s) or composite key(s).

In the world of table storage, it is important to choose the right key for scaling and efficiency purposes. Later on, we will see examples of efficient querying.

Keys for scaling

A single partition can serve at the most 500 operations per second. When we want to be able to go beyond that limit, we need a proper table storage design and have requests distributed across different partitions. Pushing too many requests to a single partition will cause throttling. Requests are throttled when the transaction rate exceeds the partition target, and these requests are "lost". To minimize the amount of throttling, implement back-off policies, and if a lot of throttling happens, you should redesign your partitioning.

We can decide to use the same PartitionKey property for all the entities in our Geotopics table. This enables us to use transactions (described later in this chapter), but the downside is that scaling is limited to one partition server. This is not a good choice where extreme workloads are expected. For geotopia, we expect a lot of topics to be inserted, updated, and deleted throughout the day. Using a single partition is not a viable option for our scenario.

Using a different PartitionKey property for each and every single entity gives us enormous scalability, as the storage system can load balance all requests to different partition servers. Thus, no throttling will occur. The downside of this approach is that querying is not efficient, as a range query will result in a full table scan and we cannot use entity-group transactions. Querying results in scans across different partitions, and when larger result sets are expected, there will be a lot of continuation tokens to take care of. A query that spans across multiple partitions can lead to server-side paging.

For our scenario, it is important to predict which access patterns there will be on our data, as follows:

- For the Geotopics table, at first we decide the username is an appropriate PartitionKey property. During the first version of Geotopia, we need to perform stress tests at the partition level to ensure the partition can provide the desired throughput of entities.

- If the stress test points out that we need to have the ability to handle more than 500 entities per second, we should revise our choice of PartitionKey. We could, for example, split up PartitionKey into more parts. Consider not having JohnDoe as a key, but also add the month to PartitionKey, which causes the entities to spread across multiple partitions throughout the year.

Keys for transactions

Transactions in the world of table storage are all about a group of entities within the same partition that need to be updated, inserted, or deleted atomically. There are a few limitations to entity-group transactions, as follows:

- A transaction can contain at most 100 entities

- The total size of the transaction can be at most 4 MB

- Within the transaction, entities must be unique (meaning, the RowKey property must be unique, as the PartitionKey property is the same)

Let's walk through a situation in the Geotopia scenario. Imagine the `Geotopics` table containing topics/comments/multimedia and the ability to have the recommendations of other users for the geotopic involved. In an ordinary database world, we would choose to have two tables—one containing the actual topics and pointers to multimedia and the other holding the total count of recommendations. Updating these two tables together could be done within a stored procedure, but this is not possible in table storage.

Because table storage is schemaless, it is possible to store different types of entities within the same table. In the `Geotopics` table, topics are stored with `PartitionKey` holding the username, and we can utilize `RowKey`, depending on the type of entity we store. An ordinary geotopic would contain a unique `RowKey` property that is based on a timestamp preceded with the subject. An entity containing the number of recommendations made by other users would have a `RowKey` property containing a timestamp, together with the subject, but also with the username of the person that actually made the recommendation. To differentiate between topics and recommendations, we prefix the `RowKey` property with the type (`T` for topic and `R` for recommendation).

The following table shows some possible entities in the `Geotopics` table:

Entity	PartitionKey	RowKey	Description
Topic	JohnDoe	TFirstPost01022 012134845	An ordinary topic with the subject "FirstPost" posted on February 1
Topic	JohnDoe	TThirdPost01022 012175000	An ordinary topic with the subject "ThirdPost" posted on the same day
Recommendation	JohnDoe	RThirdPost01022 012175000JaneDoe	JaneDoe recommends John's third post
Topic	JaneDoe	TWelcome!01022 012135000	Jane also discovered Geotopia and became a member and posted a "Welcome!" topic
Recommendation	JaneDoe	RWelcome!01022 012135000JohnDoe	John recommended Jane's first post

Because the `PartitionKey` property is the same for all the entities for both topics and recommendations, it is possible to contain create, update, and delete operations in one single transaction. A topic entity also contains the number of recommendations, while single recommendations are stored as well because we want to keep track of who actually made the recommendations. Keeping these entities together in a table in the same partition, we can make sure data is kept consistent and that the number of recommendations is equal to the number of entities containing the users that made the recommendations.

Geotopia data model

Let's take a look at a scenario in our Geotopia space. Currently, we have a storage account named **geotopia**, and we want that storage account to store my structured, NoSQL data. We are going to store typical user data altogether with some of their Facebook profiles and we are going to store geotopics (a message in the system, optionally with an image and/or video).

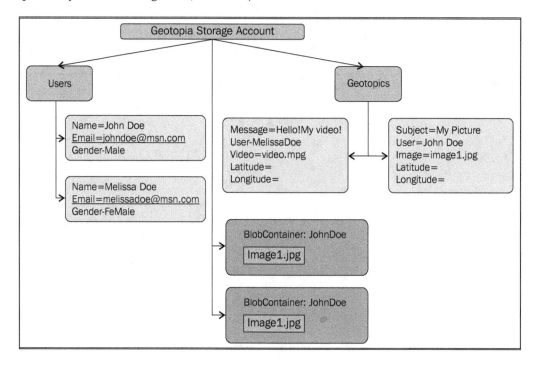

The preceding diagram depicts the initial situation with respect to the data we want to store in the Geotopia space. Users are stored together with some profile information in the user table. The PartitionKey property in the user table is the name of the user, and the RowKey property is not that important as the only important key we have here is the username. Geotopics and multimedia files (references) are stored together with the geolocation in the Geotopics table. The PartitionKey property for this table is again the username, and the RowKey property is the date and time at which the geotopic was entered. By using date and time as RowKey, we can also filter by date ranges. As a best practice, we do not store multimedia files in table storage but in blobs. In this case, to support proper partitioning, we create a blob container for every single user in Geotopia to store their files. The references in the Geotopics table to binary files point to the actual files stored in blob containers.

This data model supports the Geotopia scenario of enabling users to create a topic altogether with the possible location of the topic accompanied with some sort of media file. As a user needs to log in to the Geotopia system, the username is known in this context and correct relationships can be created (a topic has a reference to a user).

The PartitionKey property in the Geotopics table equals the username. This means that all topics posted by a user are kept together on a partition server, enabling fast querying. The RowKey property will be the subject combined with a timestamp that is generated on insert. Blobs are partitioned by the blob name.

Adding an entity

The schema for the Geotopics table is defined as a standard .NET class with some attributes to decorate the class to tell WCF Data Services that the primary key of this class consists of PartitionKey and Rowkey together, as follows:

```
[DataServiceKey("PartitionKey", "RowKey")]
public class Geotopic
{
    public string PartitionKey { get; set;}
    public string RowKey { get; set; }
    public DateTime TimeStamp { get; set; }

    public string UserName { get; set; }
    public string Video { get; set; }
    public string Image { get; set; }
```

```
    public double Latitude { get; set; }
    public double Longitude { get; set; }

    public int Recommendations { get; set; }
}

[DataServiceKey("PartitionKey", "RowKey")]
public class Recommendation
{
    public string PartitionKey { get; set; }
    public string RowKey { get; set; }
    public DateTime TimeStamp { get; set; }
}
```

The following code snippet points out how to create the `Geotopics` table and how
to add an entity to it:

```
//to use local Development Storage the connection string is
//UseDevelopmentStorage=true
//if you want to create and insert on actual WAS use a
//connection string in the format:
//DefaultEndPointsProtocol=https;AccountName=<accountname>
//;AccountKey=//<youraccountkey>

string connectionString = "UseDevelopmentStorage=true";
CloudStorageAccount account = CloudStorageAccount.
Parse(connectionString);

//now create the table if it's not there yet
CloudTableClient client = account.CreateCloudTableClient();
Client.CreateTableIfNotExist("Geotopics");

TableServiceContext context = client.GetDataServiceContext();

context.AddObject("Geotopics", new Geotopic("......."));

//also add a recommendation to the table
context.AddObject("Geotopics", new Recommendation("......."));

//save changes to the underlying table and also perform
//retries if needed.
context.SaveChangesWithRetries();
```

Try to avoid creating tables at runtime, as it has a performance penalty (because you need to check if it exists already). Creating tables is typically a matter of configuration and must be done before you deploy your application.

In the previous code fragment, two entity types were added to the same table.

To select an entity from the table, you can use the following code snippet:

```
TableServiceContext queryctx = client.GetDataServiceContext();

//use some Linq to get all the Geotopics from JohnDoe
//the result set will contain all topics and might even have
//some recommendations in it

Var geotopics = (from geotopic in queryctx.CreateQuery<Geotopic>("Geo
topics")
Where geotopic.PartitionKey="JohnDoe"
Select geotopic).AsTableServiceQuery<Geotopic>();
foreach (Geotopic geotopic in geotopics)
{
    geotopic.Subject = "generated by code";
    //the UpdateObject call will check the Etag value and see
//if it matches with the entity in the storage system on
//disk, the system only updates if it matches
    queryctx.UpdateObject(geotopic);
}
// using the batch option in the SaveChanges call makes sure
// that all the changes done in the foreach loop are treated
// a single transaction
Queryctx.SaveChangesWithRetries(SaveChangesOptions.Batch);
```

 Always create a new DataServiceContext class for a different operation.

Saving changes has different options, as shown in the following table:

SaveChangesOptions	Description
None	Every single pending create, update, or delete operation is treated as an individual request to the storage service. If an operation fails, an exception is thrown and other pending operations are not executed.
Batch	All operations, done within a certain context, are treated as a single transaction. Either all operations fail or all operations succeed.
ContinueOnError	Similar to None, although no exception is thrown on a failure and all other pending operations are still executed. For example, if 100 entities are updated and update number 10 fails, the result is that 99 entities are changed.
ReplaceOnUpdate	When entities are updated, they are updated in a "merge" fashion. Meaning, only those properties are updated that are sent in the request. Other properties are not changed. Null values are ignored.

Querying

Tables can be queried using the LINQ statements, and query results are always sorted on the primary key (PartitionKey and RowKey). You can use operators on all properties of the entity, but remember that for performance reasons, it's best to use at least the PartitionKey property. If you don't use this key, all partitions need to be queried, including a complete scan. Using the PartitionKey property (which is indexed in the partition map) enables the storage service to immediately point to the right partition.

There are a few categories in typical queries for table storage.

An example of queries that return one exact entity by specifying PartitionKey and RowKey is as follows:

```
var geotopic = (from topic in context.CreateQuery<Geotopic>
                ("Geotopics")
                Where topic.PartitionKey == "JohnDoe" &&
                topic.RowKey == "MyPicture09032012145830"
                Select topic);
```

This query returns exactly one entity, the topics regarding a picture John Doe uploaded on March 9, at 14:58:30.

Be aware that if the entity does not exist, a `DataServiceQueryException` exception is thrown.

Secondly, there are queries that return an entity or entities, which involve scanning a range.

An example of queries returning results from a single partition (row range scan), is as follows:

```
Var topics = (from topic in context.CreateQuery<Geotopic>
    ("Geotopics")
    where topic.PartitionKey = "JohnDoe" &&
    topic.Row.CompareTo("MyPicture01012012120000") >= 0 &&
    topic.Row.CompareTo("MyPicture01022012120000") <= 0 &&
    topic.Image <> ""
    select topic);
```

This query scans within the partition named `JohnDoe` and selects all the entities that involve an image but are also uploaded to Geotopia in the month of January 2012.

An example of queries returning results that span multiple partitions is as follows:

```
Var topics = (from topic in context.CreateQuery<Geotopic>
    ("Geotopics")
    Where topic.PartionKey.CompareTo("JohnDoe") >= 0 ||
    topic.PartitionKey.CompareTo("JaneDoe") >= 0 &&
    topic.Recommendations > 100
    select topic);
```

This query scans two different partitions, which belong to `JaneDoe` and `JohnDoe`, and returns only those geotopics that have a high recommendation (above 100).

An example of queries returning all entities in all partitions of a table is as follows:

```
Var topics = (from topic in context.CreateQuery<Geotopic>
    ("Geotopics")
    where topic.Recommendations > 500
    select topic);
```

This query can be a very slow one, as it is looking up all the geotopics in the `Geotopics` table that have very high recommendations (above 500). As no `PartitionKey` property is part of the LINQ query, the storage system needs to scan all partitions that belong to this storage table. In our Geotopia scenario, this can potentially be thousands and thousands of partitions, as every single user has a unique `PartitionKey`.

Obviously, queries that return a single entity are the most efficient ones with the highest performance, as both the PartitionKey and RowKey properties are provided. This lookup is comparable with the clustered indexes from the SQL Server. The performance of the range queries will vary depending on the number of entities that need to be scanned together with the number of partitions.

Query	Efficiency and performance
Provide PartitionKey and RowKey.	It looks up a single entity and is the most efficient type.
Provide PartitionKey and a range regarding RowKey (for example, subject starting with "S").	It involves a single partition but needs to scan a number of entities within the range. More entities result in lower performance.
Provide a range regarding PartitionKey (geotopics from all users that have a name with a certain length).	Its performance depends on the number of entities available in the different partitions that are involved in the query.
Provide only a range on RowKey (for example, get all the subjects between two dates).	It's inefficient, as it scans the entire table looking for the matching RowKey properties because no PartitionKey is provided.

LINQ is not optimized yet for scanning just two partitions. This will result in a full table scan (although you would not expect this). A viable workaround is to merge the separate result sets on the client side.

Continuation tokens

If a query is fired to the table and the query did not return the full set of results (this can be the case, for example when you call Take(5) to get only five rows), you can use the continuation token to make another call to the table and use the continuation token to get the next set of results. This can be very powerful to make your user interface perform well and only get those results that can be displayed on the screen (rather than getting hundreds of records). Continuation tokens are provided in case a result set contains more than 1,000 entities, when a partition boundary is crossed, when the query times out (5 seconds) and returns only a part of the required result set, or when Take(x) is used to provide the client to use pagination.

Together with the first partial results, the response also included a continuation token as part of the custom headers.

```
x-ms-continuation-NextPartitionKey
x-ms-continuation-NewRowKey
```

To retrieve the next partial results, you need to include these continuation tokens in the request as well.

Apart from accessing resources on Windows Azure storage by using the .NET storage SDK as we did before, it is also possible to use REST to make the call. The following line of code shows what a plain HTTP request looks like:

```
http://geotopia.table.core.windows.net/Geotopics?PartitionKey=
"JohnDoe"&NextPartitionKey="JohnDoe"&NextRowKey="01022012120000"
```

 Always expect continuation tokens inside your application and implement logic to handle partial result sets.

In the Geotopia case, a few dominant keys are identified. Obviously, `PartitionKey` is a dominant key as it contains the name of the user (for example `JohnDoe`). The `RowKey` property can be used to concatenate two or even more values. First of all, the actual date on which the topic was entered is combined with the subject of the topic. In this case, all topics are sorted according to `PartitionKey`, date, and subject:

```
var recentTopics = from topic in context.CreateQuery<Geotopic>
("Geotopics")
                   Where topics.PartitionKey="JohnDoe" &&
                   topic.RowKey.CompareTo("01012012") >=0
                   && topic.RowKey.CompareTo("01022012") >=0
                   select topic;
```

This LINQ query returns all the topics that John Doe posted in January 2012.

Best practices

The `DataServiceContext` class is not thread safe and it is recommended to create a new `DataServiceContext` class for every different operation. This also keeps the context from tracking lots of queries and inserts, updates, and deletions, because `DataServiceContext` keeps track of the `AddObject` and `AttachTo` operations.

Catch InvalidOperationException ("Context is already tracking a different entity with same resource URI") when calling AttachTo on an entity that has already been tracked by another context.

A query where PartitionKey and RowKey are provided (which should return only one entity) throws a DataServiceQueryException exception (Resource not found) when the entity does not exist. You can override this behavior by setting DataServiceContext.IgnoreResourceNotFoundException, which results in no exception.

Keep in mind how a single partition acts when a lot of entities are requested.

Use asynchronous operations rather than their synchronous counterparts. Asynchronous operations offer benefits when it comes to CPU and memory utilization.

Experiment with the VM size and number of VMs of your worker roles and web roles that touch your underlying storage infrastructure to find the best performing configuration. Set up a load-test infrastructure to determine the optimum instance size.

Select PartitionKey for efficient queries. Entities are sorted in ascending order of PartitionKey and RowKey. Carefully determine the keys to use in the different tables. Perform the following steps to do so:

1. First, decide which properties are important for the table. In our case, these are the name of the user (for example, JohnDoe) and the subject, together with a timestamp. It is likely that there will be a lot of querying on these properties, for example, getting all the geotopics that John Doe entered into the system during the month of December.

2. Find potential keys from these important properties.

3. Determine which one is the most important one and promote that property to be PartitionKey (if more properties are equally important, consider concatenating these).

4. Pick the next important property as RowKey (if more important properties still exist, concatenate these as well to be the RowKey property).

Table storage summary

Tables in Windows Azure provide a scalable and durable way of storing structured data, organized in rows and columns. Scaling inside WAS is based on partitions, and load balancing takes place at a partition level. Entities with the same PartitionKey property belong to the same partition on the disk, so choosing the right key is very important to designing a good data model.

Querying tables in WAS depends heavily on choosing the right keys upfront.

- Transactions can help to speed up performance and enhance throughput. Grouping and uploading large numbers of entities increases throughput and is cheaper than uploading on an entity-by-entity basis.

- When your solution demands a high level of throughput, spread your entities across several partitions. Consider using different VM sizes to enhance I/O or scale up to have, for example, multiple worker role instances divide the actual "upload work".

- The most efficient queries are those that return a single entity or a small range of entities.

- Use asynchronous operations for better scaling capabilities.

Queue usage

This section focuses on the queuing facility of the storage service. As described previously in this chapter, queues provide a reliable delivery of messages.

A closer look at the queue

In the following table, the characteristics of Windows Azure queues are listed:

Characteristic	Description
Names must be lower case	Using uppercase or lowercase characters do not affect operations on queues, though the case is preserved by the storage service.
Names are at least three and at most 63 characters long	
Names can only contain alphanumeric characters	
No ordering guarantee; based on best-effort FIFO	It is nondeterministic whether or not the messages are sorted in a FIFO order.
Delivered at least once	A message is delivered at least once. This implicitly means that it can happen that the same message appears on the queue more than once. To handle this phenomenon, your message processing needs to be idempotent (We'll see this later in this chapter).

Characteristic	Description
Locking and leasing	Default locked for 30 seconds. The maximum lock time is 7 days.
Maximum message size	64 KB.
Maximum queue size	The size of a queue is limited by the maximum size of a storage account, meaning 100 TB.
Available protocols	REST over HTTP(S), managed .NET API (storage client), Java API, PHP API, and Node.js API.
Maximum throughput	500 operations per second.
Latency	Average latency of 10 ms.
Authentication	Symmetric key or Shared Access Signatures.

Creating a queue

Creating a queue works in a similar way to creating tables. You need a
`CloudStorage` account and, instead of `CloudTableClient`, `CloudQueueClient`,
as shown in the following code snippet:

```
//to use local Development Storage the connection string would
//UseDevelopmentStorage=true
//if you want to create and insert on actual WAS use a
//connection string in the format:
//DefaultEndPointsProtocol=https;AccountName=<accountname>
//;AccountKey=//<youraccountkey>

string connectionString = "UseDevelopmentStorage=true";
CloudStorageAccount account = CloudStorageAccount.
Parse(connectionString);
//now create the table if it's not there yet
CloudQueueClient client = account.CreateQueueClient();
CloudQueue queue = client.GetQueueReference("topicsworkload");
Client.CreateQueueIfNotExists();
```

The preceding code fragment gets a reference to the designated queue and ensures the queue actually exists. After this, we can enqueue and dequeue messages.

Inserting a message

To insert a message in a queue for further processing, you need to create a `CloudQueueMessage` class, which can be a `byte[]` or a `string` datatypes:

```
//to use loca Development Storage the connection string would
//UseDevelopmentStorage=true
//if you want to create and insert on actual WAS use a
//connection string in the format:
//DefaultEndPointsProtocol=https;AccountName=<accountname>
//;AccountKey=//<youraccountkey>

string connectionString = "UseDevelopmentStorage=true";
CloudStorageAccount account = CloudStorageAccount.
Parse(connectionString);

//now create the table if it's not there yet
CloudQueueClient client = account.CreateQueueClient();
CloudQueue queue = client.GetQueueReference("topicsworkload");
Client.CreateQueueIfNotExists();

CloudQueueMessage msg = new CloudQueueMessage(
String.Format("{0};{1};{2}", topic.PartitionKey, topic.RowKey, topic.
Video);

Queue.AddMessage(msg);
```

In the preceding code fragment, we created a message from a Geotopia topic. This is only done for topics containing multimedia; other topics containing only text are inserted directly into table storage. A message is stored in the queue containing the `PartitionKey` property, the `RowKey` property, and the URI to the video.

The following diagram describes the whole scenario and shows how the workload is divided between worker and web roles:

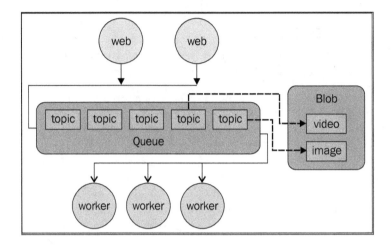

Workloads (topics) are entered by the web roles hosting, for example, Silverlight or ASP.NET clients. John Doe creates a topic, types in his message, and uploads a video.

What happens under the hood:

- The actual video is uploaded to blob storage in the `JohnDoe` container
- A message is added to the queue
- Worker roles in the background pick up the message and start processing the topic
- An entity is added to the `Geotopics` table with `JohnDoe` as `PartitionKey` by a worker role
- The entity contains the correct reference to the video uploaded in blob storage
- A thumbnail is created from the video to display a preview on the Geotopia canvas
- The entity in the table is updated to store the URI of the thumbnail

Retrieving a message

The following code fragment shows how to retrieve a single message from a queue and how to delete it:

```
//to use local Development Storage the connection string would
//UseDevelopmentStorage=true
```

```
//if you want to create and insert on actual WAS use a
//connection
string in the format:
//DefaultEndPointsProtocol=https;AccountName=<accountname>
//;AccountKey=//<youraccountkey>

string connectionString = "UseDevelopmentStorage=true";
CloudStorageAccount account = CloudStorageAccount.
Parse(connectionString);

//now create the queue if it's not there yet
CloudQueueClient client = account.CreateQueueClient();
CloudQueue queue = client.GetQueueReference("topicsworkload");
Client.CreateQueueIfNotExists();

CloudQueueMessage msg = queue.GetMessage(TimeSpan.FromMinutes(1));

//do the processing of the message, creating the thumbnail and
//updating the record in Table Storage
Queue.DeleteMessage(msg);
```

Calling `GetMessage` returns the next message from the queue. The message will be invisible to others. By default, this invisibility lasts for 30 seconds, but in our case we override this to 1 minute. Processing a video and creating a thumbnail might take longer. When the actual work is done, the message is deleted by calling `DeleteMessage`. The reason for these two steps is to prevent a message from becoming unhandled. For example, the worker role instance processing the message fails during the processing. After the failure, the visibility timeout expires at some time and makes the message visible again for other worker role instances.

Messages can also be retrieved in a batch (with a maximum of 32), minimizing transaction costs. In the following code fragment, 10 messages are retrieved in a batch and processed one by one. Setting the visibility timeout to 5 minutes means that all 10 messages get this visibility interval. When the 5 minutes are passed, every message that has not been deleted becomes visible in the queue again.

```
foreach (CloudQueueMessage message in queue.GetMessages(20, TimeSpan.
FromMinutes(5))

{

    ProcessMessage(message);
    queue.DeleteMessage(message);
}
```

In the preceding code fragment, a message is added to a queue and dequeued twice. When `msg1` is deleted, the program will throw an exception, because the message is simply not there anymore (because the time span of 30 seconds has not passed yet).

```
CloudQueueClient client = account.CreateCloudQueueClient();

CloudQueue queue = client.GetQueueReference("queue");

queue.CreateIfNotExist();

CloudQueueMessage msg = new CloudQueueMessage("Message 1");

queue.AddMessage(msg);

CloudQueueMessage msg1 = queue1.GetMessage
(TimeSpan.FromSeconds(1));      // invisible for 1 second
Thread.Sleep(2000);            // wait 2 seconds
CloudQueueMessage msg2 = queue.GetMessage
(TimeSpan.FromSeconds(30));

queue.DeleteMessage(msg1);
```

The `GetMessage` operation causes the message to "disappear" from the queue as long as the visibility time span is not elapsed. A consecutive call to `GetMessage` will cause a null value to be returned, if the queue contains no more messages.

Every `GetMessage` or `GetMessage` operation will increase the `DequeueCount` property of the specific message.

Queue operations

To get the depth of a queue (that is, the length of the queue, expressed in messages) you can call the following function:

```
CloudQueueClient client = account.CreateQueueClient();
CloudQueue queue = client.GetQueueReference("topicsworkload");
int messageCount = queue.RetrieveApproximateMessageCount();
```

> The number of messages in the queue is an approximation, because messages can be added or deleted after you get the count. To minimize the transactions to storage, you can read the `ApproximateMessageCount` property, which holds the last value retrieved by `RetrieveApproximateMessageCount`.

Removing a queue is a fairly easy exercise, as follows:

```
CloudQueueClient client = account.CreateQueueClient();
CloudQueue queue = client.GetQueueReference("topicsworkload");
Queue.Delete();
```

Beware that removing a queue means that all the messages currently in the queue are deleted as well. This action cannot be undone.

The following table lists all the members of the `CloudQueue` class:

Member	Explanation and usage
ServiceClient	The `CloudQueueClient` object.
Name	The queue name.
URI	The URI of the queue.
Attributes	Attributes of the queue, including custom metadata.

Metadata	Gets or sets metadata in the queue (name-value):
	
	`queue.Metadata.Add(new`
	`NameValueCollection()`
	`{`
	`{"Description","A queue is a queue"},`
	`{"CreatedBy","riccardo becker"},`
	`{"CreatedOn",Datetime.Now.ToString()}`
	`});`
	`queue.SetMetadata();`

ApproximateMessageCount	Gets an indication of the total number of messages in the queue.
EncodeMessage	Gets or sets the value if Base64 encoding is applied when queuing or dequeuing.
AddMessage()	Adds a message to the queue.
Clear()	Clears all the messages from the queue.
Create()	Creates the queue.
CreateIfNotExists()	Creates the queue if it does not exist yet.
Delete()	Deletes the queue.
DeleteMessage()	Removes a message from the queue.
Exists()	Indicates whether the queue exists.
FetchAttributes()	Fetches the attributes.
GetMessage()	Gets a message from the queue.

Member	Explanation and usage
GetMessages()	Gets a list of messages from the queue.
PeekMessage()	Peeks a message (preview) without dequeuing it.
PeekMessages()	Peeks a list of messages from the queue.
RetrieveApproximate MessageCount()	Retrieves an indication of the number of messages in the queue. It also sets the ApproximateMessageCount property.
SetMetadata()	Sets the metadata.
UpdateMessage()	Updates a message in the queue.

There are also asynchronous variants of AddMessage, Clear, Create, CreateIfNotExist, Delete, DeleteMessage, Exists, FetchAttributes, GetMessage, PeekMessage, SetMetadata, and UpdateMessage.

In the following table are the relevant members of the CloudQueueClient:

Member	Explanation and usage
RetryPolicy	The default RetryPolicy property for requests made by the service client. ```client.RetryPolicy = RetryPolicies.RetryExponential(10, TimeSpan.FromSeconds(2.0));``` This code snippet makes the service client retry ten times and sets a multiplier in an exponential back-off scheme.
TimeOut	Sets the server timeout.
Credentials	The credentials used for requests made through the service client.
GetQueue Reference()	Gets a reference to the designated queue. ```CloudQueue queue1 = client.GetQueueReference("queue");```

Member	Explanation and usage
`GetService Properties()`	Gets the properties, including storage analytics.
| | ```
ServiceProperties props = client.
GetServiceProperties();
ServiceProperties props = client.
GetServiceProperties();

props.Logging.LoggingOperations =
LoggingOperations.All;
props.Logging.RetentionDays = 30;

props.Metrics.MetricsLevel = MetricsLevel.
ServiceAndApi;
props.Metrics.RetentionDays = 30;
          client.SetServiceProperties(props);
``` |
| | Sets the operations to be logged and the retention days (days to keep the logs). |
| `ListQueues()` | Enumerable collections of all the queues available in the storage account. Optionally, you can add a prefix to filter queues. |

Idempotency

As we know that it is possible that the same message shows up multiple times in a queue and that "maximum once" is not guaranteed, we need to make sure our code is idempotent. Also, multiple worker roles can be busy processing the same message when the timeout of a message has passed.

That the system is idempotent means that the system remains in the same state or produces the same result when the same message is processed multiple times.

There are a few ways to achieve idempotency. You could maintain a table with message IDs and a status per message telling that the message is being processed already. This can prevent multiple worker roles from processing the same message, but this is not true idempotent software. It prevents the processing of the same message more than once.

Design and build your application in a way that processing the same message multiple times results in the same state.
```

Using blobs

In this section, we will learn how to use blob storage and how to upload and download files from blob storage. One of the requirements for Geotopia is that users must have the ability to send each other large files and be notified through Facebook or e-mail, for example. The uploaded file is stored in blob storage and the unique URI is sent to the receiver. This section contains snippets of code that demonstrate how to upload, download, and use the parallel abilities of the .NET framework.

File transfer

The Geotopia domain needs a feature that enables users to upload files such as images and video to a central place where they are stored and made available for other users.

To enable this, we have created a class called `AzureBlobUtil`, which enables uploading blobs to a designated container and downloading files to a local disk.

The following code snippet demonstrates how the `AzureBlobUtil` class can be utilized:

```
AzureBlobUtil _blobUtil = new AzureBlobUtil();

CloudStorageAccount AccountFileTransfer = CloudStorageAccount.Parse("U
seDevelopmentStorage=true");

//report back the progress of the upload
_blobUtil.TransferProgressChanged += new EventHandler<AzureBlobUtil.
BlobTransferProgressChangedEventArgs>
                (_blobUtil_TransferProgressChanged);

Uri blobUri = _blobUtil.UploadBlob(@"D:\Users\Public\Videos\Sample
Videos\Wildlife.wmv", AccountFileTransfer, "riccardobecker");

//send URI as message to facebook recipient....

Stream stream = _blobUtil.DownloadBlobAsStream(AccountFileTransfer,
blobUri.ToString());

_blobUtil.DownloadBlobAsFile(AccountFileTransfer, blobUri.ToString(),
@"D:\Users\Public\Videos\Sample Videos\Copy of Wildlife.wmv");
```

The code snippet uploads a video from the local disk to blob storage (in this case, to `DevelopmentStorage`) and downloads it again.

Uploading a file

The following code snippet demonstrates how to use the `Parallel` class to upload files. The `Parallel` class is available since C# 4.0 and allows us to enable operations such as, executing each loop in parallel, making use of the cores available on the computer (if any), and so on.

```
public Uri UploadBlob(byte[] fileContent, CloudStorageAccount account,
string facebookName)
{
BlobTransferProgressChangedEventArgs eArgs = null;
CloudBlobClient blobclient = account.CreateCloudBlobClient();

CloudBlobContainer container = blobclient.GetContainerReference
(facebookName);

container.CreateIfNotExist();
    CloudBlockBlob blob = container.GetBlockBlobReference(Guid.
NewGuid().ToString());

HashSet<string> blocklist = new HashSet<string>();
    double bytesUploaded = 0;

    #region parallel
Parallel.ForEach(GetFileBlocks(fileContent), item =>
    {
blob.PutBlock(item.Id, new MemoryStream(item.Content, false), null);

blocklist.Add(item.Id);

        bytesUploaded += item.Content.Length;
int progress = (int)((double)bytesUploaded / fileContent.Length *
100);
eArgs = new BlobTransferProgressChangedEventArgs(bytesUploaded,
fileContent.Length, progress,
        CalculateSpeed(bytesUploaded), null);

//raise the ProgressChanged event
OnTaskProgressChanged((BlobTransferProgressChangedEventArgs) eArgs);
}
    );
    #region

var blockList = blob.DownloadBlockList(BlockListingFilter.All);
```

```
    // sort the blocks by their offset. Because using Parallel
    //makes it undeterministic what the order will be
        // of the uploaded blocks
        var orderedBlockList = blockList.OrderBy(block =>
        {
        var currentOffset = this.DecodeOffset(block.Name);
            return currentOffset;
        });

        //commit the blocks in the right order
    blob.PutBlockList(orderedBlockList.Select(p => p.Name));

    return blob.Uri;
    }
```

The GetFileBlocks function is listed in the preceding code snippet. It gets the file and chops it into pieces of a maximum size. For each file block, a Parallel task is fired. The following screenshot shows that all my four cores are busy while uploading the file:

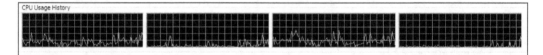

Downloading the file

The UploadBlob method returns the URI to the binary stored in blob storage. The following code snippet shows how to download the binary into a stream and save it to disk:

```
    Stream stream = DownloadBlobAsStream(account, blobUri);
    if (stream != null)
    {
    FileStream fileStream = File.Create(FileName);
    stream.Position = 0;
        stream.CopyTo(fileStream);
        fileStream.Close();
        return FileName;
    }
```

This core functionality will be at the heart of Geotopia. It enables users to upload their multimedia files into a geotopic or allows them to share files with friends.

Storage best practices

There are a lot of best practices for using blobs.

When uploading blocks or page blobs, always make sure you set the correct content type. This is crucial for clients to handle the downloaded content correctly. Setting the content type to say "video/MP4" ensures that the receiving client will correctly handle the content.

To minimize the number of storage transactions and maximize the availability of blobs (which requires a lot of money), make sure you use the `Cache-Control` header properly. Setting the `CacheControl` property ensures that static content such as HTML or pictures are cached on the client and consecutive calls to the static resource with the cache expiration will prevent clients from touching storage and costing money.

Parallelize as much as possible. When you upload large files to blob storage, use multithreading or the Parallel functionality in C# 4.0.

Pick the right blob type. Streaming contents? Choose a block blob and parallelize the upload and download. Writing multiple times to blobs and updating parts of the file? Use page blob, which allows you to update parts of the blob.

If a lot of users try to access and download the same blob, they might suffer from delays, as requests may be throttled by Windows Azure. This can be avoided by creating snapshots of the blob and offering these to users.

Create multiple snapshots and offer them to the consumers of your blob data. Snapshots are for free (as long as they are identical to the original).

Use **content delivery network (CDN)**. To decrease latency and have customers all over the world experience a top-class, high-performance delivery, make sure you check the **Enable CDN** checkbox on your storage account or hosted service.

In the following screenshot, CDN is set on a storage account named **helloworldstorage**:

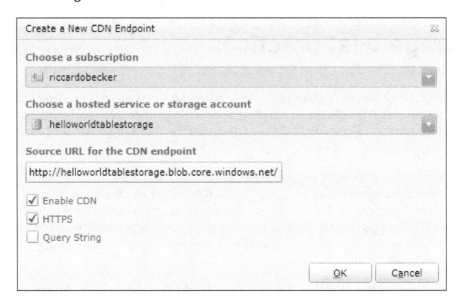

After clicking on **OK**, it can take up to an hour to have the CDN enabled worldwide. When a CDN is propagated, all public containers that are anonymously available are cached via the CDN.

The storage assets can be accessed through the ordinary `http://helloworldtablestorage.blob.core.windows.net` but also via the CDN URL — `http://az334305.vo.msecnd.net`. The `az334305` identifier is created by the platform. The URL might be different between the two, but all the locations of the containers and blobs remain the same.

Use exponential backoff

When you are reading and writing large amounts of data to your storage account and the underlying partition cannot handle your requests anymore, you will receive 503 responses (server busy, which is quite true in this case). Your application should be robust and resilient to this kind of limit and use so-called exponential backoff when retrying. **Exponential backoff** means that you increase the amount of time between retries to give the partition some time to breathe and thus smoothen the spikes in traffic to the partition. Frequent 503s mean that the application needs other approaches regarding partitioning.

In case of blobs timing out, consider using CDN. In case of tables, consider using a more narrow `PartitionKey` property (for example, partition on a customer level and not on a country level). In case of queues, increase message size and group several messages in one queue, or even better and less complex, use different queues (for example, per country level in your application, instead of one global queue receiving all your purchase orders).

Summary

In this chapter, we have learned different features from the Windows Azure Storage service. We saw how to build, operate, and manage blobs, tables, and queues, their underlying architecture, and the best practices on these subjects. We have also learned the architecture of Windows Azure Storage and how this architecture helps in maintaining availability. We learned the importance of proper partitioning and how this helps us in building responsive and scalable applications.

The next chapter digs deeper into the SQL database, the cloud variant of Microsoft SQL Server. The chapter describes how to set up and provision a SQL database, how to manage it, and how to set up a neat feature called Data Sync.

5
SQL Database

"SQL Azure is of great value to 3M because it takes the database management piece off our plate."

— Jim Graham, 3M Technical Manager

This chapter describes the cloud variant of Microsoft SQL Server. It demonstrates how to set up and provision a Windows Azure SQL Database instance server and how to manage it. It shows how to connect to SQL Azure databases and why an SQL Database is required by the Geotopia application.

Overview

Microsoft Windows Azure SQL Database is the cloud equivalent of Microsoft SQL Server (with some differences) and runs in one of the datacenters all around the world.

SQL Database and Microsoft SQL Server do have a lot of similarities but also some important differences. They both rely on the TDS interface for using T-SQL statements. Because of this similarity, it is fairly easy to switch from your traditional on-premises SQL Server to a SQL database instance on the cloud. Like other Windows Azure services, SQL Database is also a managed service that releases you from the administration burden. SQL Database is exposed as a logical database, and any physical hardware plumbing is done by the platform. Obviously, you are still responsible for managing the actual databases, logins, and users.

As with Windows Azure Storage, databases on Windows Azure are replicated automatically to uphold maximum availability. Also, load balancing and failover is part of the deal. SQL Database maintains three copies of a database inside one datacenter, to preserve availability. If it is required to replicate databases between multiple datacenters, you can set up Data Sync, which is also a Windows Azure service. This concept is explained later on in this chapter.

Setting up SQL databases

The only prerequisite for creating SQL databases on Windows Azure is that you need a Windows Azure account. When you are logged in to your `manage.windowsazure.com` portal, you see the **SQL Databases** tab on the left-hand side of the screen. Selecting that option displays the following screen:

Clicking on the **Create A SQL Database** option takes you to the next screen. On this screen, we can specify the name for our database, the edition, the maximum size, the collation, and the server. The **SERVER** option enables the creation of the database on an existing server or on a new server. In this case, we choose on a new server since we have not configured anything yet.

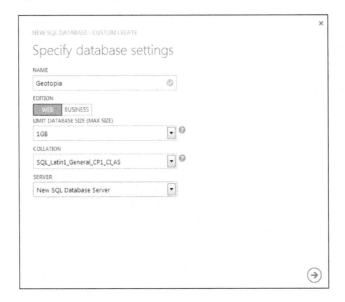

Clicking on **Next** will take us to the following screen, where we need to specify server settings:

SQL Database only supports login by username/password on the database level. For every database, you need to configure a new combination. **REGION** is an important setting, because this setting determines where the database is provisioned. Make sure you check the **Allow Windows Azure services to access the server** checkbox, if you want your cloud services to connect to the SQL database.

 Pick the location of your server carefully and use the same region as where your hosted services that use the database remain. This will save you bandwidth charges!

Guidelines

When moving to Windows Azure, it is important to keep in mind that there are certain guidelines and limitations. The following table shows a detailed description:

Guideline	Description
Drivers, libraries, and protocols	The following drivers and protocols can be used:

The following drivers and protocols can be used:

- .NET data provider for SQL Server from the .NET 3.5 framework SP1 or later
- Entity Framework, .NET 3.5 SP1 or later
- SQL Server 2008 R2 Native Client ODBC driver
- SQL Server 2008 Driver for PHP Version 1.1 or later
- SQL Server JDBC Driver 3.0
- Only TCP/IP connections
- Only port 1433

Guideline	Description
Migration	SSIS and the bulk copy utility (bcp.exe) can be used together with the SqlBulkCopy class and general INSERT scripts. RESTORE and attaching to a database is not supported.
SQL agents and jobs	SQL Database does not support agents and/or jobs.
Transactions	Opening multiple connections to different databases and using them within a TransactionScope class is not supported.
Database sizes	Every SQL Azure server can contain 149 databases (150 with the master included). Selecting an edition will set the MAXSIZE property and reaching this maximum size will disable write actions. However, you can still read from the database.
Firewall	SQL Database is only available through TCP on port 1433. This means that your local firewall or proxy must allow outbound traffic on this port. You also need to configure the firewall settings in SQL Database, as shown in the following screenshot:

Selecting the option to allow Windows Azure services to access this SQL Azure server will automatically add a new firewall rule called **MicrosoftServices**. You need this rule to enable your hosted services to connect to this server.

When you want to connect from your local SQL Server Management Studio, you also need to add a rule that matches your current IP address, in order to be able to connect. This is a preventive security measure and locks down the databases initially. Every client that wants to connect to the database must be explicitly configured in the firewall rules.

You can also use the stored procedures, firewall_rules, sp_set_firewall_rule, and sp_delete_firewall_rule, to configure the firewall settings.

Guideline	Description
Encryption	Communication between a SQL database and the outside world always requires SQL encryption.
Authentication	Only SQL Server authentication is allowed (no integrated security).
USE command	The T-SQL command, USE, to switch to databases is not supported in SQL Database. You need to create a connection string to connect directly to a different database. Connections in SQL Database are connections on a database level and not on a server level.

Go to `http://msdn.microsoft.com/en-us/library/windowsazure/ee336241.aspx`, to get an overview of all the differences and similarities between SQL Database and SQL Server.

Best practices

This section describes best practices with respect to the use of SQL Database and contains some code snippets and walkthroughs on how to implement these best practices.

Encryption and security

Encryption within Windows Azure SQL Database is the responsibility of the application, as it does not support the data encryption mechanisms for data that resides on the SQL database.

Obviously, it is not a good security approach to store passwords in source code. Store all your secrets encrypted in configuration files.

Encryption demo

To use encryption from your web or worker roles, use Pkcs12 Protected Configuration Provider, since the standard protected configuration providers in the .NET framework, for example, `RsaProtectedConfigurationProvider`, is not supported on the Windows Azure platform. If you connect to your instances of Windows Azure SQL Database from applications running on your own datacenter, it is still recommended that you use the configuration providers from the .NET framework.

To use Pkcs12 Protected Configuration Provider, you need to download it from `http://archive.msdn.microsoft.com/pkcs12protectedconfg` and open it with Visual Studio 2010. Compile and build the sources, and an installer is created and copied to the `Installer` folder. Run the `setup.exe` file that is located in this `Release` folder. After running this setup, the configuration provider is added to your **Global Assembly Cache (GAC)** and is ready for use.

To enable encryption, we need a certificate. Open a Visual Studio command prompt and perform the following steps to generate the certificate and make it available in your environment:

1. Type the following command on the command prompt and provide a strong password:

    ```
    makecert -r -pe -n "CN=Geotopia" -sky exchange "geotopia.cer" -sv
    "geotopia.pvk"

    pvk2pfx -pvk "Geotopia.pvk" -spc "Geotopia.cer" -pfx "Geotopia.
    pfx" -pi <password>
    ```

2. Import the public key into your local certificate store by starting the Microsoft Management Console, going to the **Certificates** snap-in, and importing the newly created certificate in the personal store.

3. In Visual Studio, add the certificate to the appropriate web or worker role. In this case, we will add it to the worker role, because that is the one which will be connecting to the database. You can upload the certificate to the worker role in the Windows Azure portal.

4. Add a reference in your designated project (`Geotopia.Processor` worker role, in my case) to the `PKCS12ProtectedConfigurationProvider.dll` assembly. Set the `Copy Local` property to `true`, as this assembly is needed in the package that will be deployed to Windows Azure.

5. Add the custom protected configuration provider to your configuration file. (`app.config` or `web.config`). Your configuration file should look like the following code snippet:

```
<configProtectedData>
  <providers>
    <add name="Pkcs12Provider" thumbprint="▬▬▬▬▬▬▬▬▬▬▬▬"
         type="Pkcs12ProtectedConfigurationProvider.Pkcs12ProtectedConfigurationProvider, PKCS12Protect
  </providers>
</configProtectedData>
<connectionStrings>
  <add name="GeotopiaDatabase" connectionString ="Server=tcp:▬▬▬▬.database.windows.net,1433;Datab
</connectionStrings>
```

6. Open the Visual Studio 2010 command prompt and go to the folder where the configuration file is located. If you have an `app.config` file, you need to rename it to `web.config` first, as `aspnet_regiis.exe` only works with `web.config` files. Run the following command:

    ```
    aspnet_regiis -pef "connectionStrings" "." -prov "Pkcs12Provider"
    ```

    Rename the `web.config` file to `app.config`.

7. Open the configuration file, and you can verify that the `connectionStrings` section is encrypted, as follows:

```
<connectionStrings configProtectionProvider="CustomProvider">
 <EncryptedData Type="http://www.w3.org/2001/04/xmlenc#Element"
  xmlns="http://www.w3.org/2001/04/xmlenc#">
  <EncryptionMethod Algorithm="http://www.w3.org/2001/04/xmlenc#aes192-cbc" />
  <KeyInfo xmlns="http://www.w3.org/2000/09/xmldsig#">
   <EncryptedKey xmlns="http://www.w3.org/2001/04/xmlenc#">
    <EncryptionMethod Algorithm="http://www.w3.org/2001/04/xmlenc#rsa-1_5" />
    <KeyInfo xmlns="http://www.w3.org/2000/09/xmldsig#">
     <KeyName>rsaKey</KeyName>
    </KeyInfo>
    <CipherData>
     <CipherValue>Uu1h3ru3bnVyQ48ddb9+oGUN9l/ocQe4B/9oiiZqVYvgAkgJmTXgm6946JVvdFz/NAcHgWTYq84aN3TTSLIbyOZu
    </CipherData>
   </EncryptedKey>
  </KeyInfo>
  <CipherData>
   <CipherValue>2b+50g+Ff0wktd/r9rkTgXiPGxncoSfQU6yxOtQLsTe3V0SDOknmJR4N69BOCjssvPmD8JvyD9g1OP4xqttgOd5Vvmdn
  </CipherData>
 </EncryptedData>
</connectionStrings>
```

8. To test the connection locally (running in compute emulator), you need to give `NETWORK SERVICE` permission to get to the private key in your **Certificate Manager** snap-in.

9. Test the encryption by adding the following code snippet to your worker or web role:

    ```
    Trace.WriteLine("MyConnectionString = " +

    ConfigurationManager.ConnectionStrings["GeotopiaDatabase"]);
    ```

10. The output window of the compute emulator will display the decrypted `connectionString` section with the name **GeotopiaDatabase**.

The result of the encryption process is that when somebody manages to get access to a copy of your `app.config` file, it is still not possible to get access to your instances of Windows Azure SQL Database, as the configuration string is not readable.

Data Sync

The Microsoft Sync Framework has also found its way to the cloud. Microsoft has built SQL Data Sync upon the traditional Sync Framework. With SQL Data Sync, you can easily set up and configure synchronizations between traditional SQL Server and instances of Windows Azure SQL Database or between SQL databases only.

Synchronization takes place in a so-called synchronization group. A **synchronization group** is a collection of SQL databases and SQL Server databases that are grouped together for the synchronization process.

Configuration takes place on the synchronization group level and enables you to define the following:

- Which databases, tables, and columns are synchronized
- Filters are used to define which rows are synchronized, for example filters on a country column regulate in which continent database a record needs to appear
- The synchronization direction (from the hub, to the hub, or both ways)
- How to resolve synchronization conflicts

SQL Data Sync is an easy-to-use, easy-to-provision, and easy-to-configure service that the platform offers to realize complex synchronizations. Back in the old days, you needed to create and maintain complex synchronization scripts and software, to keep your synchronization up to date.

Nowadays, you can set up complex synchronizations without writing any code and there is also no need to create and maintain hardware where your old synchronization software and backup databases were running.

Supported datatypes in Data Sync

SQL Data Sync supports only a subset of all the SQL Database data types that can be part of synchronization.

The following list contains data types that are not supported:

- `bigint`, `money`, `smallmoney`
- `Binary(50)`, `varbinary(5)`
- `SmallDateTime`
- `geography`, `geometry`
- `XmlSchemaCollection`
- `cursor`, `timestamp`, `HierarchyID`

Also `FileStream`, CLR user-defined types, and SQL user-defined types cannot be synchronized at the time of this writing.

For our Geotopia showcase, it means that the geodatatypes cannot be synchronized. An alternative would be to store geodata in plain table storage and convert it into source code.

Securing Data Sync

Data Sync offers standards encryption on different levels. This includes the following:

- All service credentials for the system databases
- All service credentials for system storage
- All user credentials for both the SQL databases and SQL Database servers
- Configuration file for the client agent
- Connections between the Data Sync service and the system databases
- Connections between the Data Sync service and system storage
- Connections between all components in the Data Sync service
- Connections between the client agent and the Data Sync service
- Connections between the Windows Azure portal and the Data Sync service

Authentication

The Data Sync service also offers different levels of authentication, including the following:

- Client agent authentication of local users with Windows user security
- The need for admin credentials when installing or accessing the client agent UI
- Authentication of the agent key of the client agent—the agent key is generated by the platform and installed on the client agent
- Client agent is authenticated by the on-premises SQL Server using the connection string that is provided by the user
- Certificates are used to authenticate connections between system components within the Data Sync service
- Access to the portal is authenticated with the Windows Live ID

Setting up a Data Sync environment

To set up a Data Sync environment, you first need to create a Data Sync Preview server. You can do this by selecting **Data Sync** on the Windows Azure portal and then by clicking on **Provision Data Sync Preview Server** to start a provisioning wizard. The wizard is then started, and after agreeing with the terms of use and selecting the appropriate subscription, the following screen is displayed:

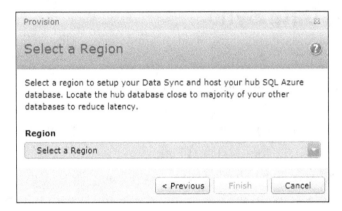

Select the region that is closest to the heart of your application. In the Geotopia case, we have the central services running in Northern Europe, so we can choose that region as well. Click on **Finish**, and the provisioning starts. After the provisioning process, the next information will be displayed on your **Data Sync** tab in the Windows Azure portal, which looks like the following screenshot:

The preceding screenshot shows that Data Sync is provisioned in my **riccardobecker** subscription in the **North Europe** region but that it has no sync groups yet.

After setting up a Data Sync Preview server in your Windows Azure portal, you need to choose whether you want the synchronization to take place between SQL databases, or between on-premise and SQL databases, as follows:

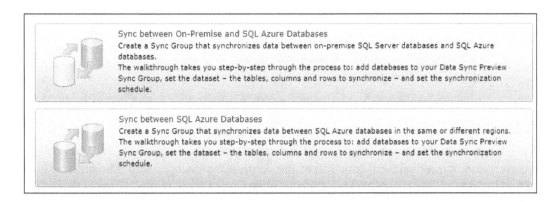

Now, we will set up synchronization between the Geotopia SQL database and other Geotopia SQL databases in other regions. By doing this, we will prepare Geotopia to be a global solution, keeping data close to the customers. By using the Traffic Manager in case of a service failure in any of the regions, we are able to uphold a highly responsive and robust service. More information on Window Azure Traffic Manager is explained in *Chapter 6*, *Key Features Explained*.

For now, select the sync between SQL Azure databases. For this scenario, we have a two-server setup, one in the North Europe region and the other in the North Central US region, as shown in the following screenshot:

Now, we want the Geotopia database in Europe to be the "central" database that works as the hub. Create a new sync group and give it a unique name (in this case, **GeotopiaSyncGroup**), as shown in the following screenshot:

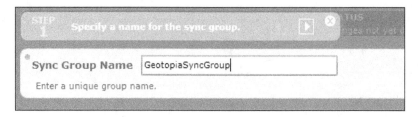

After naming your sync group, you need to add the databases that you want to sync together in the sync group. In our case, there are two databases. The first one is in Europe, which will function as the central database, or hub. The other one is located in North Central US and it will be one of the clients.

Next, add your SQL database that will be the hub (this is my North Europe Geotopia database). Next, add the SQL database(s) that you need to be part of the sync group. We added our database that is located in North Central US.

After adding the two databases, your topology looks like the one shown in the following screenshot:

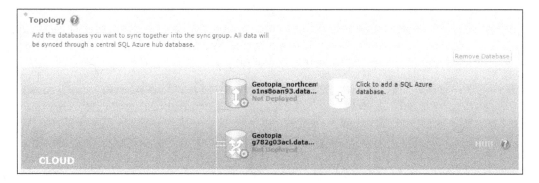

You need to choose the sync direction. There are three options, as follows:

- **Bidirectional**: Changes are synchronized between the North Central US and the North Europe databases in both directions, and the databases will be in sync. Changes to each database are synchronized with the other.

- **Sync from the Hub**: Only changes in the hub are propagated to the North Central US database.

- **Sync to the Hub**: Only changes in the North Central US database are synced to the European hub.

In this scenario, we want both databases (and later on, others) to be in sync as much as possible. The rationale behind this is that my North Europe database is also being edited and used by users in the European area. This database is not created for synchronization purposes only. So, we choose the sync direction to be bidirectional.

After both databases are added to the sync group, you need to configure **Sync Schedule** and **Conflict Resolution**, as shown in the following screenshot:

For this scenario, we have set the synchronization at **30 Minutes**, which means that after every 30 minutes, a complete synchronization cycle takes place. The **Conflict Resolution** option is set to **Hub Wins**, as that is my main environment.

Having all these set up brings us to the step to define which particular dataset is involved in the whole synchronization process. For this particular example, we will use the Geotopics table that will contain location topic information about interesting places posted by users.

In the following screenshot, you will see the selected table and the columns that need to be synchronized between hub and client(s):

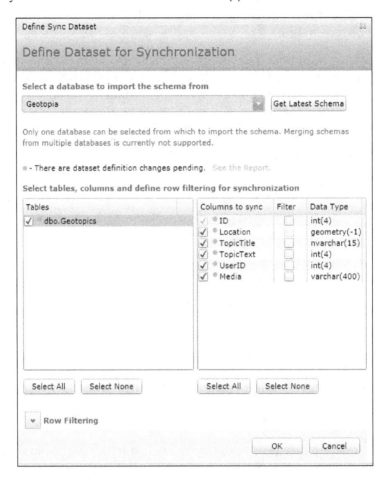

After clicking on **OK**, the synchronization setup is finished and ready to run. To enable the sync group, click on the **Deploy** button in the ribbon, and the servers start provisioning.

After the provisioning step, the syncing is in place and will take place every 30 minutes (as configured). You can also manually start the sync process by clicking on the **Sync Now** button in the ribbon of the Windows Azure portal.

Clicking on the **Sync Now** button starts the synchronization process, and after some time you can see the **Geotopics** table appear in the North Central US server space.

From the portal, select the **North Central US** server and click on **Manage**. The portal takes you to the design surface of the designated database. The following screenshot will appear.

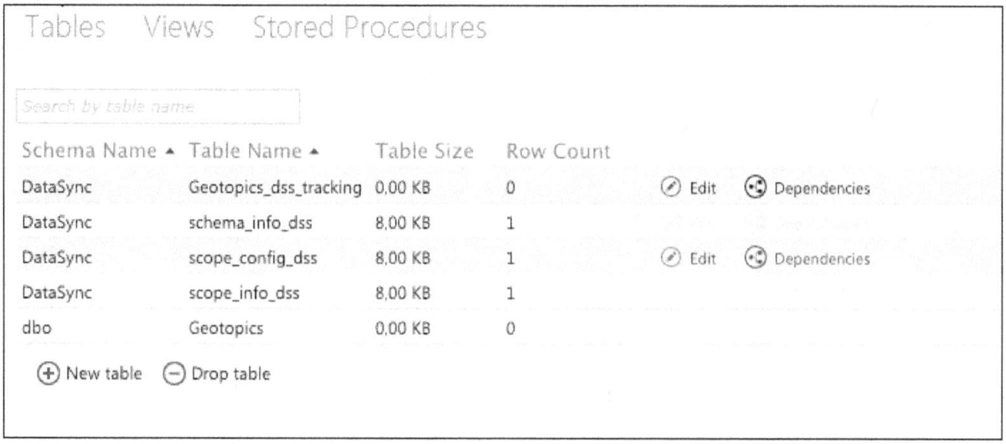

Tables   Views   Stored Procedures

Search by table name

Schema Name ▲	Table Name ▲	Table Size	Row Count		
DataSync	Geotopics_dss_tracking	0,00 KB	0	⊘ Edit	⊙ Dependencies
DataSync	schema_info_dss	8,00 KB	1		
DataSync	scope_config_dss	8,00 KB	1	⊘ Edit	⊙ Dependencies
DataSync	scope_info_dss	8,00 KB	1		
dbo	Geotopics	0,00 KB	0		

⊕ New table   ⊖ Drop table

You can see that the **Geotopics** table appears in the list, but there are also different tables concerning the Data Sync process. You do not need to touch these tables. For every table that needs to be synchronized, a new table is created. In the preceding screenshot you can see the **Geotopics_dss_tracking** table, which is created by Data Sync and contains the same information as Geotopics (which is the table to be synchronized), and additional metadata about modifications made to rows in the original table. To insert a row in the Geotopics table, enter the following query:

```
insert into Geotopics(Location, TopicTitle, UserId) values (geometry::STG
eomFromText('POINT (2.2944851 48.8582494)', 4326), 'paris', 3)
```

This query inserts a record in the `Geotopics` table. If you preview the spatial data in the SQL database portal, you will see the following screenshot:

The value in the **Geometry** column is displayed on the map and is the location of Eiffel Tower.

Summary

In this chapter, we have learned that Windows Azure SQL Database is a scalable cloud database service with high availability built on SQL Server technology. No installation, configuration, or maintenance relieves us from the heavy administration burden, so that we can focus on the application itself. We also looked at the ability to use your SQL Server expertise in the cloud variant and saw that there is no steep learning curve to work with SQL Database.

We saw how to set up a SQL Database environment in a specific region. Some guidelines and best practices have also been described along with the way to work with SQL Database from the portal environment.

Data Sync is the cloud service information synchronization service that works even in a bidirectional manner to keep databases all around the world in sync with each other. It is also possible to synchronize between on-premise and cloud-based databases, and all this can be done by configuration—no additional programming is needed. This feature relieves us from writing complex database scripts to synchronize databases, and we can easily configure it by using the Windows Azure portal. We can have fine-grained control of the synchronization on table level and even on column level and can add additional filters to synchronize only a subset of data.

The next chapter provides an overview of the different features of Windows Azure, formerly known as **AppFabric**. It demonstrates how to apply Service Bus technology and how to integrate your application with common identity providers, for example Facebook. We will also dig deeper into the caching capabilities of Windows Azure and describe how the Windows Azure Traffic Manager can help us build robust and resilient services.

6
Key Features Explained

"We live in a web of ideas, a fabric of our own making."

– *Joseph Chilton Pearce*

This chapter describes the features of Windows Azure Service Bus. Service Bus offers features that are not offered by any other cloud platform on the market. One important feature is the **Service Bus** that enables you to connect your on-premise services to Windows Azure services and beyond. The Access Control Service enables you to easily authenticate users without having to write complex authentication code ourselves. By using **Windows Identity Framework (WIF)** and supporting identity providers such as Live ID, Yahoo, and Facebook, it will be easy to use these identity providers as the main authentication mechanism in our own services.

In this chapter, we will provide a systematic guide on how to integrate with Facebook. AppFabric also contains AppFabric applications, an easy way to develop and deploy composite applications. Another interesting feature is the **caching** feature that AppFabric offers.

Service Bus

The Windows Azure Service Bus provides a hosted, secure, and widely available infrastructure for widespread communication, large-scale event distribution, naming, and service publishing. Service Bus provides connectivity options for **Windows Communication Foundation (WCF)** and other service endpoints, including **REST** endpoints, that would otherwise be difficult or impossible to reach. Endpoints can be located behind **Network Address Translation (NAT)** boundaries, or bound to frequently changing, dynamically assigned IP addresses, or both.

Getting started

To get started and use the features of Services Bus, you need to make sure you have the Windows Azure SDK installed.

Queues

Queues in the AppFabric feature (different from Table Storage queues) offer a FIFO message delivery capability. This can be an outcome for those applications that expect messages in a certain order. Just like with ordinary Azure Queues, Service Bus Queues enable the decoupling of your application components and can still function, even if some parts of the application are offline. Some differences between the two types of queues are (for example) that the Service Bus Queues can hold larger messages and can be used in conjunction with Access Control Service.

Working with queues

To create a queue, go to the Windows Azure portal and select the **Service Bus, Access Control & Caching** tab. Next, select **Service Bus**, select the namespace, and click on **New Queue**. The following screen will appear. If you did not set up a namespace earlier you need to create a namespace before you can create a queue:

There are some properties that can be configured during the setup process of a queue. Obviously, the name uniquely identifies the queue in the namespace. **Default Message Time To Live** configures messages having this default TTL. This can also be set in code and is a `TimeSpan` value.

Duplicate Detection History Time Window implicates how long the message ID (unique) of the received messages will be retained to check for duplicate messages. This property will be ignored if the **Required Duplicate Detection** option is not set.

 Keep in mind that a long detection history results in the persistency of message IDs during that period. If you process many messages, the queue size will grow and so does your bill.

When a message expires or when the limit of the queue size is reached, it will be **deadlettered**. This means that they will end up in a different queue named `$DeadLetterQueue`. Imagine a scenario where a lot of traffic in your queue results in messages in the dead letter queue. Your application should be robust and process these messages as well.

The **lock duration** property defines the duration of the lock when the `PeekLock()` method is called. The `PeekLock()` method hides a specific message from other consumers/processors until the lock duration expires. Typically, this value needs to be sufficient to process and delete the message.

A sample scenario

Remember the differences between the two queue types that Windows Azure offers, where the Service Bus queues are able to guarantee first-in first-out and to support transactions. The scenario is when a user posts a geotopic on the canvas containing text and also uploads a video by using the parallel upload functionality described in *Chapter 4*, *Storing Your Data*. What should happen next is for the **WCF** service `CreateGeotopic()` to post a message in the queue to enter the geotopic, but when the file finishes uploading, there is also a message sent to the queue. These two together should be in a single transaction. `Geotopia.Processor` processes this message but only if the media file is finished uploading. In this example, you can see how a transaction is handled and how a message can be abandoned and made available on the queue again. If the geotopic is validated as a whole (file is uploaded properly), the worker role will reroute the message to a designated audit trail queue to keep track of actions made by the system and also send to a **topic** (see next section) dedicated to keeping messages that need to be pushed to possible mobile devices. The messages in this topic will again be processed by a worker role. The reason for choosing a separate worker role is that it creates a role, a loosely-coupled solution, and possible to be fine-grained by only scaling the back-end worker role.

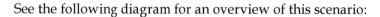

See the following diagram for an overview of this scenario:

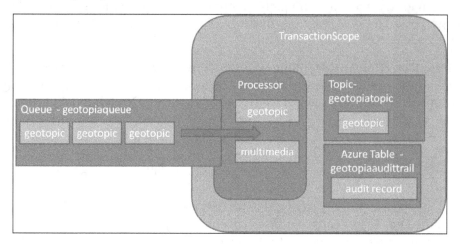

In the previous section, we already created a queue named `geotopicaqueue`. In order to work with queues, you need the service identity (in this case we use a service identity with a symmetric issuer and the key credentials) of the service namespace.

Preparing the project

In order to make use of the Service Bus capabilities, you need to add a reference to `Microsoft.ServiceBus.dll`, located in `<drive>:\Program Files\Microsoft SDKs\Windows Azure\.NET SDK\2012-06\ref`. Next, add the following `using` statements to your file:

```
using Microsoft.ServiceBus;
using Microsoft.ServiceBus.Messaging;
```

Your project is now ready to make use of Service Bus queues.

In the configuration settings of the web role project hosting the WCF services, add a new configuration setting named `ServiceBusQueue` with the following value:

```
"Endpoint=sb://<servicenamespace>.servicebus.windows.
net/;SharedSecretIssuer=<issuerName>;SharedSecretValue=<yoursecret>"
```

The properties of the queue you configured in the Windows Azure portal can also be set programmatically.

Sending messages

Messages that are sent to a Service Bus queue are instances of `BrokeredMessage`. This class contains standard properties such as `TimeToLive` and `MessageId`. An important property is `Properties`, which is of type `IDictionary<string, object>`, where you can add additional data. The body of the message can be set in the constructor of `BrokerMessage`, where the parameter must be of a type decorated with the `[Serializable]` attribute.

The following code snippet shows how to send a message of type `BrokerMessage`:

```
MessagingFactory factory = MessagingFactory.CreateFromConnectionString
(connectionString);

MessageSender sender = factory.CreateMessageSender("geotopiaqueue");


sender.Send(new BrokeredMessage(
        new Geotopic
        {
          id = id,
          subject = subject,
          text = text,
          PostToFacebook = PostToFacebook,
          accessToken = accessToken,
          MediaFile = MediaFile    //Uri of uploaded mediafile
        }));
```

As the scenario depicts a situation where two messages are expected to be sent in a certain order and to be treated as a single transaction, we need to add some more logic to the code snippet.

Right before this message is sent, the media file is uploaded by using the `BlobUtil` class we created in *Chapter 4, Storing Your Data*. Consider sending the media file together with `BrokeredMessage` if it is small enough. This might be a long-running operation, depending on the size of the file. The asynchronous upload process returns `Uri`, which is passed to `BrokeredMessage`.

The situation is:

- A multimedia file is uploaded from the client to Windows Azure Blob storage using a parallel upload (or passed on in the message). A Parallel upload is breaking up the media file in several chunks and uploading them separately by using multithreading.

- A message is sent to `geotopiaqueue`, and `Geotopia.Processor` processes the messages in the queues in a single transaction.

Receiving messages

On the other side of the Service Bus queue resides our worker role, `Geotopia.Processor`, which performs the following tasks:

- It grabs the messages from the queue

- Sends the message straight to a table in Windows Azure Storage for auditing purposes

- Creates a geotopic that can be subscribed to (see next section)

The following code snippet shows how to perform these three tasks:

```
MessagingFactory factory = MessagingFactory.CreateFromConnectionString
(connectionString);
MessageReceiver receiver =
  factory.CreateMessageReceiver("geotopiaqueue ");
BrokeredMessage receivedMessage = receiver.Receive();
try
{
    ProcessMessage(receivedMessage);
    receivedMessage.Complete();
}
catch (Exception e)
{
    receivedMessage.Abandon();
}
```

Cross-domain communication

We created a new web role in our Geotopia solution, hosting the WCF services we want to expose. As the client is a **Silverlight** one (and runs in the browser), we face **cross-domain communication**. To protect against security vulnerabilities and to prevent cross-site requests from a Silverlight client to some services (without the notice of the user), Silverlight by default allows only site-of-origin communication. A possible exploitation of a web application is **cross-site forgery**, exploits that can occur when cross-domain communication is allowed; for example, a Silverlight application sending commands to some service running on the Internet somewhere.

As we want the Geotopia Silverlight client to access the WCF service running in another domain, we need to explicitly allow cross-domain operations. This can be achieved by adding a file named `clientaccesspolicy.xml` at the root of the domain where the WCF service is hosted and allowing this cross-domain access. Another option is to add a `crossdomain.xml` file at the root where the service is hosted.

Please go to `http://msdn.microsoft.com/en-us/library/cc197955(v=vs.95).aspx` to find more details on the cross-domain communication issues.

Comparison

The following table shows the similarities and differences between Windows Azure and Service Bus queues:

Criteria	Windows Azure queue	Service Bus queue
Ordering guarantee	No, but based on best-effort first-in, first out	First-in, first-out
Delivery guarantee	At least once	At most once; use the `PeekLock()` method to ensure that no messages are missed. `PeekLock()` together with the `Complete()` method enable a two-stage receive operation.
Transaction support	No	Yes, by using `TransactionScope`
Receive Mode	Peek & Lease	Peek & Lock
		Receive & Delete
Lease/Lock duration	Between 30 seconds and 7 days	Between 60 seconds and 5 minutes
Lease/Lock granularity	Message level	Queue level
Batched Receive	Yes, by using `GetMessages(count)`	Yes, by using the prefetch property or the use of transactions
Scheduled Delivery	Yes	Yes
Automatic dead lettering	No	Yes
In-place update	Yes	No
Duplicate detection	No	Yes
WCF integration	No	Yes, through WCF bindings
WF integration	Not standard; needs a customized activity	Yes, out-of-the-box activities
Message Size	Maximum 64 KB	Maximum 256 KB
Maximum queue size	100 TB, the limits of a storage account	1, 2, 3, 4, or 5 GB; configurable
Message TTL	Maximum 7 days	Unlimited
Number of queues	Unlimited	10,000 per service namespace

Criteria	Windows Azure queue	Service Bus queue
Mgmt protocol	REST over HTTP(S)	REST over HTTPS
Runtime protocol	REST over HTTP(S)	REST over HTTPS
		TCP with TLS
Queue naming rules	Maximum of 63 characters	Maximum of 260 characters
Queue length function	Yes, value is approximate	Yes, exact value
Throughput	Maximum of 2,000 messages/second	Maximum of 2,000 messages/second
Authentication	Symmetric key	ACS claims
Role-based access control	No	Yes through ACS roles
Identity provider federation	No	Yes
Costs	$0.01 per 10,000 transactions	$ 0.01 per 10,000 transactions
Billable operations	Every call that touches "storage'"	Only Send and Receive operations
Storage costs	$0.14 per GB per month	None
ACS transaction costs	None, since ACS is not supported	$1.99 per 100,000 token requests

Background information

There are some additional characteristics of Service Bus queues that need your attention:

- In order to guarantee the FIFO mechanism, you need to use messaging sessions.
- Using Receive & Delete in Service Bus queues reduces transaction costs, since it is counted as one.
- The maximum size of a `Base64-encoded` message on the Window Azure queue is 48 KB and for standard encoding it is 64 KB.
- Sending messages to a Service Bus queue that has reached its limit will throw an exception that needs to be caught.
- When the throughput has reached its limit, the `HTTP 503` error response is returned from the Windows Azure queue service. Implement retrying logic to tackle this issue.

- Throttled requests (thus being rejected) are not billable.
- ACS transactions are based on instances of the message factory class. The received token will expire after 20 minutes, meaning that you will only need three tokens per hour of execution.

Topics and subscriptions

Topics and subscriptions can be useful in a scenario where (instead of a single consumer, in the case of queues) multiple consumers are part of the pattern. Imagine in our scenario where users want to be subscribed to topics posted by friends. In such a scenario, a subscription is created on a topic and the worker role processes it; for example, mobile clients can be push notified by the worker role.

Sending messages to a topic works in a similar way as sending messages to a Service Bus queue.

Preparing the project

In the Windows Azure portal, go to the **Service Bus, Access Control & Caching** tab. Select **Topics** and create a new topic, as shown in the following screenshot:

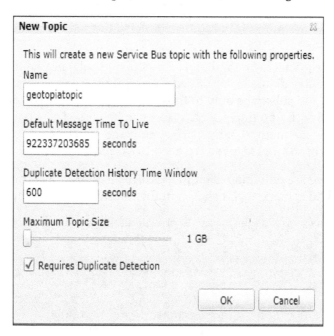

Next, click on **OK** and a new topic is created for you. The next thing you need to do is to create a subscription on this topic. To do this, select **New Subscription** and create a new subscription, as shown in the following screenshot:

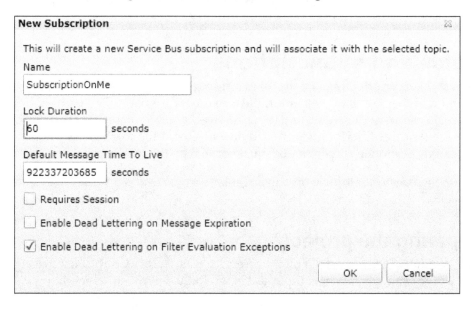

Using filters

Topics and subscriptions, by default, it is a push/subscribe mechanism where messages are made available to registered subscriptions. To actively influence the subscription (and subscribe only to those messages that are of your interest), you can create subscription filters. SqlFilter can be passed as a parameter to the CreateSubscription method of the NamespaceManager class. SqlFilter operates on the properties of the messages so we need to extend the method.

In our scenario, we are only interested in messages that are concerning a certain subject. The way to achieve this is shown in the following code snippet:

```
BrokeredMessage message = new BrokeredMessage(new Geotopic
                {
                        id = id,
                        subject = subject,
                        text = text,
                        PostToFacebook = PostToFacebook,
                        accessToken = accessToken,
                        mediaFile = fileContent
                });
//used for topics & subscriptions
message.Properties["subject"] = subject;
```

The preceding piece of code extends `BrokeredMessage` with a subject property that can be used in `SqlFilter`. A filter can only be applied in code on the subscription and not in the Windows Azure portal. This is fine, because in Geotopia, users must be able to subscribe to interesting topics, and for every topic that does not exist yet, a new subscription is made and processed by the worker role, the processor. The worker role contains the following code snippet in one of its threads:

```
Uri uri = ServiceBusEnvironment.CreateServiceUri
  ("sb", "<yournamespace>", string.Empty);
string name = "owner";
string key = "<yourkey>";
//get some credentials
TokenProvider tokenProvider =
  TokenProvider.CreateSharedSecretTokenProvider(name, key);

// Create namespace client
NamespaceManager namespaceClient = new
  NamespaceManager(ServiceBusEnvironment.CreateServiceUri
    ("sb", "geotopiaservicebus", string.Empty), tokenProvider);

MessagingFactory factory =
  MessagingFactory.Create(uri, tokenProvider);
BrokeredMessage message = new BrokeredMessage();
message.Properties["subject"] = "interestingsubject";
MessageSender sender = factory.CreateMessageSender("dataqueue");
sender.Send(message); //message is send to topic
SubscriptionDescription subDesc =
  namespaceClient.CreateSubscription("geotopiatopic",
"SubscriptionOnMe", new
  SqlFilter("subject='interestingsubject'"));

//the processing loop
while(true)
{
  MessageReceiver receiver = factory.CreateMessageReceiver
    ("geotopiatopic/subscriptions/SubscriptionOnMe");
  //it now only gets messages containing the property 'subject'
  //with the value 'interestingsubject'
  BrokeredMessage receivedMessage = receiver.Receive();
  try
  {
    ProcessMessage(receivedMessage);
    receivedMessage.Complete();
  }
  catch (Exception e)
  {
    receivedMessage.Abandon();
  }
}
```

Windows Azure Caching

Windows Azure offers caching capabilities out of the box. Caching is fast, because it is built as an in-memory (fast), distributed (running on different servers) technology.

Windows Azure Caching offers two types of cache:

- Caching deployed on a role
- Shared caching

When you decide to host caching on your Windows Azure roles, you need to pick from two deployment alternatives. The first is **dedicated caching**, where a worker role is fully dedicated to run as a caching store and its memory is used for caching. The second option is to create a **co-located** topology, meaning that a certain percentage of available memory in your roles is assigned and reserved to be used for in-memory caching purposes. Keep in mind that the second option is the most cost-effective one, as you don't have a role running just for its memory.

Shared caching is the central caching repository managed by the platform which is accessible for your hosted services. You need to register the shared caching mechanism on the portal in the **Service Bus, Access Control & Caching** section of the portal. You need to configure a namespace and the size of the cache (remember, there is money involved). This caching facility is a shared one and runs inside a multitenant environment.

Caching capabilities

Both the shared and dedicated caching offer a rich feature set. The following table depicts this:

Feature	Explanation
ASP.NET 4.0 caching providers	When you build ASP.NET 4.0 applications and deploy them on Windows Azure, the platform will install caching providers for them. This enables your ASP.NET 4.0 applications to use caching easily.
Programming model	You can use the `Microsoft.ApplicationServer.Caching` namespace to perform CRUD operations on your cache. The application using the cache is responsible for populating and reloading the cache, as the programming model is based on the cache-aside pattern. This means that initially the cache is empty and will be populated during the lifetime of the application. The application checks whether the desired data is present. If not, the application reads it from (for example) a database and inserts it into the cache.
	The caching mechanism deployed on one of your roles, whether dedicated or not, lives up to the high availability of Windows Azure. It saves copies of your items in cache, in case a role instance goes down.

Feature	Explanation
Configuration model	Configuration of caching (server side) is not relevant in the case of shared caching, as this is the standard, out-of-the-box functionality that can only vary in size, namespace, and location.
	It is possible to create named caches. Every single cache has its own configuration settings, so you can really fine-tune your caching requirements. All settings are stored in the service definition and service configuration files. As the settings of named caches are stored in JSON format, they are difficult to read.
	If one of your roles wants to access Windows Azure Cache, it needs some configuration as well. A `DataCacheFactory` object is used to return the `DataCache` objects that represent the named caches. Client cache settings are stored in the designated `app.config` or `web.config` files.
	A configuration sample is shown later on in this section, together with some code snippets.
Security model	The two types of caching (shared and role-based) have two different ways of handling security.
	Role-based caching is secured by its endpoints, and only those which are allowed to use these endpoints are permitted to touch the cache. Shared caching is secured by the use of an authentication token.
Concurrency model	As multiple clients can access and modify cache items simultaneously, there are concurrency issues to take care of; both optimistic and pessimistic concurrency models are available.
	In the optimistic concurrency model, updating any objects in the cache does not result in locks. Updating an item in the cache will only take place if Azure detects that the updated version is the same as the one that currently resides in the cache.
	When you decide to use the pessimistic concurrency model, items are locked explicitly by the cache client. When an item is locked, other lock requests are rejected by the platform. Locks need to be released by the client or after some configurable time-out, in order to prevent eternal locking.
Regions and tagging	Cached items can be grouped together in a so-called **region**. Together with additional tagging of cached items, it is possible to search for tagged items within a certain region. Creating a region results in adding cache items to be stored on a single server (analogous to partitioning). If additional backup copies are enabled, the region with all its items is also saved on a different server, to maintain availability.

Feature	Explanation
Notifications	It is possible to have your application notified by Windows Azure when cache operations occur. Cache notifications exist for both operations on regions and items. A notification is sent when `CreateRegion`, `ClearRegion`, or `RemoveRegion` is executed. The operations `AddItem`, `ReplaceItem`, and `RemoveItem` on cached items also cause notifications to be sent.
	Notifications can be scoped on the cache, region, and item level. This means you can configure them to narrow the scope of notifications and only receive those that are relevant to your applications.
	Notifications are polled by your application at a configurable interval.
Availability	To keep up the high availability you are used to on Windows Azure, configure your caching role(s) to maintain backup copies. This means that the platform replicates copies of your cache within your deployment across different fault domains.
Local caching	To minimize the number of roundtrips between cache clients and the Windows Azure cache, enable local caching. Local caching means that every cache clients maintains a reference to the item in-memory itself. Requesting that same item again will cause an object returned from the local cache instead of the role-based cache. Make sure you choose the right lifetime for your objects, otherwise you might work with outdated cached items.
Expiration and Eviction	Cache items can be removed explicitly or implicitly by expiration or eviction.
	The process of expiration means that the caching facility removes items from the cache automatically. Items will be removed after their time-out value expires, but keep in mind that locked items will not be removed even if they pass their expiration date. Upon calling the `Unlock` method, it is possible to extend the expiration date of the cached item.
	To ensure that there is sufficient memory available for caching purposes, the **least recently used** (**LRU**) eviction is supported. The process of eviction means that memory will be cleared and cached items will be evicted when certain memory thresholds are exceeded.
	By default, Shared Cache items expire after 48 hours. This behavior can be overridden by the overloads of the `Add` and `Put` methods.

Setting it up

To enable role-based caching, you need to configure it in Visual Studio. Open the **Caching** tab of the properties of your web or worker role (you decide which role is the caching one). Fill out the settings, as shown in the following screenshot:

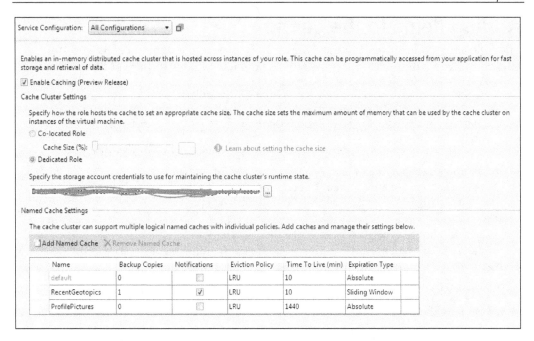

The configuration settings in this example cause the following to happen:

- Role-based caching is enabled.

- The specific role will be a dedicated role just for caching.

- Besides the default cache, there are two additional, named caches for different purposes. The first is a high-available cache for recently added geotopics with a sliding window. This means that every time an item is accessed, its expiration time is reset to the configured 10 minutes. For our geotopics, this is a good approach, since access to recently posted geotopics is heavy at first but will slow down as time passes by (and thus they will be removed from the cache eventually). The second named cache is specifically for profile pictures with a long time-to-live, as these pictures will not change too often.

Caching examples

In this section, several code snippets explain the use of Window Azure caching and clarify different features. Ensure that you get the right assemblies for Windows Azure Caching by running the following command in the Package Manager Console: `Install-Package Microsoft.WindowsAzure.Caching`. Running this command updates the designated config file for your project. Replace the `[cache cluster role name]` tag in the configuration file with the name of the role that hosts the cache.

Adding items to the cache

The following code snippet demonstrates how to access a named cache and how to add and retrieve items from it (you will see the use of tags and the sliding window):

```
DataCacheFactory cacheFactory = new DataCacheFactory();
DataCache geotopicsCache =
  cacheFactory.GetCache("RecentGeotopics"); //get reference to
  this named cache

geotopicsCache.Clear(); //clear the whole cache
DataCacheTag[] tags = new DataCacheTag[] { new
DataCacheTag("subject"), new DataCacheTag("test")};

//add a short time to live item
DataCacheItemVersion version = geotopicsCache.Add(geotopicID, new
Geotopic(), TimeSpan.FromMinutes(1)/* overrides default 10 minutes */,
tags);
//add a default item
geotopicsCache.Add("defaultTTL", new Geotopic()); //default 10 minutes

//let time pass for some minutes
DataCacheItem item = geotopicsCache.GetCacheItem(geotopicID);  //
returns null!
DataCacheItem defaultItem = geotopicsCache.GetCacheItem("defaultTTL");
//sliding window shows up

//versioning, optimistic locking
geotopicsCache.Put("defaultTTL", new Geotopic(), defaultItem.Version);
//will fail if versions are not equal!
```

Session state and output caching

Two interesting areas in which Windows Azure caching can be applied are caching the session state of ASP.NET applications and the caching of HTTP responses, for example, complete pages.

In order to use Windows Azure caching (that is, the role-based version), to maintain the session state, you need to add the following code snippet to the web.config file for your web application:

```
<sessionState mode="Custom" customProvider="AppFabricCacheSessionStor
eProvider">
  <providers>
    <add name="AppFabricCacheSessionStoreProvider"
```

```
         type="Microsoft.Web.DistributedCache.
DistributedCacheSessionStateStoreProvider, Microsoft.Web.
DistributedCache"
         cacheName="default"
         useBlobMode="true"
         dataCacheClientName="default" />
   </providers>
</sessionState>
```

The preceding XML snippet causes your web application to use the default cache that you configured on one of your roles.

To enable output caching, add the following section to your `web.config` file:

```
<caching>
  <outputCache defaultProvider="DistributedCache">
    <providers>
      <add name="DistributedCache"
     type="Microsoft.Web.DistributedCache.
DistributedCacheOutputCacheProvider, Microsoft.Web.DistributedCache"
         cacheName="default"
         dataCacheClientName="default" />
    </providers>
  </outputCache>
</caching>
```

This will enable output caching for your web application, and the default cache will be used for this. Specify a cache name, if you have set up a specific cache for output caching purposes. The pages to be cached determine how long they will remain in the cache and set the different version of the page, depending on the parameter combinations.

```
<%@ OutputCache Duration="60" VaryByParam="*" %>
```

Windows Azure Connect

Windows Azure Connect is a mechanism you can use to set up **IPsec** connections between machines in your own domain (on-premise) and web or worker roles running on Windows Azure. If these connections are set up, you can address your role instances as if they were in your own network/domain. This feature enables you to accomplish the following tasks:

- Managing and administering web and worker roles with existing management tools

- Building a distributed application where Windows Azure roles work seamlessly together with your on-premise resources, such as printers, databases, legacy systems, or other critical resources that play a viable role within your distributed application

- Domain authentication, name resolution, or other domain-wide actions

Consider the following scenario. The Geotopia worker role is built and configured to access a Microsoft SQL Server database on-premise. This is the only part of the whole solution outside the cloud. The reason for this requirement is that the local SQL Server database is used for data warehouse purposes and towards the goal of keeping this useful, analytical data inside my own environment.

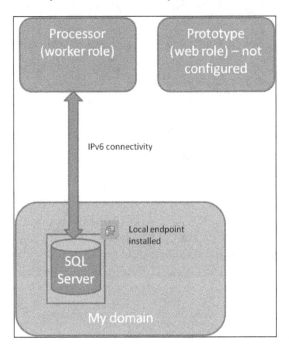

Setting it up

To set up and configure Windows Azure Connect, go to the Windows Azure portal and select **Virtual network** in the left corner of the screen. You can find the Windows Azure Connect overview under the **Connect** tab, as shown in the following screenshot:

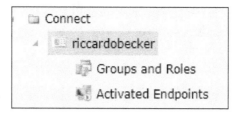

To activate Windows Azure Connect on a machine or on a virtual machine, you need to select **Install Local Endpoint** from the menu. You will now get a secure link with an **activation token**. Copy this link and run it in a browser. Running the executable file that is presented will install the local endpoint. As it contains an activation token, you cannot save the file and run it later. Windows Azure Connect will start automatically but will not operate yet, since you need to configure it first.

Enabling a web role with Connect

To connect a web role with a resource within your domain or computer, you need to configure the web role as well.

1. In the **Connect** menu, select the **Get Activation Token** option. You should see a screen similar to the one shown in the following screenshot:

2. Next, copy the activation token to your clipboard.

3. Open your web role project properties and select the **Virtual Network** tab. Select **Activate Windows Azure Connect** and paste your activation code, as shown in the following screenshot:

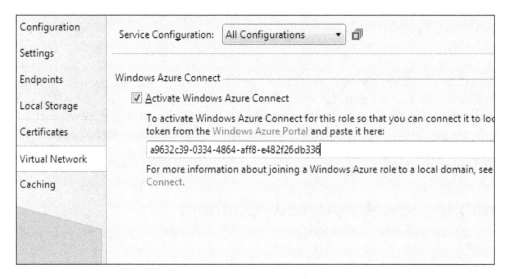

After saving these changes, you will notice that the service definition and configuration files have changed and settings with respect to Connect are added. Publish the Cloud project(s), which will appear in the Connect node in the Windows Azure portal. The name that is shown there is the machine name with the typical "RD" prefix (remember Red Dog?).

Managing Connect

Our next task is to configure the network connectivity policy. To enable connectivity between the local machine and the web and worker roles, we need to create a new endpoint group.

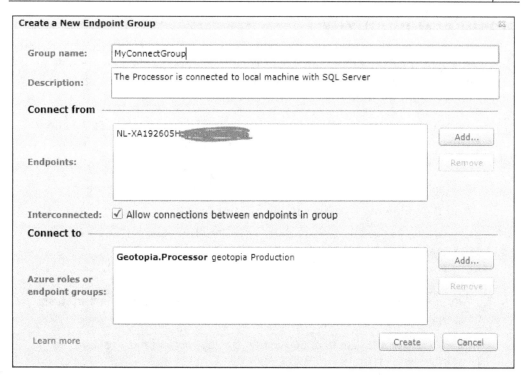

As we only need the Processor worker role to connect to the local SQL Server instance, we just add that particular role and skip the web role in the **Azure roles or endpoint groups** section. In the **Connect from** section, you can add the machines you installed as local endpoints. Click on **Create** and the group is created, and you will see that the computer is grouped together with the configured role; right-click on the **Windows Azure Connect** icon in the icon tray and select **Refresh Policy**. The Windows Azure role is automatically updated with the new policy, and this process will occur every 5 minutes.

If you redeploy your role, Windows Azure Connect will see this change and enable connectivity as soon as the role is available again. Scaling up your roles is also handled by this feature and will ensure that the new role instances are part of the group as well. Obviously, scaling down will also result in the removal of those instances from the group.

Testing connectivity

After following the preceding steps, you should have IP level connectivity between your configured roles (instances) and your local machine(s). It is now possible to communicate over **IPv6**, which is provided by Connect and secured with IPsec. This enables communication through firewalls and NATs.

By default, Windows Azure roles do not allow incoming ping requests. To allow your role to accept these requests, you can add a .cmd file to your role project. Perform the following steps to accomplish this goal:

1. Add a file with the extension .cmd to your Visual Studio project.

2. Add the following two lines to the file and save it:

```
netsh advfirewall firewall add rule="Allow ping" dir=in
action=allow enable=yes protocol=icmpv6:128, any

exit /b 0
```

3. Add a section to the service definition file that will create a start-up task:

```
<Startup>

<Task commandLine="Startup.cmd" executionContext="elevated"
taskType="simple"/>

</Startup>
```

4. Verify that the **Copy Always** setting is selected for the .cmd file to ensure that the file is always copied and that the Publish process copies the file to the root folder for the deployment.

5. Deploy the solution to Windows Azure.

After deployment, the start-up process of the role is executed, and pinging the role is allowed. In addition, logging in remotely on the worker role instance and pinging the local machine from there is possible.

Other Connect capabilities

Common scenarios are the ones described earlier, building hybrid solutions where cloud and on-premise resources are brought together. Besides this, it is also possible to join roles to an on-premise AD domain. Also for administrating purposes, you could use Connect to enable the use of remote event viewing or for other remoting purposes.

Another neat application of Windows Azure Connect is to connect your devices in a group to enable your laptop, home server, and desktop at work to be connected and to enable the sharing of data and the use of your home printer or other peripherals.

Access Control Service

The **Access Control Service (ACS)** feature of AppFabric is a service that enables an easy way to authenticate and authorize users who want to make use of your services. It isolates authentication and authorization logic from your core code and relieves you from the burden of maintaining your own identity store. ACS simplifies the process of integrating known identity providers with your solution. This section shows how to set up ACS and how to use Facebook as your main identity provider.

Getting started

In order to make use of ACS, you need to do some setting up in the Windows Azure portal.

To prepare your account to make use of ACS, follow the ensuing steps to set it up:

1. Browse to your Windows Azure portal environment and select the **Service Bus, Access Control & Caching** tab from the ribbon.

2. Select **Access Control** and click on **New** to create a new Access Control namespace.

3. Fill out the details and find a unique namespace identifier, as shown in the following screenshot:

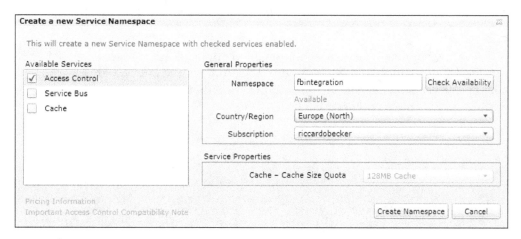

4. Select **Create Namespace**, and after some time, your namespace is provisioned.

5. Now that your namespace is created, you need to manage it. Select the newly created namespace and select **Access Control Service**.

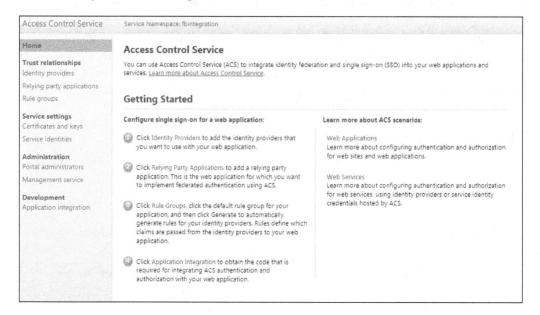

6. There are some important parts on this screen to enable ACS and make use of it. Now that your ACS is enabled, it is time to register your application on Facebook.

As we want Geotopia to be a Facebook-enabled application that uses Facebook as its identity provider, we need to register Geotopia at the `www.Facebook.com/developers` website. Registering your application there will result in `AppID` and `AppSecret`, which we will need later on.

The registration screen looks similar to the one shown in the following screenshot:

Now that we have our ACS set up and have created a Facebook application, it is time to bring these two together and enable our Geotopia application to allow users to log in with their Facebook credentials.

Adding an identity provider

First, we need to add an identity provider by using the screen shown in the following screenshot. Click on **Identity Providers** and select **Add**.

Select the **Facebook application** option and click on **Next**. This will take you to a screen where you need the information you got by registering your application on the www.Facebook.com/developers site.

Adding a relying party

Since our Geotopia application relies on claims, it is called a relying party. A relying party is an application that is claims-aware. Adding a relying party is done by configuration in the Windows Azure portal and is shown in the following screenshot:

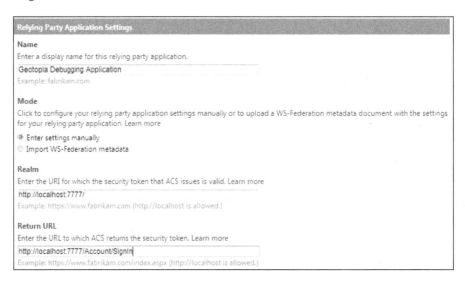

Leave the **Mode** option as is, but setting the **Realm** and **Return URL** is very important to be able to incorporate federated authentication by using ACS. Configuring the relying party here means that our Geotopia application trusts an ACS service namespace.

The **Realm** property tells us for which URI the tokens issued by the ACS are valid. In our case, since we are still building the application, we refer to localhost, to be able to test locally. Setting **Realm** to http://localhost:7777 implies that, only for the given URI, the claims that ACS issues are valid. Setting **Return URL** defines where the tokens for the relying party are returned.

Optionally, you can also define an **Error URL**. ACS redirects users to this specific URL in case an error occurs.

Enter your specific details in the screen, as shown in the previous screenshot.

Application integration

The next thing we need to do is to recover the **WS-Federation metadata** location. We need this property later on when we enable our application with ACS and integrate it with Facebook. You can find this value in the **Development – Application** tab.

In the **Rules** tab, it is possible to transform the claims we receive from Facebook to our own format. For the purpose of this book, we just leave it as is and get the raw Facebook claim.

Endpoint Reference	
Management Service	https://fbintegration.accesscontrol.windows.net/v2/mgmt/service
Management Portal	https://fbintegration.accesscontrol.windows.net/
OAuth WRAP	https://fbintegration.accesscontrol.windows.net/WRAPv0.9
OAuth2	https://fbintegration.accesscontrol.windows.net/v2/OAuth2-13
WS-Federation Metadata	https://fbintegration.accesscontrol.windows.net/FederationMetadata/2007-06/FederationMetadata.xml
WS-Metadata Exchange	https://fbintegration.accesscontrol.windows.net/v2/wstrust/mex

Integrating with Facebook

All the prerequisites are set right now. We added a Facebook application and got AppID and AppSecret. Next, we configured ACS, created a namespace, and added a relying party and Facebook as identity provider. The next step is to change our Geotopia application and enable it to make use of Facebook's login mechanism and get the claims in our application.

Make sure you have the Windows Identity Framework runtime installed, together with the Windows Identity SDK. We need these for the next steps.

To incorporate Facebook integration in our Geotopia application, perform the following steps:

1. Add an STS Reference to your web role web application by right-clicking on the project.

2. The **Federation Utility** wizard starts automatically; fill out the appropriate values specific to your application, as shown in the following screenshot:

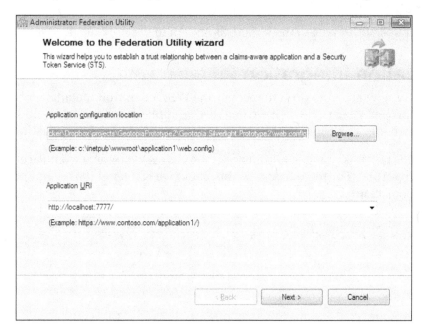

3. The application configuration location is automatically filled and points to your `web.config` file. For **Application URI**, you need to enter the details as configured in the **Relying Party** tab of the Windows Azure portal, as shown in the *Adding a relying party* section in this chapter. Click on **Next**, and you will be notified about the fact that your application is not hosted on a secure HTTPS connection, but for now, we can ignore this message.

4. The wizard takes you to the next screen, where you need to select your **Security Token Service**. Since we already have one (ACS will provide us with tokens), enter the value from the **Application Integration** tab, as shown in the following screenshot:

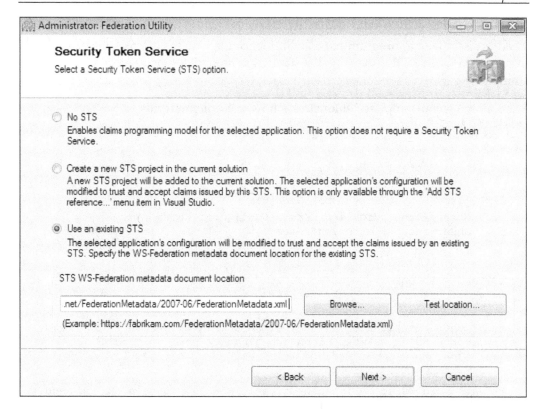

5. Click on **Next** and confirm the screens about **certificate chain validation**, security **token encryption**, and **offered claims** with the default values. Finally, click on **Finish** on the **Summary** screen. You can schedule a task here that refreshes the metadata document every day.

6. The `FederationMetadata.xml` file is added to your solution in a separate solution folder.

The magic happens when you run your cloud solution. The Silverlight application is launched and hosted on `http://localhost:7777`, as configured in the project properties. Make sure this address is identical to the one that is configured as the **Realm** in the relying party. Running your application takes you to the login page for Facebook, and after logging in, your application asks for your permission about you and your friends list.

Allow this, and you will be taken back to the return URL configured in the relying party configuration.

Using FederatedAuthentication

There is also a way to programmatically influence the way the callback mechanism is executed. You can do this by using the static class named `FederatedAuthentication` from the `Microsoft.IdentityModel.Web` namespace in your `global.asax` file.

The following code snippet demonstrates how to implement this:

```
protected void Application_Start()
{
    AreaRegistration.RegisterAllAreas();
    RegisterGlobalFilters(GlobalFilters.Filters);
    RegisterRoutes(RouteTable.Routes);
    FederatedAuthentication.ServiceConfigurationCreated +=
        OnServiceConfigurationCreated;
}

private void OnServiceConfigurationCreated(object sender,
ServiceConfigurationCreatedEventArgs e)
{
FederatedAuthentication.WSFederationAuthenticationModule. SignedIn +=
new EventHandler(WSFederationAuthenticationModule_SignedIn);
}

private void WSFederationAuthenticationModule_SignedIn(object sender,
EventArgs e)
{
    HttpContext.Current.Response.Redirect("/Facebook/Index");
}
```

The `SignedIn` event is fired when you log in through the Facebook login mechanism. The `Redirect` method calls the `Index` action in the MVC3 `FacebookController` class. As we defined the `e-mail`, `user_about_me`, `read_friendlists`, and `publish_stream` application permissions in the configuration of the identity provider, it is possible to get information from the logged in user and display it in our Geotopia web application and also post a message on the wall of the user. In our scenario, we create a separate Facebook view that displays information about the user and their friends (we want them to be invited to Geotopia as well!) and the ability to post geotopics in the Geotopia application and also as a post on the wall. The next section demonstrates how this can be achieved.

Displaying information about me

After we are redirected to the `Facebook/Index` URL in the
`WSFederationAuthenticationModule_SignedIn` event, we call the **GraphAPI**
from Facebook. For more information on the GraphAPI, please refer to
`https://developers.Facebook.com/docs/reference/api/`.

To use the Graph API from Facebook, you need the access token. This can be
retrieved as shown in the following code snippet:

```
var claimsPrincipal = Thread.CurrentPrincipal as IClaimsPrincipal;
var claimsIdentity = (IClaimsIdentity)claimsPrincipal.Identity;
var accessToken = (from claim in claimsIdentity.Claims
where claim.ClaimType == "http://www.Facebook.com/claims/AccessToken"
    select (string)claim.Value).FirstOrDefault();


//Now that we have the access token we can make webcalls to get //
information about "me".
private Hashtable GraphAPI(Uri uri, string accessToken)
{
UriBuilder builder = new UriBuilder(uri);
    if (!string.IsNullOrEmpty(builder.Query))
    {
        builder.Query += "&";
    }

builder.Query += "access_token=" + accessToken;
JavaScriptSerializer jsSerializer = new JavaScriptSerializer();

    using (WebClient client = new WebClient())
    {
        string data = client.DownloadString(builder.ToString());
return (jsSerializer.Deserialize(data, typeof(Hashtable)) as
Hashtable);
    }
}
```

The `Index` method of the Facebook controller returns the Facebook view and passes
on the information about "me" to be displayed.

```
return View(GraphAPI(new Uri("https://graph.Facebook.com/me"),
accessToken));
```

Traffic Manager

The **Windows Azure Traffic Manager (WATM)** enables you to configure and control how user traffic is distributed to your hosted services. You can use the Traffic Manager to create an application that services users all around the world while still upholding performance and availability and being robust and resilient. Based on a policy that you configure, the WATM routes traffic to the correct hosted service. Under the hood, **DNS** is used to route traffic to the correct service, and the WATM is not an additional entity that sits in the middle of all that user traffic. The WATM is enabled and configured from the Windows Azure portal. In the following diagram, the process of routing traffic is displayed:

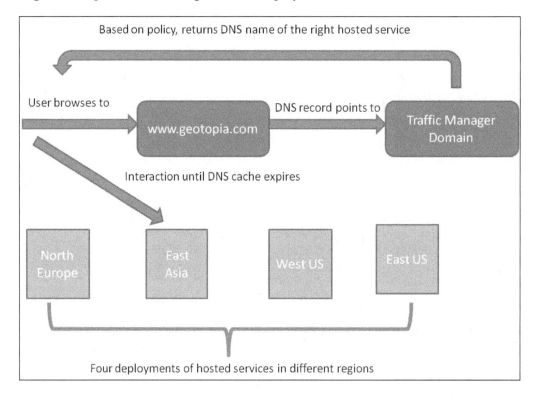

The detailed flow is as follows:

- The user browses to the appropriate domain name (www.geotopia.com). Obviously, this domain name needs to be reserved at some domain name registrar.

- Our DNS record for the Geotopia domain refers to the Traffic Manager domain which is configured in the Windows Azure portal.

- Based on the applied policy (load balance method and monitoring status), the Traffic Manager returns the IP address of the chosen hosted service to the user.

- The user calls the hosted service directly, using its IP address. The domain and IP address are cached on the client, so the user keeps interacting with the hosted service until the local DNS cache expires.

- If the DNS cache expires, the whole process starts again and may result in another IP address!

Setting it up

Setting up the WATM is done by configuration in the Windows Azure portal.

1. Browse to your portal and click on the **Virtual Network** tab on the ribbon, which will open the following screen:

2. From the preceding screen, you can click on **Create** to set up a new policy for WATM, as follows:

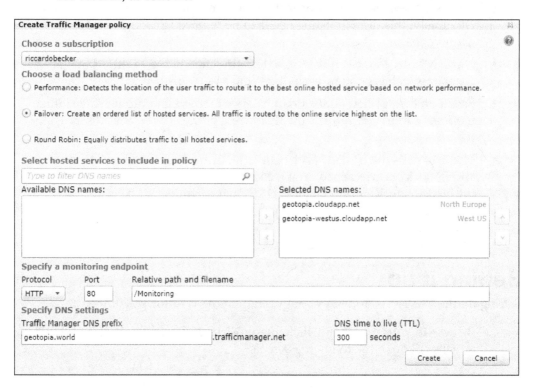

This screen allows you to set up a new policy for Traffic Manager. In our scenario, we are interested in a failover load balancing method. This enables Geotopia to become a robust and resilient solution that has high availability. When either one of my hosted services in the North Europe region or the West US region is unavailable for any reason, WATM ensures that traffic is rerouted to the other hosted service, allowing my application to be available even in case of a major event. The rerouting is based on the next highest service in the list in case a service fails. In our case, we have the solution running in two different datacenters and if either one of them goes down, the next will service the user request. Copy the rest of the settings as shown in the previous screenshot. Click on **Create** to actually create and set up the policy.

After creating the policy, you can review the policy in the **Traffic Manager | Policies** tab.

Round robin

Besides a failover balancing method, there is also the round robin way of load balancing. Choosing this method means that all traffic is equally distributed over the hosted services that are included in the policy.

What happens when a round robin policy is set up?

1. A user accesses the domain, `www.geotopia.com`. The configured Traffic Manager actually receives the incoming request.

2. In the round robin policy, a list of hosted services is created. The Traffic Manager keeps track of the service that received the last request.

3. The Traffic Manager sends the next hosted service in line back to the client.

4. The Traffic Manager remembers this hosted service as being the one that serviced the last traffic.

5. The next request follows this sequence again.

Performance

The performance load balancing policy routes the traffic to the closest hosted service. The Traffic Manager knows the origin of the request. To define what the closest hosted service is, a network performance table containing round-trip times is created and maintained. The table is updated at fixed intervals.

The following events take place when a performance policy is created:

1. Traffic Manager determines the round trip times between different locations in the world and the Windows Azure datacenters. All this happens under the hood and cannot be influenced. These round-trip times are kept in a network performance table.

2. A user accesses the domain, and therefore, Traffic Manager receives the request.

3. Traffic Manager determines, by querying the network performance table, the best performing hosted service to handle this specific request. The best performing hosted service is the one with the lowest round-trip time, not necessarily the closest one.

4. Traffic Manager returns the DNS name of the hosted service with the best round-trip time.

5. The client calls the hosted service that is chosen by the Traffic Manager.

Keep in mind that the time-to-live on a client machine determines how long the DNS entries are cached. As long as the cache is not expired, requests will be sent to the same hosted service (since the IP address of the hosted service is resolved from the local DNS cache).

Failover

The following events take place when a failover policy is created:

1. A failover policy routes the traffic to the next cloud service in line. It iterates a table from the top down, containing all the cloud services that are part of the policy. It continues to iterate until it finds a service that is not offline. The Traffic Manager receives a request from a user that browses to the Geotopia portal.

2. The Traffic Manager iterates the ordered list of the cloud services being part of the policy and determines which is the first in the list that is online.

3. The DNS entry of the first online cloud service is returned to the user.

4. The client calls the IP address of the first-in-line, online cloud service.

Testing the policies

In order to test different policies, you need to take a few steps. In case of the failover scenario, perform the following steps:

1. Bring up all your hosted services. In my scenario, we have two hosted services — one running in North Europe and the other running in West US. This is the ideal scenario where every run is normal.

2. Open a command prompt and use the `nslookup` command to verify the primary hosted service in use:

```
Administrator: Visual Studio Command Prompt (2010)

D:\>nslookup geotopia.world.trafficmanager.net
Server:   UnKnown
Address:  10.20.63.98

Non-authoritative answer:
Name:     geotopia.cloudapp.net
Address:  168.63.40.152
Aliases:  geotopia.world.trafficmanager.net


D:\>
```

3. Now, bring down the primary hosted service. You can do this by stopping the primary hosted service in the Windows Azure portal.

4. Now use the `nslookup` command again, and the result should point to the next hosted service in line, in this scenario, to the one deployed in the West US region. This is displayed in the following screenshot:

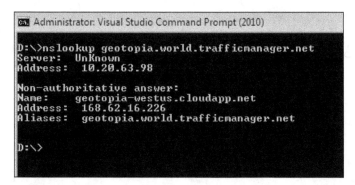

5. To test the WATM policy based on round robin, follow the exact steps as described earlier, but then without bringing down one of the services.

6. When the TTL expires, the `nslookup` command will return a different hosted service than before:

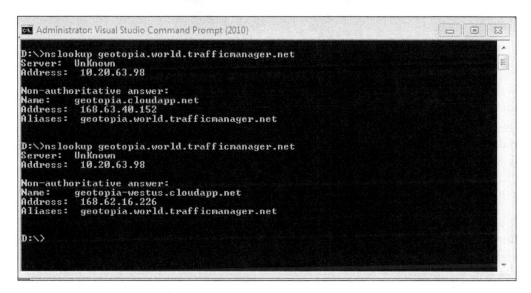

Testing your Traffic Manager based on performance is a bit tougher to accomplish. You need to set up different clients all around the world (running in Azure, of course!) to simulate diverse user traffic that all call the hosted service through www.geotopia.com. There are third-party tools available that can support you with doing this.

Failover scenario

Bringing the WATM together with SQL Azure Data Sync offers a great combination for failover. In the following diagram, you can see these two brought together:

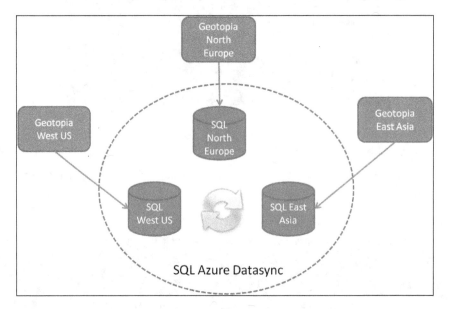

The complete set of Geotopia services contained in a hosted service is deployed in different regions with at least two instances of every role to uphold the basic SLA that the platform offers. Every hosted service has its own connection string and connects to its own, co-located SQL Azure database to minimize latency and reduce bandwidth costs.

There are an equal number of SQL Azure databases, all deployed in the same datacenters as their accompanying hosted service. The SQL Azure databases are kept in sync by using SQL Azure Data Sync, as explained in the previous chapter.

It is possible to define three different policies to support all scenarios:

- **Failover**: To make sure that Geotopia is never unreachable in case of a major event. Traffic is rerouted to the next hosted service in line to handle user requests, until the hosted service is back up again. Data Sync will keep the databases synchronized.
- **Round robin**: To distribute traffic equally around hosted services.
- **Performance**: To get the most out of the application by having the Traffic Manager select the best performing hosted service based on network performance.

Summary

In this chapter, we saw that AppFabric offers some very interesting features. We also saw how to set up Service Bus queuing and how to send and receive messages to and from it. In addition, topics and subscriptions were explained, together with some code snippets.

We learned how we can add caching capabilities to our application quickly and how to fine-tune this. We demonstrated the configuration of Windows Azure caching and saw how to programmatically use caching features.

The next subject covered was the Windows Azure Connect feature. This is an interesting method to build hybrid cloud solutions that mix web and worker roles together with local, on-premise servers, virtual machines, or anything else that has an IP address.

We also covered the Access Control Service that is part of AppFabric and we saw how to build a claims-aware application and how to integrate our solution with an Identity Provider, such as Facebook.

Finally, we went through the Windows Azure Traffic Manager and saw how some interesting scenarios can be created to offer the best for our clients and uphold the high performance and failover standards we have for our applications.

The next chapter will walk you through the different billing aspects of Windows Azure. As you pay per use, you will also need to pay extra attention to the resources you are going to use on the Windows Azure platform.

7
The Billing Aspects of Windows Azure

"My doctor gave me six months to live, but when I couldn't pay the bill he gave me six months more."

— Walter Matthau, actor

This chapter describes the different aspects of billing on Windows Azure. It gives an insight into the basic billing details of the different Windows Azure components. It explains the Windows Azure Pricing Calculator, different purchase options, different member offers, and free trials. It also focuses on how to program in a cost-effective manner and provides some tips and tricks on how to keep the bill as low as possible while still delivering the value we want to deliver.

Basic billing details

In this section, we will learn the basics of the billing model of Windows Azure. We will see that not everything is billed in the same way and that there are differences between the features of the platform.

Compute

We are charged for the compute hours when our application is deployed on Azure. The hours are calculated in clock hours, for example, from 10:00 pm till 10:59 pm. Keep in mind that we are billed for the hours our services are deployed and not for the hours our services are running. Suspended cloud services still appear on the bill.

Don't assume we are only billed for the running hours, because a lot of my colleagues were unhappily surprised by a bill even when their web role instances were in suspended mode. Remember that even when our application is not running, it is still deployed and Microsoft has to create a virtual machine for the designated role. It is always a good practice to make sure our roles are undeployed if we do not need them. This can reduce costs, especially during development and testing phases. Partial hours (for example, thirty minutes) are rounded up to a full hour.

In the following table, the costs per hour are listed based on the basic plan (pay as you go):

VM Size	Number of Cores	Memory	Charges	Local Storage	Allocated Bandwidth
Extra Small	Shared	768 MB	$ 0.02 per hour	~19 GB	5 Mbps
Small	1	1.75 GB	$ 0.12 per hour	~224 GB	100 Mbps
Medium	2	3.5 GB	$ 0.24 per hour	~489 GB	200 Mbps
Large	4	7 GB	$ 0.48 per hour	~1 TB	400 Mbps
Extra Large	8	14 GB	$ 0.96 per hour	~2 TB	800 Mbps

Keep in mind that for the VM role, local disk storage is less than that in the preceding table, since the operating system requires more space.

As mentioned before, computing is charged by the compute hour, and all compute hours are presented on our bill as small instance hours. As we can see in the table, the prices of the VM sizes (besides Extra Small) are the prices of a Small instance multiplied by the number of cores. Since computing is charged by the clock hour, each time we deploy a service, we are charged for at least one hour. If an instance of a role is deployed for less than five minutes in an hour, there will be no charges for that role in that hour.

Windows Azure SQL databases

Windows Azure SQL databases are billed monthly based on the size of the database. At the time of writing, there are two editions available:

* Web Edition, which supports up to 5 GB
* Business Edition, which supports up to 150 GB

The charges for the different databases are listed as follows:

Size	Charges
Up to 100 MB	Flat rate of $4.995 per month
Above 100 MB up to 1 GB	Flat rate of $9.99 per month
Above 1 GB up to 10 GB	$9.99 for the first GB and an additional $3.996 per extra GB
Above 10 GB up to 50 GB	$45.954 for the first 10 GB and an additional $1.998 per extra GB
Above 50 GB up to 150 GB	$125.874 for the first 50 GB and an additional $0.999 per extra GB

We are charged at a monthly rate for each Azure database we use, but the fee is calculated on a daily basis.

For example, if you have a 20 GB database up and running for seven days, within one month, you will be charged:

- $ 45.954 for the first 10 GB
- $1.998 per GB for the next 10 GB for the period of 7 days (10 * $1.998 / 31 days * 7 days), which adds up to $4.51, bringing the total that month to $45.954 + $4.51, which is $50.464

Storage

Storage is billed as per average daily amount of GB stored in any of the storage areas (table, blob, or queue). For example, if you have 100 GB stored for the whole month in blob storage, you are charged for 100 * $0.125, which amounts to $12.50. If you have the same amount of data but only for one day, you are charged $12.50 divided by 31, which would be around $0.40.

Remember that besides being charged for the amounts of gigabytes, you are also charged for each storage operation. These are charged at $0.01 per 100,000 transactions.

Bandwidth

Microsoft decided that uploading data to any of its datacenters is free of charge. Outbound data transfers are charged per GB. For the European and North American regions, the charges are $0.12 per GB, while for the Asia Pacific regions, the charges are $0.19 per GB.

Bandwidth is not charged if you transfer data between cloud services, SQL databases, or other Windows Azure features within the same datacenter. At the time of this writing, there are the following datacenters: North Europe, West Europe, Southeast Asia, East Asia, North Central US, South Central US, West US, and East US.

Content delivery network

All requests to the Content delivery network are billed as well as the bandwidth that is needed for the transfer of the data. The charges are the same as ordinary bandwidth charges. Keep in mind that the charges of data transfer are based on the location of the datacenter and not the user.

It is not possible to control which locations deliver what content. You should carefully analyze your bill for CDN charges, since you are not in charge and if your solution serves a lot of people in the Asia Pacific regions, you might be surprised (or shocked) by the costs.

Users are redirected to the closest CDN nodes, where closest means those with the fastest network access. When a node is down, data is served for another location, such as Northern Europe. When a user tries to open a video and the file is not available yet on the CDN node, an ordinary request to blob storage is made to transfer the data from the original datacenter to the CDN node (charged separately).

Cache

The billing aspects of the cache are a fixed fee per month per cache size and additional bandwidth costs if the cache is accessed from outside the datacenter.

In the following table, the prices are listed based on the standard pay-as-you-go fees and are applicable to the shared caching facility of Windows Azure:

Cache size	Fee
128 MB	$45
256 MB	$55
512 MB	$75
1 GB	$110
2 GB	$180
4 GB	$325

After you provision a cache with a size of, say, 128 MB, the system will limit the amount of data in your cache. It might be possible that at a certain point there is more data in the cache than you subscribed for, but this will be temporary. Windows Azure will delete data from your cache until it is below its threshold again. Windows Azure also might limit the number of transactions made, the amount of data transferred, or the number of concurrent connections, to ensure a fair use policy.

The following table lists the thresholds beyond which the system will raise exceptions. According to Microsoft's pricing pages (http://www.windowsazure.com/en-us/pricing/details/#caching), these numbers are an estimation:

Cache	Number of transactions per hour	Data per hour	Concurrent connections
128 MB	400,000	1,400 MB	10
256 MB	800,000	2,800 MB	10
512 MB	1,600,000	5,600 MB	20
1 GB	3,200,000	11,200 MB	40
2 GB	6,400,000	22,400 MB	80
4 GB	12,800,000	44,800 MB	160

The role-based caching discussed in *Chapter 6, Key Features Explained*, is billed the same way as compute hours, together with additional bandwidth costs if the caching facility is being accessed from outside the datacenter in which the role is running.

Service Bus

You will be charged $0.01 per 10,000 messages (send or receive) and $0.10 per 100 hours of relaying. Both messages sent to and delivered by the service bus will be included in the total number of messages. Relay hours are charged from the time of creation until the time of deletion and are rounded up to the whole hour. Besides paying for messages and relaying, you will have additional data transfer fees.

Access Control Service

Access Control Service (ACS) is a service offered by Windows Azure that enables authenticating users without building this authentication code. ACS integrates with common identity providers such as Windows Live ID, Google, and Facebook as well as Active Directory. The billing model for access control is fairly simple. You will be charged for the number of transactions and bandwidth. The standard pricing for ACS is $1.99 per 100,000 transactions.

Pricing

This section shows how to use the Microsoft calculator to estimate your costs and how to get the cheapest offer for your needs. Also, the different purchase options and member offers are explained.

Calculator

In the following figure, you can see a fictional usage scenario at a high level. The service utilized three small instances (1 web role instance and 2 worker role instances), a 5-GB SQL Azure database, 1,000 GB of blob storage, and an additional 400 GB of outbound data transfer. At a glance, you can see that the price will be around $468, but you can also immediately see that you would benefit from a 6-month plan, since it would save you around 14 percent.

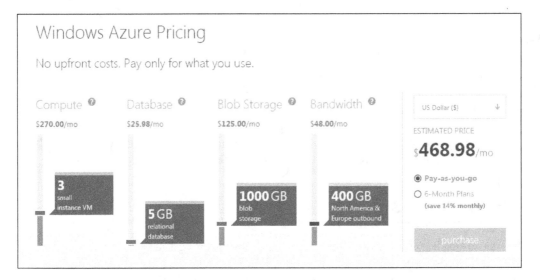

This is the compact view of the calculator and can be used to give us an indication of the costs. To get a more detailed and fine-grained overview of estimated costs, you can use the Full Pricing Calculator, which enables you to tweak every single concept of Azure that you will be billed for. Also for more complex scenarios, we should use this extended calculator.

It enables you to specify the following:

- Exactly how many instances of any VM size will be used
- The size and the number of SQL Azure databases
- The amount in GB stored and the number of storage transactions

- The estimated bandwidth for each tariff area
- Number of Service Bus messages and relaying hours
- The estimated CDN bandwidth for each tariff region
- The number of access control transactions
- The size of the cache

Again, in this scenario you immediately see whether or not it is cheaper to buy a 6-month plan.

Purchase options

Microsoft offers two purchase options — pay-as-you-go and a 6-month plan. Pay-as-you-go is where you pay for what you use, with no commitment. Microsoft offers high discounts if you decide to buy one of the 6-month plans. This plan offers a 20 percent discount on computing fees and up to 33 percent on storage fees. When your usage exceeds the plan, you will be charged at normal pay-as-you-go tariffs.

Member offers

MSDN subscribers, MPN members, or BizSpark members get free access to Windows Azure resources as part of the membership.

MSDN subscribers

If you or your company are already MSDN subscribers, you will have free access to Azure resources.

The following table lists the benefits for a Visual Studio Ultimate with MSDN. The benefits for MSDN subscribers are sufficient to enable some exploration of the Windows Azure features and get familiar with it.

Azure Resource	Benefit
Compute	1,500 hours of the small instance compute size
CDN	2,000,000 transactions
Storage	30 GB
Storage transactions	4,000,000
SQL Azure	5 GB web edition
ACS transactions	500,000
Caching	128 MB
Data transfer	35 GB

MPN members

For Microsoft Partner Network members, there are two distinctive offers (besides the normal ones, of course); Cloud Essentials and Cloud Accelerate.

Cloud Essentials

When your business is not cloud ready yet, you can make use of this offer to quickly get access to different resources for free. There are some requirements for enrolling in the Cloud Essentials pack:

- Signing the Microsoft Online Services Partner Agreement and completing training and assessment
- A membership in a Microsoft Partner Network Competency
- To have closed three cloud deals with a minimum of 150 total licenses prior to the enrollment
- After successfully enrolling into the Cloud Essentials program, closing three more cloud deals within the next 12 months, to continue to benefit from the program

Besides Windows Azure offerings, there are others as well, and they are listed in the following table:

Offer	Description
Microsoft Office 365	250 licenses
Windows Intune	Subscription for 25 PCs
Dynamics CRM Online	250 licenses
Windows Azure	375 hours of small compute instance
	20 GB of storage
	250,000 storage transactions
	SQL Azure Web Edition 1 GB database
	100,000 ACS transactions
	128 MB cache
	25 GB data transfer

Cloud Accelerate

When your company is already doing business in the cloud, you can qualify for the Accelerate program and get additional benefits. To qualify for this program, you need to enroll in the Essentials program first. Besides the benefits from the Essentials program, you get some additional interesting features, such as the following:

- You get listed as an Accelerate partner on the Pinpoint marketplace and the Office 365 marketplace
- 20 advisory hours
- Cloud Accelerate logo
- Additional access to training resources

Obviously, the requirements for this program are more stringent than for Cloud Essentials. First, you need to get the Essentials pack and meet those requirements. Secondly, you need to get your application certified as being platform ready. Thirdly, you need to agree to a certain sales commitment, and last but not least, you need to provide three customer references.

BizSpark members

Members of the BizSpark program get the Azure benefits through their Ultimate MSDN subscription. This means that the offerings for BizSpark members are the same as the ones for Ultimate MSDN subscribers. This offer is described in the previous sections.

How much we use

Now that the prices are clear, the big question is how we can predict the costs. We do not want to be surprised with a high bill at the end of the month, so it is important for us to be able to estimate the costs per billing period. As described in the previous sections, a few costs are hard to estimate. These are bandwidth, transactions, and the amount of data stored. Predicting the costs of compute power is fairly simple, at least, if your deployment is a flat deployment with no auto scaling implemented (see *Chapter 8*, *Windows Azure Patterns*, for auto scaling using the Enterprise Library).

Bandwidth is only charged when data is accessed from outside the datacenter. Hosted services deployed in the same datacenter, using storage, will not cause any bandwidth charges.

Every REST request to any of the storage concepts (not SQL Database) will cause a storage transaction (which is billable).

Everything that is stored in your storage accounts will be added up to measure storage costs.

Bandwidth

As described before, bandwidth is only charged when it goes beyond the datacenter boundaries. Choose the location of your storage account carefully. Even better, use affinity groups to ensure that hosted services and the storage account are co-located. Accessing storage will result in storage transactions, and the location where the REST request is coming from is not important.

When a user requests a blob from CDN and the blob is not on the CDN node yet, it will be transferred by the system. This will result in a single storage transaction, together with bandwidth charges. This will also occur when the time-to-live of the blob has expired, so make sure the TTL is not too tight, since it will cause additional bandwidth and storage transactions to be billed.

In the following figures, you can see some scenarios that will clarify when you are and aren't charged.

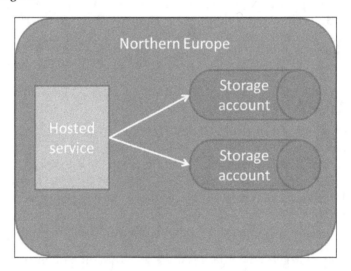

A hosted service touching two different storage accounts within the same Northern Europe datacenter will not cause any bandwidth charges, but only storage transactions.

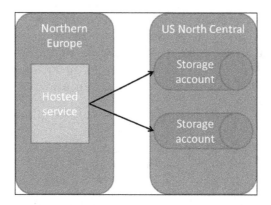

A hosted service running in the Northern Europe region and accessing data located in the US North Central region will incur bandwidth charges (since they are not in the same datacenter). Storage transactions will also be billed.

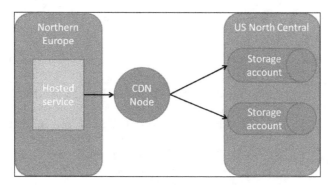

A cloud service, running in the Northern Europe region and accessing data from a CDN node located in Europe somewhere, will result in exactly one storage transaction and bandwidth charges depending on the number of gigabytes. Data is being served to the original storage accounts located in the US North Central region, causing a transfer of a blob from storage to the CDN node.

What is counted as a transaction

The basics are simple—every single REST call to some storage entity will be counted as one storage transaction. Obviously, you will only be charged for successful transactions.

Since every REST call is counted as a transaction, a query resulting in continuation tokens will also result in multiple transactions. Every continuation will also count as a single transaction. For example, getting 5,000 records from a table will cause the initial REST request to add one transaction and the four REST requests; using the continuation tokens will cause an additional four transactions.

Batched operations are pretty efficient, since you can get or update multiple entities in a single transaction (only causing one storage transaction to be billed). The `GetMessages` operation can get up to 32 messages in a single operation. `Entity Group Transactions` can perform an atomic transaction with a maximum of 100 entities but cause only one storage transaction to be accrued.

REST calls made yourself are easier to track than REST calls that are made by Storage Client Library. It is hard to guess what happens under the hood of the Storage Client Library and how certain calls are translated in how many storage transactions.

In the following table, different impacts on storage transactions and sizes in different Storage Client Library calls are listed.

Scenario	Impact
Uploading a blob of 100 MB	By default, the blob will be broken into 4 MB blocks, resulting in 25 blocks. Every block will be uploaded with the `PutBlock` REST call, resulting in 25 storage transactions with an additional transaction because of the `PutBlockList` command, which will commit all the blocks uploaded before. The block size can be changed with the `WriteBlockSizeInBytes` objects of the `CloudBloblClient` class.
Querying a table	Querying a table using the `CloudTableQuery` class implicitly results in the use of continuation tokens, and therefore, in performing multiple REST requests to the table.
SaveChanges to a table	`AddObject`, `UpdateObject`, or `DeleteObject` will only reflect the context. The actions are flushed to the underlying Azure table when `SaveChanges` is called. All pending actions are flushed to the storage service, using its corresponding REST call. So, every single change to the context will result in one storage transaction added to your bill. The exception is when you use batching, which will flush all changes at once to the underlying service, only counting for one storage transaction.
GetBlob, PutBlob	Result in one transaction.

Scenario	Impact
Querying a table getting a single entity	Results in one transaction.
Querying a table getting multiple entities	Results in one transaction (will be more if continuation tokens are available).
Putting and getting a message from queue	Results in one transaction.

How to reduce the number of transactions

There are different ways of reducing transactions, but we will illustrate a few examples in this section.

Back in the old days (pre-Azure, ancient times), we had MSMQ. Some Windows Service handles messages appearing in those queues would constantly poll the queues to see if some new message had appeared.

Now, in Azure times, polling a queue (or peeking) counts as a transaction, so imagine what the financial consequences are of polling every 2 seconds for a whole month.

1800 transactions per hour * 24 * 30 = 1, 296, 000 storage transactions per month, and this will result in 1,296,000 / 100,000 = \$0.13 for just polling a queue for a month. Imagine how this will add up if you have different instances of worker roles doing the same thing for many different queues.

Have a look at the following code snippet, which is the Run() method of a worker role doing a lot of intensive processing on a queue:

```
//doing some intensive and expensive queuing in a worker role
public override void Run()
{
    CloudStorageAccount account = CloudStorageAccount.
DevelopmentStorage;

    CloudQueueClient client = account.CreateQueueClient();
    CloudQueue queue = client.GetQueueReference("expensivequeue");
    Client.CreateQueueIfNotExists();

    While(true)
    {
```

```
            CloudQueueMessage message = queue.GetMessage();
            if(message != null)
            {
                    //process it
                    Process(message);
                    Queue.DeleteMessage(message);
            }
        }
    }
```

At first, there is nothing special about this little piece of code, but wait—this worker will continuously take a message from the queue, and if there is one available, process it and finally delete it.

A queue can handle up to 500 transactions per second, but let's assume in this example, because of some processing time, this little piece of code is only able to handle 100 messages per second (and 100 deletions, of course!).

This code snippet will add up to: 200 transactions per second (100 `GetMessage` transactions and 100 `DeleteMessage` transactions) * 60 second * 60 minutes * 24 hours * 30 days = 518,400,000 transactions per month! This amounts to $5.18 a month.

> We should be glad we used `DevelopmentStorage` in this code example, otherwise we would have to pay!

You can eliminate storage transactions by putting a `Thread.Sleep()` statement inside the `while` loop to delay the polling if there is no message available. A sleeping period of 100 milliseconds will drastically reduce the storage transaction bill. After all, this will cause the worker role only to touch the queue ten times per second (20, if there are messages that are processed and deleted as well), instead of 200 times.

Implement a back-off inside your worker role to enhance the sleeping period when no messages are in the queue.

Have a look at the following code snippet:

```
    TimeSpan maximumDelay = TimeSpan.FromMinutes(10);

    TimeSpan currentDelay;

        public override void Run()
        {
```

```
        CloudStorageAccount account = CloudStorageAccount.
DevelopmentStorageAccount;
        CloudQueueClient client = account.CreateCloudQueueClient();
        CloudQueue queue = client.GetQueueReference("messages");
        queue.CreateIfNotExist();

        //initially wait for 100 milliseconds if no msg is found
        currentDelay = TimeSpan.FromMilliseconds(100);

        while (true)
        {
          CloudQueueMessage msg = queue.GetMessage();
          if (msg != null)
          {
            ProcessMessage(msg);
            queue.DeleteMessage(msg);
            currentDelay = TimeSpan.FromMilliseconds(100);
          }
          else
          {
            Thread.Sleep(currentDelay);
            if (currentDelay < maximumDelay)
              currentDelay = currentDelay.Add(currentDelay);
            Trace.WriteLine(String.Format("Currently backing off for
{0} seconds",                                currentDelay.TotalSeconds.
ToString()));

          }

        }
      }
```

What happens in this code snippet is that every time when no message is available,
the thread sleep will take longer and longer (actually, it doubles each time),
up to more than 10 minutes. This will drastically reduce the number of storage
transactions, especially compared with the previous snippets. When a message
is found on the queue, the back-off delay is reset to 100 milliseconds, because
it is reasonable to expect that more messages will appear on the queue.

In the output of Compute Emulator, you can see this backing off mechanism work. Look at the following screenshot:

```
[MonAgentHost] Output: Agent will exit when
[MonAgentHost] Output: Monitoring Agent Start
[Diagnostics]: Starting configuration channel
Currently backing off for 6,4 seconds
Currently backing off for 12,8 seconds
Currently backing off for 25,6 seconds
Currently backing off for 51,2 seconds
[Diagnostics]: Checking for configuration up
[Diagnostics]: Signalling process restart on
[MonAgentHost] Output: Exiting the monitorin
[MonAgentHost] Output: Monitoring Agent Stop
[Diagnostics] Information: Diagnostic proces
[Diagnostics] Information: D:\Users\RIBECKER
[Diagnostics] Information: d:\users\ribecker
\monitor\MonAgentHost.exe -LocalPath "D:\Use
"D:\Users\RIBECKER\AppData\Local\dftmp\Resou
\RIBECKER\AppData\Local\dftmp\Resources\ce84
ShutDown-2492945bf2bb49f1b16edcf4bb07fb10 -I
[MonAgentHost] Output: Agent will exit when
[MonAgentHost] Output: Will signal WADM-Start
[MonAgentHost] Output: Registered as an event
[MonAgentHost] Output: Agent will exit when
[MonAgentHost] Output: Monitoring Agent Start
[Diagnostics]: Starting configuration channe
Currently backing off for 102,4 seconds
[Diagnostics]: Checking for configuration up
[Diagnostics]: Checking for configuration up
Currently backing off for 204,8 seconds
[Diagnostics]: Checking for configuration up
```

Another cost-effective measure is to pay close attention to your diagnostics and logging.

With Windows Azure Diagnostics, you can collect a lot of useful diagnostic information from your deployments and instances. But, the downside is that every gathered metric will be copied to a storage account you configure. For monitoring and performance measuring, this mechanism works fine, but when running in a production environment, there is no need to turn on intensive diagnostics (you can do this remotely, in case of incidents). In the code snippet, a sampling rate of 120 seconds is used, since in a production environment, we need to see trends in our applications and taking a snapshot every few minutes or hours does not tell us much about the application's performance.

See the following code snippet:

```
public override bool OnStart()
{
// Get the Role instance Diagnostics configuration.
var diagConfig = DiagnosticMonitor.GetDefaultInitialConfiguration();

   var procTimeConfig = new PerformanceCounterConfiguration();
procTimeConfig.CounterSpecifier = @"\Processor(*)\% Processor Time";
procTimeConfig.SampleRate = system.TimeSpan.FromSeconds(120);
        diagConfig.PerformanceCounters.DataSources.Add(procTimeConfig);

var diskBytesConfig = new PerformanceCounterConfiguration();
diskBytesConfig.CounterSpecifier = @"\LogicalDisk(*)\Disk Bytes/sec";

diskBytesConfig.SampleRate = System.TimeSpan.FromSeconds(120);
        diagConfig.PerformanceCounters.DataSources.Add(diskBytesConfig);

var workingSetConfig = new PerformanceCounterConfiguration();
workingSetConfig.CounterSpecifier =        @"\Process(" + System.
Diagnostics.Process. GetCurrentProcess().ProcessName + @")\Working
Set";

workingSetConfig.SampleRate = System.TimeSpan.FromSeconds(120);
        diagConfig.PerformanceCounters.DataSources.
Add(workingSetConfig);
        diagConfig.PerformanceCounters.ScheduledTransferPeriod =
TimeSpan.FromMinutes(5);

DiagnosticMonitor.Start("Microsoft.WindowsAzure.Plugins.Diagnostics.
ConnectionString", diagConfig);

return base.OnStart();

}
```

The preceding code snippet initializes the worker role to start gathering diagnostics information on three different performance counters. The sampling interval is set to 120 seconds, which means that every two minutes, three storage transactions are being made.

Diagnostics information in stored is a table called `WADPerformanceCountersTable`. There are a lot of tools out there that can help you analyze the trends of your performance counters, for example, Cloud Storage Studio 2 from Cerebrata. The following figure is a snapshot from the performance counter, Processor Time. This performance counter can give one insight into how busy their worker role is.

From the preceding figure, you can see that this worker role is working, but not very hard, so there is no action needed for scaling up or otherwise.

 The sampling rate was set to 1 second to create this figure.

When are transactions billed

In the previous section, we explained what exactly storage transactions are. Not all of the storage transactions will actually be counted towards billing.

The following table lists all scenarios in which no storage transaction and/ or bandwidth is charged:

Scenario	Explanation
Prior to authentication failure	The system is not able to authenticate the request because of bad HTTPS headers or malformed URLs.
Authentication failure	Authentication fails because the provided account key is invalid.

Scenario	Explanation
An anonymous request	A request without signature not being a GET request will not result in a storage transaction.
Quota limit	When your storage action results in exceeding the 100 TB limit per storage account, the system will only allow read and delete actions.
Getting a non-existent blob from a non-existent container	Trying to get a blob from a container that is just not there (no blob or no container).
Timeouts	The system timing out will not result in a transaction.

Obviously, every successful transaction will be added to your bill. However, some actions performed on the storage system might fail but still count as a transaction (or more than one). The following table lists several of these scenarios:

Scenario	Impact
ETag matching	A storage operation failing because of a conditional ETag operation will still count as one storage transaction (you did touch the storage after all).
Add an existing entity	Trying to add an entity that is already there will result in a 409 failure but still counts as a storage transaction.
Updating a non-existing entity	Trying to update an entity that is not there will result in a 404 (not found) failure but still counts as a storage transaction.
A valid SAS	Providing a valid Shared Access Signature when the container or specific blob does not exist will still count as one storage transaction.

It is a good practice to keep in mind what might happen under the hood of the specific Storage Client library classes. Remember that storage transactions have nothing to do with the number of entities, messages, or megabytes, but only with the corresponding REST requests made to the storage service. If you specifically want to control the number of transactions, use the REST interface only (will be more work), instead of the Storage Client library.

Estimate capacity

To get a good grip on your needed storage capacity, you need to understand the basic billing principles of storage, as described in the first section of this chapter. Secondly, you need to understand how much data is actually stored and what aspects of storage consume storage space. The following table lists which assets of storage consume disk space and how this can be calculated. Some might be unexpected!

Storage Asset	Calculation
A block blob	The size of a blob is calculated as: *124 bytes + 2* length (blob name) + for each metadata (3 bytes + length (metadata name) + length (value)) + 8 bytes + number of blocks * block id size + size in bytes* This is explained in more detail as follows: • 124 bytes is the overhead for a blob with some metadata. • The blob name is stored as Unicode so the length of the blob name in bytes is doubled. • For each instance of metadata, the length of the name and the length of the value add up to the size of the blob. The block list adds another 8 bytes. • Number of blocks multiplied with the block ID size. • Size of the data in both committed and uncommitted blocks. Uncommitted blocks that are not committed within a week, will be discarded by the system and will stop accruing charges.
A page blob	The size of a page blob is calculated slightly differently: *124 bytes + 2 * length (blob name) + for each metadata (3 bytes + length (metadata name)) + length (value) + number of non-consecutive page ranges * 12 bytes + size in bytes* • The metadata part of the calculation for a page blob is identical to a block blob • The number of non-consecutive page ranges, multiplied by 12 bytes, is also added to the size of the page blob • The total size of the data, in bytes, of all the stored pages is also added to the total size of the page blob
A blob container	The size of a blob container (with nothing in it) can be calculated as follows: *2* Length (ContainerName) + 48 bytes + for each metadata (3 bytes + length (metadata)) + for each signed identifier (512 bytes)* This is explained in more detail as follows: • 48 bytes is the overhead for each container containing metadata • ContainerName is stored as Unicode, which causes the duplication • For every piece of metadata, the length of the name and the length of the string value are stored • Signed identifier includes name, expiry time, start time, and information around permissions

Storage Asset	Calculation
A table	A table consumes the following amount of storage: • 12-bytes overhead for each table of metadata • The length of the table name multiplied by two, because of Unicode

An entity	An entity consumes the following in terms of storage:
	
	• 4 bytes of overhead for each entity, because of metadata
	
	• The length of the PartitionKey and RowKey multiplied by two, because of Unicode
	
	• For every property, an overhead of 8-bytes plus the name of the property multiplied by the Unicode factor 2 plus the size of the property type
	
	• Property types:
	
	    String: *number of characters * 2 bytes + 4 bytes for length of string*
	
	    DateTime: 8 bytes
	
	    GUID: 16 bytes
	
	    Double: 8 bytes
	
	    Int: 4 bytes
	
	    Int64: 8 bytes
	
	    Bool: 1 byte
	
	    Binary: 4 bytes for the length and the size of the value in bytes

A queue	A queue consumes the following storage: • 24 bytes of overhead for metadata • For each piece of metadata stored, the length of the name and the length of the value is multiplied by two
A message	A message takes 12 bytes of overhead for metadata purposes (for example, for Creation Time and Invisibility Time) plus the length of the message. Keep in mind that objects being serialized suffer around a 33 percent penalty because of Base64 encoding.

Implementing your own billing tracker

Last year, Microsoft released Windows Azure Storage Analytics, which performs logging and provides metrics on different levels for a specific storage account. The logging and metrics information can be used to find out how many storage transactions you actually performed. This feature of the platform gives you all the information to build your own billing tracker that analyzes this storage analytical information.

Enabling analytics

To turn on Storage Analytics for each service (blob, table, and queue), you must specifically set this in code or use REST requests.

In the following code snippet, everything is explicitly turned on for every service:

```
CloudStorageAccount account = CloudStorageAccount.
DevelopmentStorageAccount;

        CloudBlobClient blobClient = account.CreateCloudBlobClient();
        CloudQueueClient queueClient = account.CreateCloudQueueClient();
        CloudTableClient tableClient = account.CreateCloudTableClient();

        blobClient.SetServiceProperties(new ServiceProperties()
          {
            DefaultServiceVersion = "1.0",
            Logging = new LoggingProperties()
              {
                LoggingOperations = LoggingOperations.All,
                RetentionDays = 7
              },
            Metrics = new MetricsProperties()
            {
              MetricsLevel = MetricsLevel.ServiceAndApi,
              RetentionDays = 7
            }
          });

        queueClient.SetServiceProperties(new ServiceProperties()
        {
          DefaultServiceVersion = "1.0",
          Logging = new LoggingProperties()
          {
            LoggingOperations = LoggingOperations.All,
            RetentionDays = 7
          },
          Metrics = new MetricsProperties()
          {
            MetricsLevel = MetricsLevel.ServiceAndApi,
            RetentionDays = 7
          }
        });
```

```
tableClient.SetServiceProperties(new ServiceProperties()
{
  DefaultServiceVersion = "1.0",
  Logging = new LoggingProperties()
  {
    LoggingOperations = LoggingOperations.All,
    RetentionDays = 7
  },
  Metrics = new MetricsProperties()
  {
    MetricsLevel = MetricsLevel.ServiceAndApi,
    RetentionDays = 7
  }
});
```

In the preceding code snippet, we start logging all the operations on all three storage services and keep the data for 7 days. There is a limit of 20 TB on the analytical data per storage account. The log will contain detailed information for authenticated requests and successful anonymous requests.

Logs are stored in a block blob in an anonymous container, **$logs**, which is created when analytics is enabled. This container cannot be deleted, but its contents can. All metrics data is stored in two separate tables per service, containing capacity information and transaction information.

The following figure displays how storage analytics is organized in terms of table and blob storage. The following snapshot is taken from Cloud Storage Studio 2 by Cerebrata.

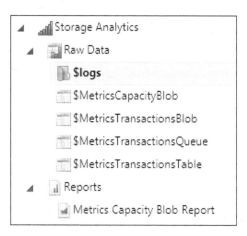

There are two different types of tables. First, there are the ones that contain the transaction information. In the preceding figure, you see the tables **$MetricsTransactionsBlob**, **$MetricsTransactionsQueue**, and **$MetricsTransactionsTable**. Second, there are the ones that contain capacity information that covers all usage data around storage. Version 1.0 of analytics only supports capacity data from blob storage.

Request logging

Both authenticated and anonymous requests are logged inside analytics. Requests made by the Analytics Service itself are obviously not logged.

Type of request	Logged
Authenticated	• Successful requests
	• Failed requests, such as timeout, throttling, and authorization
	• Both successful and failed requests that use a SAS
	• Requests to analytics data itself
Anonymous	• Successful requests
	• Server errors
	• Timeout error
	• 304 failure (Not modified)

All the requests described in the preceding table are logged in a block blob called **$logs** (see previous figure). When you open up the **$logs** block blob, you can see a structured tree as displayed in the following figure:

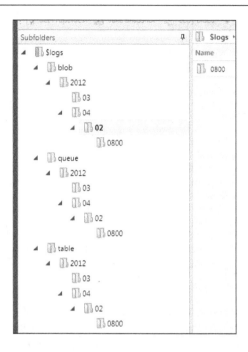

$logs is structured in a tree, and you can drill down from a service (blob, queue, or table) right down until the specified hour. Analytics are stored and grouped on an hourly level.

> Please keep in mind that the **$logs** container is not listed in a `ListContainers` request. We can access it directly or use a third-party tool to unveil the log secrets.

A log file called `000000.log`, in the folder **0800**, logged on April 2, 2012 for a queue service in the Geotopia storage account, can be accessed by REST at the following URL:

```
http://geotopia.blob.core.windows.net/$logs/
queue/2012/04/02/0800/000000.log
```

These logs contain every single transaction that happened on the different storage services. In the different `MetricsTransactions` tables, things are more summarized, and you are better able to analyze these figures.

Example transactions

In the following figure, you can see an example of transactions logged in the `$MetricsTransactionsBlob` table, where the results are narrowed to a certain hour:

PartitionKey	RowKey	Timestamp	TotalRequests	TotalBillableRequ	TotalIngress	TotalEgress	Availability
20120402T0800	system;All	2012-04-02T09:18:29.6505250Z	9	9	21437	1700	100
20120402T0800	user;All	2012-04-02T09:18:29.4504294Z	31	31	9295	35198	100
20120402T0800	user;GetBlob	2012-04-02T09:18:29.6505250Z	4	4	1129	17915	100
20120402T0800	user;GetContainerACL	2012-04-02T09:18:29.4504294Z	7	7	1841	1985	100
20120402T0800	user;GetContainerMetadata	2012-04-02T09:18:29.4504294Z	1	1	280	190	100
20120402T0800	user;ListBlobs	2012-04-02T09:18:29.4504294Z	18	18	5758	13149	100
20120402T0800	user;ListContainers	2012-04-02T09:18:29.4504294Z	1	1	287	1959	100

Taking a closer look at these records, we can see that the system executed nine transactions in this timespan of one hour. These transactions all resulted in billable requests, as you can see in the fifth column.

With respect to transactions being the result of user interaction, you can see that every single hour there is one record available in the table, summarizing what happened in that specific hour. In this example, you see the record with **RowKey user;All**, showing a total of 31 requests, and below that record are the detailed transactions. Listing blobs and containers all result in requests that are billable. The column **TotalEgress** displays how many data transfer bytes were involved in the specific request.

The following figure displays a sample of the queue services and some specific operations:

PartitionKey	RowKey	Timestamp	TotalRequests	TotalBillableRequ	TotalIngress	TotalEgress	Availability
20120329T1500	user;All	2012-03-29T16:20:17.1161488Z	20	20	8158	5156	100
20120329T1500	user;CreateQueue	2012-03-29T16:20:17.1161488Z	1	1	294	126	100
20120329T1500	user;GetMessage	2012-03-29T16:20:17.1161488Z	12	12	3428	2580	100
20120329T1500	user;GetQueueServiceProperties	2012-03-29T16:20:17.1161488Z	2	2	532	1116	100
20120329T1500	user;SetQueueServiceProperties	2012-03-29T16:20:17.1161488Z	5	5	3904	1334	100

In this snapshot, you can see that the summary record is there again. Besides that, the creation of a queue resulted in a billable transaction with some egress, and getting twelve messages (one-by-one) resulted in twelve transactions and some bandwidth. Even turning on this Storage Analytics feature resulted in some billable transactions.

Blob capacity

As we described before, only capacity information for the blob is available at the time of writing (tables and queues will probably follow soon). In general, you can say that blob storage will probably have the highest impact on your monthly bill, so being able to get the figures around blob capacity will help you build your own billing tracker and keep a close eye on your bill.

In the following figure, you can see a snapshot of my blob analytics data:

PartitionKey	RowKey	Timestamp	Capacity	ContainerCount	ObjectCount
20120330T0000	analytics	2012-03-30T01:21:11.4757180Z	76811	1	34
20120330T0000	data	2012-03-30T01:21:11.6295593Z	128571	7	7
20120331T0000	analytics	2012-03-31T01:19:38.2256071Z	76811	1	34
20120331T0000	data	2012-03-31T01:19:38.5829026Z	128571	7	7
20120401T0000	analytics	2012-04-01T01:19:39.5393374Z	76811	1	34
20120401T0000	data	2012-04-01T01:19:39.8759800Z	128571	7	7
20120402T0000	analytics	2012-04-02T01:18:28.7349723Z	76811	1	34
20120402T0000	data	2012-04-02T01:18:28.6610420Z	128571	7	7

This screenshot tells us that there are two records every hour on the blob capacity metrics—one record telling us how much data is involved with analytics data (which you also have to pay for, of course) and the other records telling us how much of our own data usage is being billed.

The **Capacity** column displays how many bytes are involved.

Since every request made to the storage service is logged by Storage Analytics, including status, number of bytes involved, and whether or not the request was billable, you have all the information in your hands to build a real-time billing tracker. It can help you investigate your specific usage on the storage service, but most of all, it can help you find out how to improve your storage architecture and where you can save money.

In the following table, the specific operations that are logged by the analytics service are listed; these are the operations that you can expect to appear in the corresponding analytics tables.

Service	Operation
Blob	• `AcquireLease`
	• `BreakLease`
	• `ClearPage`
	• `CopyBlob`
	• `CreateContainer`
	• `DeleteBlob`
	• `DeleteContainer`
	• `GetBlob`
	• `GetBlobMetadata`
	• `GetBlobProperties`
	• `GetBlockList`
	• `GetContainerACL`
	• `GetContainerMetadata`
	• `GetContainerProperties`
	• `GetLeaseInfo`
	• `GetPageRegions`
	• `LeaseBlob`
	• `ListBlobs`
	• `ListContainers`
	• `PutBlob`
	• `PutBlockList`
	• `PutBlock`
	• `PutPage`
	• `ReleaseLease`
	• `RenewLease`
	• `SetBlobMetadata`
	• `SetBlobProperties`
	• `SetContainerACL`
	• `SetContainerMetadata`
	• `SnapshotBlob`
	• `SetBlobServiceProperties`
	• `GetBlobServiceProperties`

Service	Operation
Table	• EntityGroupTransaction
	• CreateTable
	• DeleteTable
	• DeleteEntity
	• InsertEntity
	• InsertOrMergeEntity
	• InsertOrReplaceEntity
	• QueryEntity
	• QueryEntities
	• QueryTable
	• QueryTables
	• UpdateEntity
	• MergeEntity
	• SetTableServiceProperties
	• GetTableServiceProperties
Queue	• CreateQueue
	• DeleteQueue
	• DeleteMessage
	• GetQueueMetadata
	• GetQueue
	• GetMessage
	• GetMessages
	• ListQueues
	• PeekMessage
	• PeekMessages
	• PutMessage
	• SetQueueMetadata
	• SetQueueServiceProperties
	• GetQueueServiceProperties
	• UpdateMessage

There is a lot more to say about analytics, but that is beyond the scope of the book. Check `http://msdn.microsoft.com/en-us/library/windowsazure/hh343270.aspx` to find out in greater detail about the Storage Analytics Server and the format of the different logs in `$logs`, what exactly is logged, and the different properties that are available.

Summary

In this chapter, we saw in great detail the billing aspects of Windows Azure. We outlined what concepts of Windows Azure are billable and how these are billed, ranging from paying per usage to per month.

Then, we saw how we could use the calculator that Microsoft provides on its website to estimate your Azure costs in great detail. We saw what the purchase options are and what specific member offerings Microsoft has.

We drilled down to the hardest to predict costs of Windows Azure—bandwidth and transaction. These sections outlined in great detail what exactly a transaction is, when it is billable, and when bandwidth is charged. Later on, we provided details on how to estimate the capacity we need on our different storage services.

In the last part of the chapter, we saw how we could get a good grip on and view of our Azure costs (at least, everything that has to do with storage) on a daily basis by using Storage Analytics. We saw some examples of analytics data, how to read it, and to find out what exactly appears on your bill.

The next chapter will provide an overview of some common Windows Azure patterns and will explain in detail how to enable auto scaling in your cloud services.

8
Windows Azure Patterns

"A cloud does not know why it moves in just such a direction and at such a speed...
It feels an impulse...this is the place to go now. But the sky knows the reasons
and the patterns behind all clouds, and you will know, too, when you lift yourself
high enough to see beyond horizons."

— Richard Bach

In this chapter, we will consider some common scenarios with respect to cloud
development, focusing on **autoscaling**, the application of Enterprise Library in
Windows Azure, and a security pattern.

Enterprise Library for Windows Azure

This section focuses on applying Enterprise Library functionality in a Windows
Azure scenario. First, it describes at a high level what Enterprise Library is and
how ready it is for the Windows Azure platform. In the second part of the chapter
it highlights how to apply these features in a Windows Azure scenario and what is
added to Enterprise Library to solve specific Windows Azure problems. In the last
part of the chapter, we will demonstrate how we can solve the problem of automatic
scaling inside the Geotopia scenario. It is expected that the load on Geotopia will
grow over time, and we will outline a growth scenario combined with unexpected
spikes in the load on the system and how these different growth patterns can be
supported with Enterprise Library.

EntLib and Azure compatibility

The latest release of Enterprise Library by the patterns and practices group of Microsoft is Version 5.0, as of this writing. This version consists of features that are configurable and easy to embed in your own solution. Enterprise Library makes it easier and centralizes the use of typical functionality, such as logging and exception handling, and provides a common framework for these tasks. Roughly, Enterprise Library can be divided into application blocks and core infrastructure blocks. Every block is built to solve a specific problem in your development. Enterprise Library tries to solve the following:

- **Consistency**: All blocks are consistently designed and follow the same implementation structures

- **Extensibility**: Every block has different extension points available, where you can plug in your own custom code to alter the standard behavior to your needs

- **Integration**: All blocks are designed and built to collaborate and be easy to use together

EntLib Integration Pack

The Integration Pack for Windows Azure extends Enterprise Library with additional features focusing on Windows Azure applications. There are two new application blocks added, namely the **Autoscaling Application Block** and the **Transient Fault Handling Application Block**. Besides the new application blocks, there are additional new features:

- **Blob configuration**: The ability to store configuration files in blob storage, enabling modifications to your configurations without redeploying

- **PowerShell Cmdlets**: This is used to administer and edit settings from the Autoscaling Application Block directly from PowerShell

- **Protected configuration provider**: This enables encryption of your configuration files, or parts of it

This section will demonstrate the use of both new application blocks and will show code samples of all the features in the Integration Pack. The main focus will be on the Autoscaling Application Block since it is an important aspect for Geotopia.

Autoscaling

This section outlines the growth scenario for Geotopia. The prognosis is that the number of users will grow exponentially, so that the need for Windows Azure resources will do the same. Besides this steady growth, there will also be unexpected spikes in the load on the system. For both scenarios, we need to add additional features to the core of Geotopia, in order to serve our customers at any time, at the high standards we have for the platform.

Transient fault handling

Operations can fail because of unexpected conditions that affect your services on Windows Azure. Conditions such as network issues (latency and timeouts) or your service being unavailable can be overcome by applying retry policies on the applications. These unexpected conditions resulting in errors are called transient faults.

Blob configuration

Blob Configuration enables you to store your configuration settings for the Enterprise Library settings in blob storage. Changing your configuration when your solution is live can be done without redeploying.

PowerShell Cmdlets

The Integration Pack contains a complete set of PowerShell cmdlets that can be used to administer the Autoscaling Application Block.

Protected configuration provider

To help secure information located in configuration files, use the protected configuration provider to make (parts of) your configuration unreadable by humans and ensure that connection strings or username/password combinations are encrypted sufficiently.

Windows Azure autoscaling

The Windows Azure Autoscaling Application Block (WASABi) adds automatic scaling to your Windows Azure application based on specific rules that you can configure. Scaling in the world of Windows Azure mostly means adding or removing instances of the same role, but also throttling is a mechanism to help handle more load than expected. Throttling is the process of turning off features in your application or service to ensure that it doesn't overload and can continue to perform important tasks during busy times.

WASABi allows you to define your own rules on how your application can automatically scale up or scale down, to minimize your operational costs on Windows Azure while still being able to service all your users and uphold availability. An excellent side effect of autoscaling is that manual tasks for operators are minimized.

The autoscaling application block supports two types of rules:

1. **Reactive rules**: Rules that fire based on metrics or variables that you define
2. **Constraint rules**: Rules that control the minimum and maximum number of instances of your roles involved

Growth model

The following figure shows how the exponential growth scenario causes an exponential load on the system.

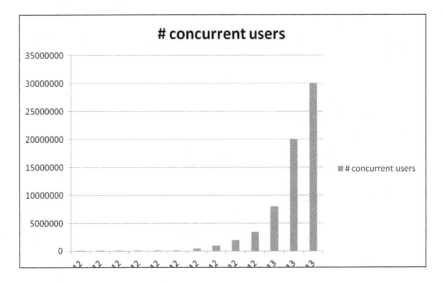

The previous figure sketches exponential growth from less than 100 concurrent users in March of 2012 to a stunning 30 million users in the same month a year later (I know, it's an optimistic scenario!).

Besides this natural growth caused by success of the platform, there will also be unexpected spikes in concurrent users on the system. These unexpected spikes can be caused by compelling events in the news, such as the Super Bowl or the European Soccer Championship. Also, other local events can cause sudden spikes. The following figure shows what these unpredicted spikes look like:

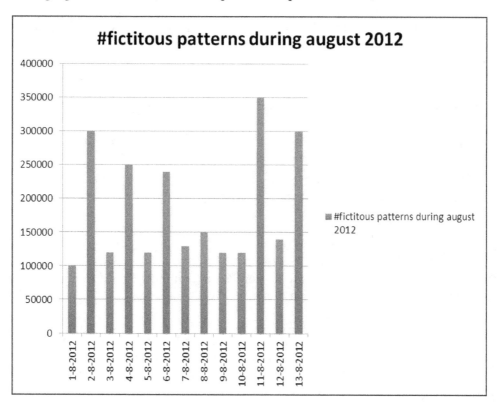

In summary, due to expected growth (linear or nonlinear) and unexpected spikes, we need a mechanism that scales the system up and down depending on the demand. The Autoscaling Application Block (WASABi) from Enterprise Library helps you add automatic scaling to your application.

From the two types of spikes, a few scenarios arise on the Geotopia domain regarding scaling issues.

- The average growth on the platform is exponential and will occur over time. This involves both the web and worker roles.

- A thorough analysis of usage patterns concluded that on Mondays there is an above average use of the platform, possibly to let everyone know what interesting places were visited during the weekend.

- The administrator of Geotopia wants to manage the autoscaling preferences by using PowerShell cmdlets.

- Enable throttling for short peaks. This is a good choice since there will be no scaling action, and therefore, no additional costs. If the peak remains over hours or even days, there will be scaling involved, because the level of service would go down.

- We want scaling (both up and down) to happen on a few specific performance counters and want to make sure we fully use the compute hours we pay for.

Applying WASABi

To make use of the Autoscaling Application Block, you need to add it to your project first. You can use NuGet to perform this task.

In the **Package Manage Console** type:

`Install-Package EnterpriseLibrary.WindowsAzure.Autoscaling` and press *Enter*. The correct assemblies are added to your project and the Application Block is technically ready to use. The following sections involve configuration and the defining of rules.

This chapter demonstrates how to use the WASABi Application Block to enable your application to handle predicted growth and unexpected spikes.

Key concepts of WASABi

WASABi contains some key concepts that together make up the autoscaling block. In the next figure, you can see the important parts of the application block and how the collaboration between the Geotopia solution and WASABi takes place. In summary:

- The scaling worker acts as the host for the autoscaling block. This can be any type of application, but we want the scaling features to be independent of some on-premises application or Windows Service.

- The scaling worker reads the needed information from Windows Azure storage about the rules and the topology of the deployments on Windows Azure (subscription ID, X.509 management certificate, and so on) to be able to use the Service Management API to perform scaling actions.

- The scaling worker detects when a rule is fired and scales up or down the affected roles.

- The web and worker roles write their performance counter data into the `WADPerformanceCounter` table in table storage.

- The developer or IT pro needs to define the rules and create the topology of your Windows Azure environment that needs to be scaled and/or throttled.

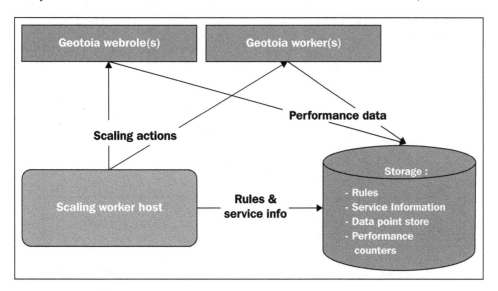

Configure autoscaling

After installing WASABi by using NuGet, the worker role needs to be configured with autoscaling settings. The most efficient and least error-prone way to do this is by using the **Enterprise Library Configuration** tool. Right-click on the `app.config` file in your worker role and select **Edit Configuration File**. In the tool, add an **Autoscaling Settings** block to your configuration file. This can be achieved by selecting **Add Autoscaling Settings** in the **Blocks** menu.

Furthermore, configure the application block, as shown in the following screenshot:

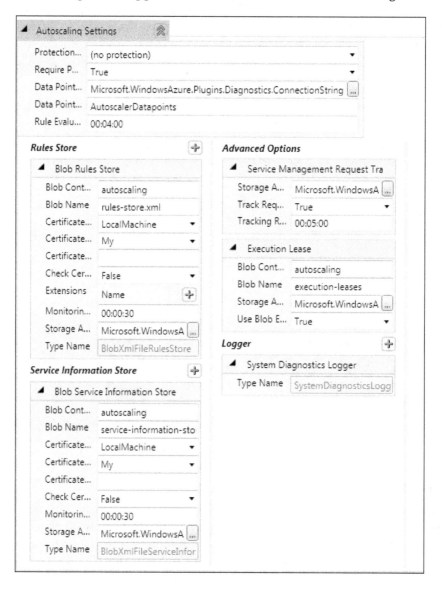

You can leave all the default settings as is, but only set the appropriate storage account, where the rules store, the service information store, the leases, and tracking of service management requests (in a separate queue in the configured storage account) details are persisted. The only property that you configured so far is the storage account (four times), and the rest of the properties can be left as default. Save your work, and your `app.config` file is modified in the appropriate way.

Worker host

A new worker role is created to host the Autoscaling Application Block.

Add the WASABi Application Block to your designated project using NuGet. In **Package Manage Console**, type: `Install-Package EnterpriseLibrary`. `WindowsAzure.Autoscaling` and press *Enter*. The NuGet command is executed and the worker role is prepared to turn into an autoscaling application.

Add the following snippet to your `WorkerRole.cs` file at the class level.

```
private Autoscaler autoscaler;
```

Next, add the following code to the `OnStart` method of your worker role:

```
CloudStorageAccount csa = CloudStorageAccount.Parse(
    RoleEnvironment.GetConfigurationSettingValue(
    "CloudStorageAccount");

DiagnosticMonitorConfiguration dmc =
    DiagnosticMonitor.GetDefaultInitialConfiguration();

dmc.Logs.BufferQuotaInMB = 4;
dmc.Logs.ScheduledTransferPeriod = TimeSpan.FromMinutes(1);
dmc.Logs.ScheduledTransferLogLevelFilter = LogLevel.Verbose;
DiagnosticMonitor.Start("Microsoft.WindowsAzure.Plugins.
    Diagnostics.ConnectionString", dmc);

autoscaler =
    EnterpriseLibraryContainer.Current.GetInstance<Autoscaler>();

autoscaler.Start();
```

When the worker role is started, it also starts the autoscaler.

Setting rules

We concluded in the growth model earlier in this chapter that we need to use both constraint and reactive rules.

Constraint rules

Constraint rules are rules that enable you to minimize and maximize the number of instances of any of your roles, based on a timetable. To meet the standard SLA, one of the constraint rules for all my roles is to set the minimum number of instances to 2. Setting a maximum threshold on the number of instances will make sure that the autoscaler will not go above this maximum. Use this maximum setting to avoid running out of money.

To set these constraint rules, modify `RulesStore.xml` (we need to add it to your project first, and later on, save it in the configured blob container). `RulesStore.xml` contains both the constraint and reactive rules. We will see an example next:

The constraint rules we define, based on findings in the growth model, are:

- Every Monday there is an above average use of the platform. To service this additional load, both web and worker roles instances need to be doubled.

- To meet the Azure SLA, we need a minimum instance count of 2 for each role.

To set these rules, open `RulesStore.xml` and add the following elements to the XML file:

```
<constraintRules>
<rule name="SLARule" description="Make sure to meet the Azure sla"
  rank="10" enabled="true">
  <actions>
    <range target="AllRolesForSLA" min="2" max="10"/>
  </actions>
</rule>
</constraintRules>
```

This snippet of XML creates a constraint rule that is applied to a target called `AllRolesForSLA`. This is a scale group that is defined in `ServiceInformationStore.xml`, as follows:

```
<scaleGroups>
<scaleGroup name="AllRolesForSLA">
  <roles>
    <role roleAlias="Geotopia.Processor" ratio="1"/>
    <role roleAlias="Geotopia.Silverlight.Prototype2" ratio="1"/>
  </roles>
</scaleGroup>
</scaleGroups>
```

The scale group contains two roles: the `Geotopia.Processor` and the `Geotopia.Silverlight.Prototype2` roles. These role aliases need to correspond with the exact names of the roles that need to be scaled.

 Ratios defined in the `scaleGroup` element determine how scaling is performed. A ratio of 1 does not additionally affect the scaling algorithm.

The following table lists how scaling is performed based on ratios for the different rule types. Constraint rules help you control the number of instances to remain in a certain range of values (for example, a minimum of two and a maximum of 10). Obviously, a constraint rule always overrules a reactive one (since these cause the autoscaling actions eventually). A reactive rule is a rule that is fired when some metric exceeds its threshold (for example, when the average CPU utilization of the last hour exceeds 75 percent).

Rule	Scaling algorithm
Constraint rule	`Minimum role count = ratio * minimum instance count in rule`
	`Maximum role count = ratio * maximum count in rule`
Reactive rule with incremental instance count	`Role instance count = current instance count + (increment * ratio)`
Reactive rule with proportional instance count	`Role instance count = current instance count + (current instance count * increment * ratio)`

Reactive rules

Reactive rules use values that are extracted from metrics such as memory usage, or CPU utilization, or from your own metrics, and that are meaningful for your application domain. In the Geotopia case, this could be the number of logged-in users or number of unprocessed topics that are waiting to be processed.

Every metric is stored in Azure table storage as a generic data point. These metrics are gathered by the application block and written to Windows Azure Storage as a data point. A data point is defined as follows:

```
public class DataPoint
{
/// <summary>
  /// Gets or sets the source for the data point.
  /// </summary>
  public string Source { get; set; }

  /// <summary>
  /// Gets or sets the type of data point.
  /// </summary>
  public string Type { get; set; }

  /// <summary>
```

```
    /// Gets or sets the name of the data point.
    /// </summary>
    public string Name { get; set; }

    /// <summary>
    /// Gets or sets the value.
    /// </summary>
    public double Value { get; set; }

    /// <summary>
    /// Gets or sets the creation time.
    /// </summary>
    public DateTimeOffset CreationTime { get; set; }

    /// <summary>
    /// Gets or sets the time represented by the data point.
    /// </summary>
    public DateTimeOffset DataTimestamp { get; set; }
}
```

A data point holds the value of a metric and a timestamp indicating when this data point was collected by the application block. Reactive rules typically use statistical functions on a range of data points to calculate values such as average and maximum. The reactive rule compares the calculated values with a threshold value configured in the rule store. The outcome of the comparison (for example, the average CPU utilization of role X in the last 10 minutes is above the threshold of 75 percent) can result in a scaling action. In this case, the action is probably a scale up by one or more instances.

Besides scaling actions, it is also possible to handle the unexpected load variations by application throttling. Throttling is a technique used to temporarily disable operations in your application instead of performing costly scaling operations.

Throttling

We want to add throttling to Geotopia.Processor as we do not want to scale it up regularly (also done in stabilizer, described in the The *stabilizer* section). Besides setting cool-down periods to prevent Geotopia.Processor from scaling up actively, we also enable throttling.

Throttling is a logic that is not provided by the application block but is more something that can be enabled from reactive rules. When a rule fires, it can change configuration settings for your role. Your role needs to detect these changes using the RoleEnvironment.Changed event and act properly to throttle any actions handled by the role.

Consider the following three reactive rules:

```
<rule name="Heavy CPU" enabled="true" rank="10">
<when>
  <greaterOrEqual operand="CPU_Last_15Minutes" than="0.8"/>
</when>
<actions>
  <changeSetting target="Geotopia.Processor"
    settingName="ThrottlingMode" value="OnlyUrgentTasks"/>
</actions>
</rule>

<rule name="Medium CPU" enabled="true" rank="20">
<when>
  <greaterOrEqual operand="CPU_Last_15Minutes" than="0.5"/>
</when>
<actions>
  <changeSetting target="Geotopia.Processor"
    settingName="ThrottlingMode" value="SkipLowPriorityTasks"/>
</actions>
</rule>

<rule name="Normal CPU" enabled="true" rank="30">
<when>
  <lessOrEqual operand="CPU_Last_15Minutes" than="0.5"/>
</when>
<actions>
  <changeSetting target="Geotopia.Processor"
    settingName="ThrottlingMode" value="Normal"/>
</actions>
</rule>
```

These three reactive rules are ranked in order to make sure the proper action is taken. In this scenario the following throttling logic is defined:

- When the average CPU utilization of the last 15 minutes of the role Geotopia.Processor is below 50 percent, Geotopia.Processor is set to its normal behavior and handles all the work that is available

- When the average CPU utilization of the last 15 minutes of the role is above 50 percent, some throttling is done and an application setting is changed

- When the average CPU utilization of the last 15 minutes is above 80 percent, all work is turned off, except for the most urgent tasks

Ranking prevents the last two rules from being fired consecutively.

When either one of the rules is fired, the configuration setting ThrottlingMode is changed. To enable the Geotopia.Processor worker role to respond to this change, we add the following code snippet to the RoleEnviromentChanged() event handler (this event is fired after a change in the configuration of your role instance is applied)

```
private void RoleEnvironmentChanged(object sender,
RoleEnvironmentChangedEventArgs e)
{
  var ThrottlingMode =
    RoleEnvironment.GetConfigurationSettingValue
      ("ThrottlingMode");

  switch (ThrottlingMode)
  {
    case "Normal":
    //read messages from every requests queue
    break;
    case "SkipLowPriorityTasks":
    //stop reading messages from the LowPriorityQueue
    break;
    case "OnlyUrgentTasks":
    //stop reading messages from the LowPriorityQueue and
    //MediumPriorityQueue
    break;
    default:
    break;
  }
}
```

When the application block sets a new value for the ThrottlingMode setting, the next code handles this change. In the switch statement, you can implement logic (or set some global variables) to do the throttling. In this case, the worker role stops getting messages from designated queues to get rid of some heavy burden, until the throttling is stopped when one of the reactive rules instruct it.

 Verify that the new configuration setting ThrottlingMode is added to both the service definition and configuration files of your cloud project.

Service information store

Besides the scale group, the service information store also contains information that the autoscaler needs to be able to use the service management API.

See the following XML snippet for what the service information store might look like:

```xml
<?xmlversion="1.0" encoding="utf-8"?>
<serviceModelxmlns="http://schemas.microsoft.com/practices/2011/
  entlib/autoscaling/serviceModel">
<stabilizerscaleUpCooldown="00:20:00" scaleDownCooldown="00:15:00"
  scaleUpOnlyInFirstMinutesOfHour="30"
  scaleDownOnlyInLastMinutesOfHour="30"
  notificationsCooldown="00:25:00">

  <roleroleAlias="TestWorkerRole" scaleUpCooldown="00:18:00"
    scaleDownCooldown="00:18:00" />
  <groupgroupName="AllRolesForSLA" scaleUpCooldown ="00:01:00"
    scaleDownCooldown="00:01:00"/>
  <roleroleAlias="HighCPUWorkerRole" scaleUpCooldown="00:18:00"
    scaleDownCooldown="00:18:00" />

</stabilizer>
<scaleGroups>
  <scaleGroupname="AllRolesForSLA">
  <roles>
    <roleroleAlias="Geotopia.Processor" ratio="1"/>
    <roleroleAlias="Geotopia.Silverlight.Prototype2" ratio="1"/>
  </roles>
  </scaleGroup>
</scaleGroups>

<subscriptions>
  <subscriptionname="your Subscription"
    subscriptionId="yoursubscriptionid"
    certificateThumbprint="thumbprint"
    certificateStoreLocation="LocalMachine"
    certificateStoreName="My">
  <services>
    <servicednsPrefix="geotopia" slot="Production"
      scalingMode="ScaleAndNotify"
      notificationRecipients="riccardobecker@msn.com">
    <roles>
```

```
      <rolealias="Geotopia.Silverlight.Prototype2"
        roleName="Geotopia.Silverlight.Prototype2"
        wadStorageAccountName="wadStorageAccount"/>
      <rolealias="Geotopia.Processor"
        roleName="Geotopia.Processor"
        wadStorageAccountName="wadStorageAccount"/>
    </roles>
    </service>
  </services>

  <storageAccounts>
  <storageAccountalias="wadStorageAccount"
    connectionString="DefaultEndpointsProtocol=https;
    AccountName={YOURACCOUNTNAME};AccountKey={YOURACCOUNTKEY}">
  <queues>
    <queuealias="PerfTestQueue" queueName="perftestqueue"/>
  </queues>

  </storageAccount>

  </storageAccounts>
  </subscription>
</subscriptions>
</serviceModel>
```

The previous snippet defines one scale group that is affected by the constraint rule defined earlier in this chapter. This rule is to make sure that at least two instances of the roles are deployed.

Next, the subscription is defined; be aware that the subscription ID and the certificate are very important. The certificate needs to be uploaded as a management certificate to the Windows Azure portal (to make sure service management API calls are authenticated), but the certificate also needs to be deployed to the hosted service itself. This needs to be a `.pfx` certificate, where the private key is also uploaded to the portal. Finally, the thumbprint of the certificate needs to be in the service configuration file of the worker role hosting the autoscaling block. Go to `http://msdn.microsoft.com/en-us/library/gg465712.aspx` to find out in detail about this process. The scenario we see here is a single worker role handling autoscaling of one hosted service only. To be more efficient, it is also possible to have this worker role handle multiple hosted services located in multiple subscriptions and add autoscaling capabilities to them. This way, you can share your autoscaler host with multiple hosted services, to be cost effective. In other words, you don't have to have a single autoscale worker for every subscription and/or hosted service.

The Windows Azure hosted service now looks as follows, with the autoscaler worker role and the Geotopia web role:

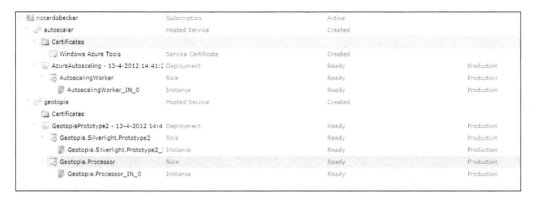

After a few minutes the magic happens. The autoscaling block starts evaluating rules defined in the rule store and detects that SLARule comes into play, since the web and worker roles in the Geotopia-hosted service are only running one instance each. Under the hood, the autoscaling blocks do the following:

- The Windows Azure applications being *autoscale-enabled* capture their configured performance data in memory and push these records every configured interval to Windows Azure storage.

- The application block gathers this data from WADPerformanceCountersTable and saves these records in the data points store.

- The application block also collects other metrics data (besides performance counter data), such as queue length and instance count, and saves it to the data points store.

- All the applicable rules are run by the evaluator through the configuration.

- The evaluator gets the data points needed, at a specific time, from the data points store.

- The stabilizer finally decides whether or not scaling operations are executed, for example, depending on cool-down periods. The stabilizer is an important component of WASABi and prevents the autoscaler from being a bit too reactive and responds to every rule immediately. The stabilizer uses the cool-down periods to ensure that the rule is still applicable after some configured interval. For example, the CPU rule comes into play because the metrics cause this rule to fire, but the stabilizer uses the cool-down period to ease the scaling and reinstate the CPU rule during this period.

These actions result in scaling up my two roles to two instances each.

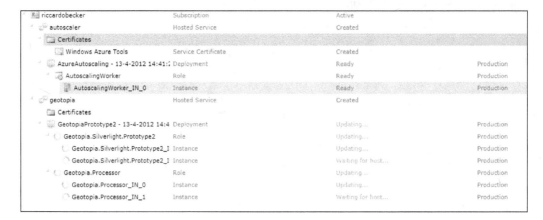

The following section describes core components from the autoscaling block to give a good overview of how the block operates.

Metronome

The metronome class is at the heart of the system. It acts as a scheduler and performs actions at configured intervals. Every activity that the autoscaling block performs is launched by the metronome. The metronome uses a lease on a blob to ensure that only one instance of the metronome (singleton) is running.

The metronome schedules activities that evaluate rules, tracking requests, and data point collection.

Data collection

To be able to evaluate reactive rules, it needs to get a hold on data point values. A data point can be any of the following sources:

- Performance counter data from the WADPerformanceCountersTable table that holds the performance counters from the affected roles. The roles need to be configured to store these counters.

- Metrics about storage, including queues, blobs, and tables. The autoscaling block is able to get the length of any queue to act upon.

- The block can act on transaction statistics and capacity data (described in *Chapter 7, The Billing Aspects of Windows Azure*).

- Custom metrics from your own application. In the case of Geotopia, this could be the number of logged-in users, for example.

Data points store

The data collector activities executed by the metronome store data points in the data points store. The rule evaluator queries this table to evaluate the reactive rules defined in the rules store.

Rule evaluation

Rule evaluation is also executed by the metronome. Every time the evaluator runs, it checks the rules store and finds out if any of the defined rules apply.

 The rules are kept in memory by the application block but it checks periodically (configurable) if any changes to the rules store took place.

The evaluator queries the data points store and calculates (if applicable) any aggregate functions defined in the rules store. The evaluator also resolves conflicting rules before taking any scaling actions.

Conflicting rules

If any of the rules conflict, there is logic available to tell the application block how to solve these conflicts.

First of all, a constraint rule always overrides a reactive rule. Imagine having defined a constraint rule defining a minimum of two instances and a maximum of ten instances. The reactive rules can only act within this range. If this did not take place, it would be possible that a reactive rule would result in more than the upper limit of ten instances, the number we configured earlier in the constraint rules section. This comes with a price!

When constraint rules overlap, that rule with the highest rank defined in the rules store wins. Rules with equal rank are handled in order of appearance.

When reactive rules overlap or conflict, that rule with the highest rank wins (the same approach as constraint rules). If rules have the same rank, the rule resulting in the largest scaling action (the most instances scaling up or least instances scaling down) will be executed.

The scaler

The scaler encapsulates the service management API and is responsible for the scaling actions that add or remove instances of roles. The scaler also contains the stabilizer, which prevents the application from scaling up and down too frequently (for example, scaling down while the scaling up action is not even finished). The scaler also writes messages to the tracking queue (if configured) to create a sort of audit trail on the scaling operations. If configured, the scaler can send e-mails with scaling actions.

The tracker

The tracker keeps track of all the scaling operations carried out by the scaler. The tracker is also initiated by the metronome and checks to see which scaling operation is finished and then logs the details of the scaling operation and removes the message from the queue. When the autoscaler performs a scaling action (using the service management API asynchronous **Change Deployment Configuration** operation), a request ID is returned. The status of the scaling operation can be tracked with this request ID. The tracker uses the GetOperation method and request ID to track the status of the scaling actions.

The stabilizer

The stabilizer is a component of WASABi that prevents the application block from reacting instantly when rules are met. Imagine that a rule results in a scaling up action and a few minutes later, the same or another rule will result in a scaling down action. Since we are billed per hour, it would be cost-effective to scale up early in the hour and scale down late in the hour. To make sure that scaling is really needed, the stabilizer can take so called cool-down periods into account. These periods can be defined in the service information store. The following XML snippet is an example:

```
<stabilizer scaleUpCooldown="00:20:00" scaleDownCooldown="00:15:00"
scaleUpOnlyInFirstMinutesOfHour="30"
scaleDownOnlyInLastMinutesOfHour="10"
notificationsCooldown="00:25:00">

  <role roleAlias="Geotopia.Processor" scaleUpCooldown="02:00:00"
    scaleDownCooldown="00:10"
    scaleUpOnlyInFirstMinutesOfHour="30"
    scaleDownOnlyInLastMinutesOfHour="30"/>

  <role roleAlias="Geotopia.Silverlight.Prototype2"
    scaleUpCooldown="00:05:00" scaleDownCooldown="01:00:00"/>

</stabilizer>
```

The preceding code snippet defines default cool-down periods of 20 minutes for scaling up and 30 minutes for scaling down. It also configures scaling up to only take place in the first 30 minutes of an hour and scaling down to only take place in the last 10 minutes of an hour. The `notificationsCooldown` setting is to define how often notifications are sent (if the scaling mode is set to `Notify` or `ScaleAndNotify` in the service information store). Setting this timespan to 25 minutes results in the application block waiting for this period before sending the next notification for the same role.

These default settings can be overridden on a per-role basis. In the XML snippet, you can see that, for `Geotopia.Processor`, the cool-down period for scaling up is set to two hours, since the processor is handling asynchronous work. This work can take some time, but it is background processing with no need for the user to see what is happening. The sense of urgency and responsiveness for this role is less important than for the web frontend. Also, scaling down can take place earlier.

The web frontend has a more strict cool-down strategy, since it scales up after a timespan of five minutes. This is because we don't want users to be confronted with a less responsive user interface, as that would scare them off. Also, the scaling down period takes longer.

The settings you can define on a role basis can also be defined on groups.

Customizing WASABi

As with Enterprise Library, the Autoscaling Application Block offers developers the ability to extend the default behavior. The block offers several built-in extension points.

To create custom actions (besides the ones that the application block offers), you need to execute three steps:

1. Deserialize the additional, custom-made configuration settings.
2. Create the actual custom action.
3. Adjust the rules to make use of the custom action.

For this example, we don't need any additional configuration settings, and I'll just show how to create a custom action and how to use it.

In the Geotopia area, we want to make sure that our costs are not running out of control. Therefore, we want our scaling actions to be accompanied with a notification sent to us by e-mail, showing the impact of the scaling action on our bill.

The following code snippet shows how to create a custom action as well as all the other plumbing that is needed.

First of all, you need to define a new XML element that describes the custom action.

```
[XmlRoot(ElementName = "emailAction",
  Namespace = "http://Geotopia/NotifyEmail")]

public class NotifyEmailActionElement: ReactiveRuleActionElement
{
  [XmlAttribute("email")]
  public string EmailAddress{ get; set; }

    public override ReactiveRuleAction CreateAction()
    {
      return new NotifyEmailAction
      {
        EmailAddress= this.EmailAddress
      };

  }
}
```

This code snippet enables the use of additional XML snippets in the rule store definition, adding the ability to add this as an action.

The action is coded in the following snippets, including the action result (the actual execution of the action).

```
public class NotifyEmailAction: ReactiveRuleAction
{
public string EmailAddress{ get; set; }

  public NotifyEmailAction()
  {

  }

  public override IEnumerable<RuleEvaluationResult>
    GetResults(ReactiveRule forRule,
    IRuleEvaluationContext context)
  {
    return new[]
    {
      new NotifyEmailActionResult(forRule)
      {
        EmailAddress= this.EmailAddress
      }
```

```
    };
  }
}

public class NotifyEmailActionResult: ExecuteActionResult
{
  public IEmailHelperemailHelper;

  public string EmailAddress;

  public NotifyEmailActionResult(Rule sourceRule)
    : base(sourceRule)
  {
    this.emailHelper=
      EnterpriseLibraryContainer.Current.
      GetInstance<IEmailHelper>();
  }

  public override string Description
  {
    get
    {
      return "An actionresult that sends an email";
    }
  }

  public override void Execute(IRuleEvaluationContext context)
  {
    this.EmailHelper.SendMessage("riccardobecker@geotopia.nl");
  }
}

public interface IEmailHelper
{
  void SendMessage(string emailAddress);
}

public class EmailHelper: IEmailHelper
{
  public void SendMessage(string emailAddress)
  {
    Console.WriteLine("need to build the actual
      emailhelper first");
  }
}
```

Make sure the assembly containing the preceding code is deployed along with the application block.

Besides building custom actions it is also possible to create custom operands (for example, the current number of logged-in users), custom stores (for example, in a SQL Azure database), and custom logging (for example, to Windows Azure Tables).

Blob configuration

The integration pack also offers the ability to store the autoscaling settings in blob storage. This takes away the configuration from your standard `app.config` or `web.config` file and moves it to blob storage. The main advantage is that you can change the configuration settings without redeploying your solution.

Add the configuration extensions to your designated project using NuGet. In **Package Manage Console**, type:
`Install-Package EnterpriseLibrary.WindowsAzure.Configuration` and press *Enter*. The correct assemblies are added to your project and the application block is ready to use.

Your project is now ready to use the blob configuration store. To enable this, right-click on the `app.config` or `web.config` file of the project, which hosts the autoscaler.

Now, follow these steps to implement this feature:

1. Choose **Edit Configuration File**.
2. In the **Enterprise Library Configuration** tool, select **Blocks** and add **Configuration Settings**.
3. Add a new source called **Blob Configuration Source**.

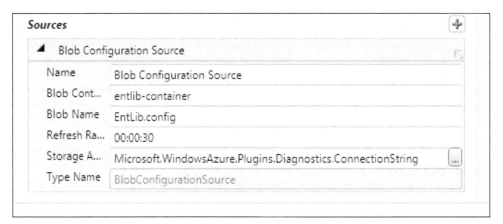

4. Make sure to properly configure your storage account; in this example, it is taken from the service configuration file.

5. Set **Blob Configuration Source** as the **Selected Source**, as in the following screenshot:

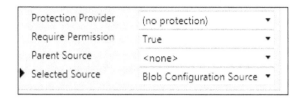

6. Now, the configuration block is configured to take the autoscaling settings from a blob instead of the default app or `web.config` file.

7. Save the settings from the Autoscaling Application Block in a separate file called `entlib.config`, and upload it to the appropriate container.

8. Starting the autoscaler now takes the settings from blob storage and it is configured to reread the contents every 30 seconds.

PowerShell cmdlets

The WASABi block offers different PowerShell commands to manage the Autoscaling Application Block from your PowerShell console. This enables administrators to manage the settings for your autoscaling environment. As we saw before, configuring rules straight into the XML and uploading it to blob storage is more of a developer's job. The PowerShell cmdlets that are provided enable administrators to configure autoscaling as well, but they do not need Visual Studio or other developer tools to achieve this.

To use the cmdlets, go to `http://www.microsoft.com/download/en/details.aspx?id=28189`, download the `WASABiCmdlets.exe` file, and execute it. Make sure the assembly containing the cmdlets is in a location where PowerShell is able to find it. By default on a Windows 7 machine, this location is `Documents/WindowsPowershell` and all of its subfolders.

The block offers the following PowerShell cmdlets:

- `Disable-ScalingRule`
- `Enable-ScalingRule`
- `Disable-ScalingRuleEvaluation`
- `Enable-ScalingRuleEvaluation`
- `Get-ScalingRule`

- `Get-ScalingStore`
- `Set-ScalingStore`
- `Protect-ScalingStore`
- `Unprotect-ScalingStore`
- `Set-ScalingRuleRank`
- `Set-ScalingStabilizerConfig`

For detailed information on the cmdlets, run the PowerShell host and the `get-help` command with the `-detailed` flag.

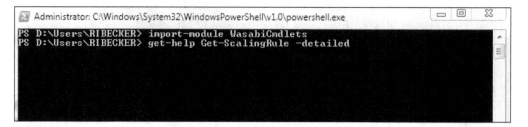

Transient fault handling

There is no typical distinction between transient faults or "ordinary" faults. For example, a database connection to SQL Azure is dropped for a specific reason. This can be caused by an application error but also by actions performed by the fabric controller that decided to break the connection.

The Transient Fault Handling Application Block

The Transient Fault Handling Application Block contains logic to manage and handle these faults.

The application block contains logic to detect transient faults for common services. This is called "detection strategies". The strategies are capable of identifying whether an exception is caused by transient faults. There are detection strategies for SQL Azure, Service Bus, Windows Azure Storage, and caching services. In this chapter, I will explain a typical storage scenario in conjunction with this application block.

The block also enables the definition of retry strategies to create a consistent approach of handling transient faults. Retry strategies can be configured to occur at specific intervals.

- **Fixed**: For example, retry a certain action every second.

- **Incremental**: Retry a certain action where the time between retries grows incrementally. For example, retry the action after 1 second, then after 3, then after 5, and so on.

- **Random exponential**: Retry the action after an interval that increases exponentially with a random modifier between the retries.

- Retry the action after an exponential time with a random interval.

Every strategy needs to define a maximum number of retries.

In line with the way application blocks work, you can define your own retry strategy if the existing ones do not meet your requirements.

Applying transient fault handling

To make use of the application block, you need to add the application block to your project first. You can use NuGet to perform this task.

Add the Transient Fault Handling application block to your designated project using NuGet. In the **Package Manage Console**, type: `Install-Package EnterpriseLibrary.WindowsAzure.TransientFaultHandling` and press *Enter*. The correct assemblies are added to your project, and the application block is ready to use.

This section demonstrates how to use the block on Windows Azure storage transient faults. The following code snippet shows how to use the Enterprise Library infrastructure to create the appropriate `objects:objects`. The storage client libraries already contain retrying logic; this snippet just demonstrates the use.

```
//use the default retryCount, interval and increment, can be
//overridden
var retryStrategy =
  newIncremental(Incremental.DefaultClientRetryCount,
  Incremental.DefaultRetryInterval,
  Incremental.DefaultRetryIncrement);

//we want to handle Azure storage transient faults.
var retryPolicy =
  new RetryPolicy<StorageTransientErrorDetectionStrategy>
  (retryStrategy);

//i want to track the retries
retryPolicy.Retrying += (sender, arguments) =>
{
```

```
    var msg = String.Format("Retry - Count:{0}, Delay:{1},
    Exception:{2}", arguments.CurrentRetryCount, arguments.Delay,
    arguments.LastException);
    Console.WriteLine(msg, "Information");
};

CloudStorageAccount account =
    CloudStorageAccount.Parse(connectionString);

//now create the table if it's not there yet
CloudTableClient client = account.CreateCloudTableClient();

try
{
// Do some work that may result in a transient fault.
    retryPolicy.ExecuteAction(
    () =>
      {
        // Call a method that uses Windows Azure storage and
        //which maythrow a transient exception.
          client.CreateTableIfNotExist("Geotopics");
      });
}
catch (Exception ex)
{
//All the retries failed.
    Console.WriteLine(ex.Message);
}
```

What happens in the code snippet is that the `CreateTableIfNotExist` method is called inside a block that handles transient faults. By default, there are a few exceptions marked as transient, and these are defined in the Enterprise Library.

These are:

- `WebExceptionStatus.ProtocolError`
- `WebExceptionStatus.ConnectionClosed`
- `StorageErrorCodeStrings.InternalError`
- `StorageErrorCodeStrings.ServerBusy`
- `StorageErrorCodeStrings.OperationTimedOut`
- `TableErrorCodeStrings.TableServerOutOfMemory`
- `StorageErrorCode.ServiceInternalError`
- `StorageErrorCode.ServiceTimeout`
- `TimeoutException`

You can manually add new exceptions to be considered as transient faults, if you edit the sourcefile `StorageTransientErrorDetectionStrategy.cs` and add exceptions to be considered as transient faults in the method `CheckIsTransient`.

Consider the following code addition to the first lines of the `CheckIsTransient` method:

```
if (ex is Exception)
{
return true;
}
```

This means that every single exception is considered to be a transient fault. If you throw an exception in the `ExecuteAction` block, you can test how this application block works. By default, you will see a linear retry strategy, where one second is added every time to the retry interval and the `retrycount` is `10`.

So far, we saw some nice features from the Enterprise Library extensions for Windows Azure. Besides these, we also take a look at a generic security pattern that can help us to be more *secure* and that demonstrates a nice pattern.

The Gatekeeper pattern

The Gatekeeper pattern is a design pattern that describes a way of brokering access to your storage. This is a typical security best practice and serves to minimize the attack surface of your roles. This is done by communicating over internal channels and only to other roles that are part of the pattern.

The Gatekeeper pattern takes two roles that play the gatekeeping game. There is one internet-facing web role that handles requests from users—in our scenario, requests to create a geotopic. The Gatekeeper is suspicious and does not trust any requests it receives. The Gatekeeper validates the input and runs in partial trust. When some hacker manages to successfully attack the web role, there is no sensitive data there. The keys to access confidential data in Windows Azure storage are kept somewhere else.

This is done by the KeyMaster, a worker role that only communicates with the Gatekeeper web role and declines all other incoming requests. The communication between the Gatekeeper and the KeyMaster takes place on an internal endpoint. Internal endpoints can only be used by roles from the same hosted service. The KeyMaster has storage account information available in its service configuration file.

Consider the following figure, which illustrates the Gatekeeper pattern:

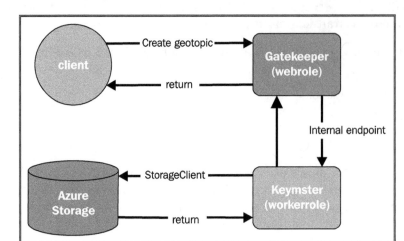

The figure depicts the following steps:

- The client calls the WCF service hosted in the web role to create a geotopic
- The Gatekeeper web role has no knowledge of storage accounts and just calls the KeyMaster on an internal endpoint
- The KeyMaster knows what storage account and storage table to modify and does the actual insertion of data
- The client only receives a return value indicating a failure or success

The KeyMaster

The KeyMaster is implemented in a worker role. The following code snippet demonstrates how to host a service in a worker role on an internal endpoint:

```
NetTcpBinding binding = new NetTcpBinding(SecurityMode.None);
// define an internal endpoint for inter-role traffic
RoleInstanceEndpoint internalEndPoint =
  RoleEnvironment.CurrentRoleInstance.InstanceEndpoints["
  InternalEndpoint"];

serviceHost = new ServiceHost(typeof(InternalGeotopicService));
  serviceHost.AddServiceEndpoint(
  typeof(IInternalGeotopicService),
  binding, string.Format("net.tcp://{0}/InternalEndpoint",
  internalEndPoint.IPEndpoint));
```

```
// create channel factory for inter-role communication

WorkerRole.factory = new
  ChannelFactory<IInternalGeotopicService>(binding);

try
{
  serviceHost.Open();
  Trace.TraceInformation("Geotopiaservice host
    started successfully.");
}
catch (TimeoutException timeoutException)
{
  Trace.TraceError("The service operation timed out. {0}",
    timeoutException.Message);
}
catch (CommunicationException communicationException)
{
  Trace.TraceError("Could not start Geotopiaservice host. {0}",
    communicationException.Message);
}
```

This code runs in the `OnStart()` method of the worker role. The internal endpoint is configured as shown in the following screenshot:

The code combined with the configuration of the internal endpoint results in a service running in the development fabric at the address `net.tcp://127.255.0.1:20000/InternalEndpoint`.

In turn, the Gatekeeper hosts a WCF service that is externally available for clients. This WCF service implements an interface called **IGeotopicService**. The actual implementation of the WCF service is shown in the following code snippet:

```
foreach (RoleInstance roleInst in RoleEnvironment.CurrentRoleInstance.
Role.Instances)
{
```

```
    Trace.WriteLine("Instance ID: " + roleInst.Id);
    foreach (RoleInstanceEndpoint roleInstEndpoint in
      roleInst.InstanceEndpoints.Values)
    {
      Trace.WriteLine("Instance endpoint IP address and port: " +
        roleInstEndpoint.IPEndpoint);
      CallInstanceEndpoint("InternalEndpoint", geotopic);
    }
  }
}
```

This piece of code iterates through all the instances of the current role and finds all the endpoints defined. For every endpoint (in this case only the one that defines the internal endpoint), it calls the `CallInstanceEndpoint` method. This method is shown in the following snippet:

```
var instance = RoleEnvironment.Roles["KeyMaster"].Instances.
FirstOrDefault();

if (instance != null)
{
  // get the endpoint
  var endpoint =
    instance.InstanceEndpoints[endpointName].IPEndpoint;

  if (endpoint != null)
  {
    string address;
    ChannelFactory<IInternalGeotopicService> factory;

    if (endpointName.ToLower().Contains("http"))
    {
      address = string.Format(@"http://{0}/BackEndService.svc",
        endpoint.ToString());

      factory = new ChannelFactory<IInternalGeotopicService>(new
        BasicHttpBinding(), address);
    }
```

```
else
{
  address = string.Format(@"net.tcp://{0}/InternalEndpoint",
    endpoint.ToString());

  factory = new ChannelFactory<IInternalGeotopicService>(new
    NetTcpBinding()
  {
    Security = new NetTcpSecurity()
    {
      Mode = SecurityMode.None
    }
  },
  address);
}

var channel = factory.CreateChannel();

try
{
  channel.AddGeotopic(new Geotopic());
  factory.Close();
}
finally
{
  if (factory.State != CommunicationState.Closed)
  {
    factory.Abort();
  }
}
```

The code first gets the instance of the KeyMaster role running in the hosted service. Next, it gets the internal endpoint and uses it to compile the address string that is needed to create ChannelFactory. Finally, a channel is opened and the actual call to AddGeotopic is made.

Summary

This chapter extensively describes the use of Enterprise Library in your Windows Azure environment. It outlines in detail what additions are made that resulted in the Enterprise Library Integration Pack for Windows Azure. A detailed autoscaling scenario is explained through code samples and snippets. The internal use of the Autoscaling Application Block is explained, as is how to apply this in the Geotopia scenario. Several circumstances describe when the application needs to be scaled, sometimes through constraint rules and sometimes by using reactive rules, which act on performance metrics. The phenomenon of throttling is explained and so is how to use it in your own application.

Analogous to the traditional Enterprise Library, the Enterprise Library Integration Pack is highly extensible, and this chapter also shows how to extend the pack by demonstrating a new action. Next, the chapter explains how to save the configuration settings of the Autoscaling Application Block in blob storage. This enables updates to the autoscaling configuration without the need to redeploy your application, since the block periodically reads the configurations settings and reconfigures the complete block, if necessary.

The last section describes what transient fault handling is and how you can use it to implement retry logic to overcome transient errors.

The final section of the chapter describes a security pattern called Gatekeeper that increases the security level of your application. It splits the responsibility of writing data to storage and separates it into a worker role. The frontend WCF service communicates with the worker role by using internal endpoints.

9
Application Lifecycle Management

"If you aren't doing ALM today and software is important to your business, you need to start thinking about how to get transparency, how to get understanding of the application process flow, and to think of software as a business process."

— *Dave West, Forrester*

This chapter describes an approach on how to manage the application lifecycle in the Windows Azure environment. First, it describes what **Application Lifecycle Management (ALM)** is all about, and in the second part of the chapter, we focus on specific ALM activities when developing and running applications on Windows Azure and how to use Team Foundation Server for the same.

ALM overview

ALM is much more than the software development lifecycle. ALM is all about the complete lifecycle of an application, starting from the initial idea and ending at the last time the application is used. Roughly, ALM can be divided into three major areas:

- **Governance**: This is is a continuous process that spans the whole lifecycle.
- **Development**: This starts when the original idea is designed and lasts until the product goes live. During the lifecycle, development will still play a role in bug fixes, patches, or enhancements.
- **Operations**: This maintains the application and starts before going live (for example, to perform tests) and lasts until the end of the life of the application.

Governance

Governance spans the whole lifecycle and contains different activities, such as the development of a business case (for example, is this project or service worth making?) or project portfolio management (centralized management of processes, methods, and tools for running projects). Before we start building Geotopia, we need to find out if we can earn money with it (or have other non-financial benefits). Once the business case is approved, we need to create a project team with a project manager, architects, developers, and testers.

Development

The business case is approved, and we can finally start developing the first version of Geotopia. Since we want and need to be agile (requirements are constantly changing and we want to be flexible), we decide to realize the prototype of Geotopia in several iterations or sprints. After building and delivering the first version, we can go live and attract new users to our application.

Operations

We want Geotopia to be a high performing and robust system. To achieve these non-functional requirements, we need to monitor and maintain Geotopia. During this stage, we already start testing Geotopia before deployment. After the deployment, **Operations** is responsible for patching and updating Geotopia.

The following figure shows how these three areas are related to each other:

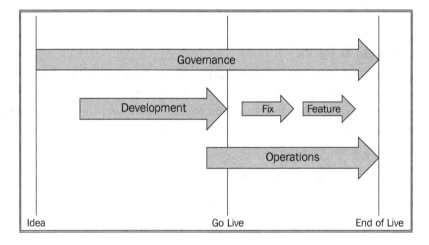

ALM tooling

ALM is all about collaboration and how we work together as a team. It's not about tools but about a mindset—about being flexible while staying in control. Everybody in the team is part of this collaboration.

Though ALM is not about tools, they can help reach the goal of ultimate collaboration.

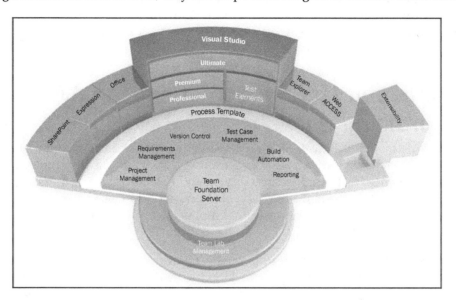

Microsoft Visual Studio Team Foundation Server 2010 (TFS) is the collaboration platform at the core of Microsoft's Application Lifecycle Management solution. Team Foundation Server automates the software delivery process and provides the tools to manage the software developments project of Geotopia. TFS enables everyone on the team to work together more effectively, be more agile, and deliver better quality software. Project artifacts and data from work item tracking, source control, builds, and testing tools are stored in a data warehouse, and reporting and dashboarding provide us with historical trending, traceability, and real-time visibility into quality and progress against business drivers and opportunities.

By using the suite of tools in Visual Studio Ultimate in combination with Visual Studio Team Foundation Server, we can apply proven practices to manage Geotopia's application lifecycle. Using these tools, we can better understand customer needs and more effectively design, implement, and deploy our code. We can trace requirements to checked-in code, builds, and test results.

Planning and tracking

Using Visual Studio ALM management, we can manage customer needs more effectively. We can create high-level plans that break our projects down into potentially shippable increments, and we can create detailed plans to execute shorter iterations in which we develop those increments. Because we develop a detailed plan at the start of each iteration, we are more certain of how the plan progresses with each milestone we reach. When we finish each iteration, we can refine the high-level plan based on what we have learned during the iteration. We can also reschedule any work that was not completed.

Writing, unit testing, debugging, analyzing, and profiling

To make sure that the application or database code modifications meet our goals and do not break other parts of Geotopia, we use Visual Studio Premium or Ultimate to perform common tasks that include implementing features, fixing bugs, and coding. Developers perform design, development, and test tasks repeatedly over an iteration. The integration amongst the components of Visual Studio enables us to perform tasks such as:

- Associating code changes with specific tasks and bugs to create traceability. This creates the possibility to track back why certain changes have taken place.

- Identifying tests that must be run if a particular change is made. This can be achieved by associating tests with a `changeset`.

- Planning and tracking our progress against our schedule and project/ iteration plan. This can be done in close collaboration with tools such as Excel or Microsoft Project.

Build

With TFS **Build**, we can create build definitions to automate compiling code, running associated tests, performing code analysis, releasing continuous builds, and publishing build reports. To build a version of Geotopia, we create a build definition to specify what projects to build, what triggers a build to run, what automated tests (unit, coded UI) to run, and where to deploy the output. Deployment to Windows Azure can be automated as well, running tests at night and fully undeploy, which include, deleting deployments to reduce costs. All information is stored in the data warehouse, from which it is retrieved when a build runs. After the build, data about the build results is stored back in the warehouse, so that it is available through build reports.

The following figure shows the three main phases of building an application:

Defining a Build

In the Build definition, we define exactly what needs to be built by the build server of Visual Studio Team Foundation Server (or the online TFS). We also configure when the build needs to take place. Initially, we decide to run a nightly build, meaning every night the build process is automatically executed. When we get close to the first deployment of Geotopia, we switch from nightly build to continuous integration. This means that upon every check-in of source files in the version control system of TFS, the complete solution is built. In the build definition, we also configure what tests to run. During the first iterations of Geotopia, we mostly run system and unit tests, but later on we can also run coded UI tests. The last important piece of the build definition is to decide where to copy the output of the build process. Since we want to automatically deploy to Windows Azure as the final step in a successful build, we need to decide on how to deploy new versions of Geotopia. During development, this is not that important, but after Geotopia is commercially available, updating and patching the application is a delicate process that needs a good approach. There are several ways to update our existing and running Geotopia application:

- Full deployment: This type of deployment completely deletes the current deployment. The underlying virtual machines are allocated and a deployment is created from the binaries and configuration files. A full deployment can be executed from Visual Studio or on the Windows Azure portal. Remember that a full deployment takes more time to finish than other methods described here. Geotopia will be unavailable during a full deployment.

- In-place upgrade: An in-place upgrade means that Windows Azure updates the running role instances accordingly, with the number of upgrade domains as defined in the configuration file of the cloud service. Instances of Geotopia running in the same upgrade domain are stopped, updated, and brought back to running state again. Windows Azure then moves on to the next upgrade domain.

- Staged deployment: A staged deployment means that Geotopia is first deployed to the staging slot while the current version of Geotopia is still up and running. When deployment to the staging slot is successful and some last tests are done, we swap the **Virtual IP (VIP)** to promote the staging environment to production. The production environment will be demoted to be the staging environment. Swapping deployments can be achieved by using the Service Management API or in the Windows Azure portal by simply pressing the **Swap** button.

- Web deployment: With Web deployment, changed binaries are pushed directly to a running instance of a web role (web deployment of a worker role is not possible). The changes are immediately copied to the virtual machine where the web role is running and can only be performed on single instances of a web role. To use web deployment, remote desktop must be enabled.

The Virtual IP address assigned to a deployment will not change during its lifetime. Even swapping between staging and production does not change the VIPs. Only when a deployment is deleted, will the VIP become available again for other deployments.

Queue build

In the defining build step, we created a build. Now, it is time to execute the defined build. For Geotopia, we find it desirable to have a constant quality check on our software. Therefore, we decided to create a build with a **Continuous Integration** trigger. This means that upon every check-in, a build is started. In this way, we can keep track of the software quality during the day. The build is triggered and executed every time somebody from the team checks in on a source file. To uphold the quality before a build is fired, we could set the check-in policy of our project to testing policy. This means that every time a file is checked in, a set of tests is run and the results of these tests need to be positive before the system checks the file(s) in. At this time, we know for sure that the Continuous Integration build is successful because our test set is executed prior to the build.

We could also decide to build our solution manually or by scheduling it.

Review build

When the Continuous Integration build is completed successfully, we can review the build results by double-clicking the build in the build explorer. In the build report, we have several options:

- Open the drop folder of the build where all the binaries were dropped by the build

- Rate the build quality

- Delete the build

- Get a detailed insight on all the steps that were taken by the build and see the possible errors that occurred during the build

Application Lifecycle Management on Windows Azure

Performing ALM in a Windows Azure environment adds additional needs to our ALM approach. While the core is still Team Foundation Server combined with Visual Studio, new aspects arise. Before describing the specifics of ALM on Windows Azure, a list of the characteristics of the Windows Azure platform is shown as follows:

- Cloud services (application level) allow deploying to two identical but independent environments; the **staging** and the **production** environment. The word "Production" implies that it's a more mature and better environment than "Staging", but this is not the case. The staging slot is very useful as a test bed for Geotopia services before going live in a production slot. Going live is just a click away by swapping the virtual IPs of both the environments. Therefore, we can go live without having to perform a possibly cumbersome deployment directly into production, but rather have it tested in the staging environment first. Use the staging slot only for a smoke test to verify that the crucial parts of Geotopia work. After this verification, execute a VIP swap.

- Guest OS versions (on Windows Azure where Geotopia is deployed) are identical for every instance. The OS version is configurable and every instance will be built with the same image. The result of this approach is that test, acceptance, and production environments are identical. In on-premise situations, this is very hard to realize.

- Windows Azure applications can be developed and run locally on developers' machines by using emulators. The Windows Azure compute and storage emulator enables us to run, test, debug, and fine-tune our Geotopia solution, using Windows Azure Storage Services locally before deploying Geotopia as a hosted service to Windows Azure.

A typical deployment scenario while developing and testing Geotopia is:

- Local development in emulated environments as part of the Windows Azure SDK.
- A mix of local and Windows Azure. Move emulated storage to Windows Azure. Developers can work on the same data sources.
- Set up a different cloud service to do functional testing and user acceptance testing.
- Move everything to staging environment(s) and perform a smoke test
- Swap from staging to production and go live.

To set up a professional and sustainable ALM around Geotopia and Windows Azure, we need to support the following processes and roles:

- Developer
- Automated Tests
- Build
- Deployment
- Acceptance Tests
- Operations

The steps defined as follows show how to go from team development and local testing on the development machines straight up to building, deployment, and finishing in a release drop that provides environments with a running version of Geotopia.

Step 1: Team development

The team implements the requested features and specifies test cases. Locally, inside compute and storage emulation, developers dry run **CodedUI** tests (customize code to handle different environments) and associate CodedUI tests with a **Microsoft Test Manager (MTM)** test case. Then, we execute the automated test cases from MTM. As soon as possible, move from emulated storage to Windows Azure storage, because of differences in environments, but using the same test-development data. Also, focus on tracing and Windows Azure diagnostics for testing and operation of the Geotopia application.

Step 2: Build, Unit test, Deploy, UItest flow, and manual test

During a "formal" build (not daily or continuous), for example, a sprint review build, we deploy the application automatically to the staging slot. This can be achieved by using PowerShell commands or using build tasks. First, compile the unit test and create the deployment packages and configuration files for different environments (test, production). After deployment, automated platform/staging tests are run. These are CodedUI tests that verify the installation and stability on the Windows Azure environment. During the build, build verification tests are executed, and after deployment, environment verification tests are run. If these are all successful, we can use VIP swap to swap the staging and production slots for additional manual testing.

Step 3: Release drop

The package created during the build is reused in different Windows Azure subscriptions (testers and developers don't have the security keys for this environment).

The following image depicts a scenario where multiple subscriptions are used for the complete lifecycle of Geotopia:

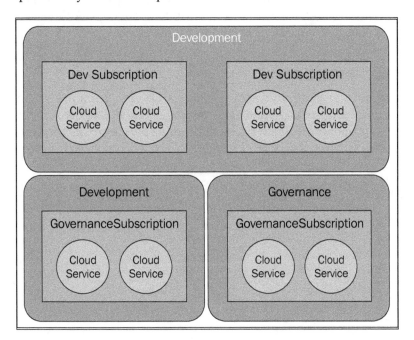

At Geotopia, we decided to separate environments and make every department responsible for their own bills. The development department has two subscriptions, one for development purposes and one for testing purposes. The operations department is responsible for the production environment of Geotopia and strictly monitors this subscription and the cloud services and other Windows Azure assets running on it. For marketing, prototyping, and demoing purposes, Geotopia decided to set up a governance environment, which is completely disconnected and has no role in the development-test-acceptance-production process.

Because the different environments are separated, it is possible to separate the management of the environments as well. Developers can play around and create sandboxes, being part of the development subscription. Testers control their own environments since they do not want developers to be able to make last minute changes. The operations team only has a single subscription in which Geotopia runs and services many users all around the world.

Configuration files differ, especially storage connection strings. Usually only operators have access to the storage keys for the production environment, which makes it impossible for others to use production storage during testing activities by accident. Customers execute their acceptance tests against the staging environment of the production subscription. By using Microsoft Test Manager (MTM), we can execute manual tests, automated tests, and fuzz tests while still being connected with the TFS repository. This still gives the possibility of providing rich bug reports to our team. When acceptance testing is done and approved, Geotopia is manually swapped from staging to production, and Geotopia is live.

Step 4: Operations

The goal of application monitoring is to answer a simple question—is Geotopia running efficiently within its defined SLA parameters and without errors? If the answer is no, our operations team needs to be made aware of this condition as soon as possible.

Summary

In this chapter, we learned that Application Lifecycle Management is all about governance, development, and operations. We learned what tooling is available and how Team Foundation Server can help us set up an ALM environment and how to define and run Builds. We described what roles are involved in realizing Geotopia and what the overall process looks like to get from development to a formal release of Geotopia, all in an automated way by using Team Foundation Server.

We also saw an example of how to set up and create different Windows Azure subscriptions all with their own purpose of development, testing, and operations.

In the next chapter, we will learn all about the Security Development Lifecycle and how to create awareness on the topic of security and make it an integral part of your ALM, with a special focus on the security topics in the Windows Azure context.

10
Windows Azure Security

"The mantra of any good security engineer is: "Security is a not a product, but a process." It's more than designing strong cryptography into a system; it's designing the entire system such that all security measures, including cryptography, work together."

— Bruce Schneier, Security Guru and Chief Security Technology Officer of BT

This chapter focuses on Microsoft **Security Development Lifecycle (SDL)**, with respect to cloud computing in general and with special attention to Windows Azure. The SDL is a process that can be (or should be) part of your software development process. It creates awareness on the topic *security* throughout the whole project, from requirements up to release. Microsoft created process guidance on the SDL, released whitepapers, and created tooling, so that you can quickly adopt this process into your own development process. This chapter contains:

- Core concepts of SDL
- Security roles involved in projects
- Activities to be performed in the SDL
- The SDL again, but focused on the Windows Azure platform

Security development lifecycle

The security development lifecycle is a security process that can be embedded in any of the development processes that are available nowadays. It helps to create security awareness in your team or department. By formalizing *security* and making it a part of daily activities, a culture is created in which security is an important part of the project just like testing or designing. Microsoft uses SDL to make sure security and privacy are upheld in their software. Analogous to reducing bugs in testing, SDL's main interest is to reduce vulnerabilities in software. What is special about SDL is that it introduces the importance of security and privacy in all phases of your development process.

SDL defines a number of activities and attaches these to the phases of the development process. An important part of SDL is that you should focus on the quality of the output required at the end of each phase. The next sections will dig deeper into the specifics of SDL in the various project phases and what activities should be undertaken to comply with SDL.

Security roles

The SDL also contains criteria and job descriptions of the security roles needed throughout the project(s).

- **Reviewer**: The reviewer oversees the security issues and privacy concerns and needs to have the mandate to accept or reject security plans. They need to be an SME (Subject Matter Expert) and part of the project team, play the role of auditor, and should review each phase of the development process to verify that all activities are done and all output criteria are met.

- **Team Champion**: There should be an SME on the project team, responsible for the addressing of security and privacy issues in the project but also for reporting and meeting with the reviewer mentioned earlier.

Security maturity

As adding something *new* and *formal* to your projects and development process can be a harsh and time-consuming activity, Microsoft created the **SDL Optimization Model** to overcome this. The model focuses on five capabilities and groups of activities that are similar to phases in a typical development process. To reach a high level of security maturity, it is vital that you enrich your development lifecycle at every stage or phase with the typical security and privacy activities and formalize them (for example, add them to your Team System template). Following the pragmatic approach of SDL and training your people can quickly get your organization and projects from a low level of maturity to a higher one.

Security activities

To be compliant with the SDL, you need to perform at least the 16 mandatory activities. Of course, you are free to add other security or privacy activities. These 16 mandatory activities are:

- Training
- Security
- Quality Gates/Bug Bars
- Security and privacy risk assessment
- Design requirements
- Attack surface reduction
- Threat modeling
- Use approved tools
- Deprecate unsafe functions
- Static analysis
- Dynamic program analysis
- Fuzz testing
- Threat model and attack surface review
- Incident response plan
- Final security review
- Release/Archive

These activities will be explained later in the chapter.

Training

Team members of the projects that need to comply with SD need to be trained and should at least have applicable knowledge of the following subjects. The following table shows what areas and subjects should be covered by the training:

Area	Subjects
Security design	Attack surface reduction (reduce entry points)
	Defense in depth (multiple threat mitigations)
	Principle of least privilege (run with the fewest possible permissions)

Area	Subjects
Threat modeling	Overview, design implications of a threat model, and coding constraints
Secure coding	Cross-site scripting, SQL injection, cryptography, buffer overruns, integer arithmetic errors, and other common security pitfalls
Security testing	Testing methods and assessments
Privacy	Best practices on privacy design, assessment, privacy testing, development, and design

Requirements

After having your personnel trained on security and privacy areas, you should be able to follow the practices Microsoft describes in SDL. There are four SDL practices that need to be executed in the requirements or design phase.

- **Security requirements**: It is very important that requirements be defined as early as possible, so that the involved security people can identify and integrate security and privacy early in the project. At this point, minimum security and privacy requirements can be described for the application or applications that need to run in some operational environment. This is also the right moment to use work item tracking in Visual Studio Team System to keep track of security and privacy issues.

- **Specify bug tracking tool**: This step involves selecting and implementing a tracking system that enables us to enter, administer, filter and track security bugs or breaches. A good candidate would be Visual Studio Team System.

- **Quality gates**: Define the minimum acceptable levels of security and privacy quality, so that the development team can identity and fix security bugs and privacy issues. For example, all compiler warnings need to be triaged and fixed, or explicitly suppressed, before the code can be checked in into Team System source control. Setting these quality gates (a formal gate that every piece of code needs to go through) is part of the project but the gates need to be approved by the security reviewer or advisor. A bug bar is also a quality gate and provides an indication about the minimum security vulnerabilities that need to be fixed prior to release.

- **Security and privacy risk assessment**: These two assessments are mandatory and should identify and describe, on a functional level, what aspects of the code need heavy reviewing. These assessments should include the following:

  - What parts of the project require threat models prior to release?
  - What parts of the project require security design reviews prior to release?

  - ○ What parts of the project require penetration testing?
  - ○ What additional analysis or testing (if any) is proposed by the security advisor?
  - ○ What is the scope of fuzz testing requirements?
  - ○ What is the privacy impact rating?

- **P1**: High privacy risk, for things such as changing settings or installing software
- **P2**: Moderate privacy risk, for things such as clicking a link and going to an external website
- **P3**: Low risk

Design

After the requirements phase and the definition of security requirements, quality gates, and performing the security and privacy risk assessment, the next three activities can be performed during the design phase:

- **Design requirements**: Identifying and mitigating security and privacy issues as early as possible will save time and money. Create security and privacy design specifications (security or privacy features that are directly exposed to users), specification review, and minimal cryptographic design requirements.

- **Attack surface reduction**: Reduce the attack surface by giving attackers less opportunity to misuse a vulnerability by applying the principle of least privilege.

- **Threat modeling**: An activity to identity security impact(s) of a design considering the planned operational environment. It is a joint activity for the whole team and the initial security analysis task.

Implementation

After training, requirements, and design, the project moves into the implementation phase, where the actual software is built. The development team decides what best practices to use throughout the project, including tooling:

- **Approved tools**: The project team defines a list of approved tools and their security impact. The list should be checked and mandated by the security advisor. Using the latest versions of the tooling mostly gives the team the best security analysis functionality.

- **Deprecate unsafe functions**: The project team defines a *black list* of SDKs and APIs—specifically on a function, class, or unit level—that are considered to be unsafe. These banned components should be identified prior to checking in code, or at least prior to release, by the use of code analysis tools.

- **Static analysis**: Always perform static analysis of all source code in the project(s). It enables the enforcement of secure coding policies but cannot compete with manual code reviewing. Static code analysis can only cover predefined rules and will not identify rare and complex security issues.

Verification

During verification, the follow three activities need to be performed:

- **Dynamic program analysis**: This is the process of the verification of software during runtime. There is tooling available that can monitor application behavior over time that checks memory leaks, buffer overruns, and other security problems.

- **Fuzz testing**: Fuzz testing is the process of presenting random data to your application and verifying the robustness of your application.

- **Threat model and attack surface review**: After completing the source code, it is a good practice to repeat the threat model and attack surface activities to verify that changes in the design of the implementation did not affect the system on a security or privacy level and that newly introduced attack surfaces have been identified and mitigated.

Release

Prior to the release, there are three last activities that need to be performed to comply with the SDL:

- **Incident Response Plan (IRP)**: An IRP contains an approach on how to respond to new threats that arise after releasing your software. What team is lined up to tackle these new threats and come up with a service pack? What authorized people can be contacted to make crucial decisions? What third-party tooling is used by your software and how is this contract organized?

- **Final Security Review**: A final check of all the security activities performed during the project. The security advisor executes this activity and is assisted by the project team. It is definitely not a re-run of all the activities but merely an examination of threat models and output of tooling and the results of quality gates. This Final Security Review (FSR) can lead to the disapproval of the project and there will be no release!

- **Release and Archive**: After successfully complying with the SDL and having the security advisor certify that security requirements are met and all components with Privacy Impact Rating P1 are satisfied, the software can be released. Part of this last SDL activity is to archive and store all relevant data for servicing the software after release. This includes documentation created in previous steps, such as designs, code, threat models, ERPs, and so on.

SDL in Windows Azure

The following section shows how the SDL can be applied to Windows Azure projects in particular. The approach does not change, but there are some caveats and differences between them.

Requirements

As we know, Microsoft is in charge of the physical hardware infrastructure of Windows Azure, so you don't need to look after this. This will give you time to focus on the application layer in particular and apply common SDL practices in our Windows Azure project(s). Using SDL will make you feel comfortable, because it is a proven approach that is also used during the actual realization of Windows Azure itself. Some common attack surfaces disappeared due to abstractions of infrastructure and operating system. Although designing and building for the cloud might be slightly different it does not change the security and privacy requirements much. You can make use of **Windows Identity Framework** for authentication and authorization. Use **Active Directory Federation Services** to make your identity store (Active Directory) available in the cloud as well. The best practice for security and Windows Azure is that you fully utilize the power that Windows Azure offers on a security perspective. Use strong encryption for high privacy risk data and do not store any keys in Windows Azure storage. The platform offers some basic denial of service preventions and request throttling.

Design

The design phase of SDL in Windows Azure-related projects differs from traditional development processes. The Windows Azure framework is new, different, and offers possibilities—but it can also introduce some caveats. Trust levels of roles are new, and the best way to deal with this is to use the least privileges wherever possible.

The Windows Azure Storage Services, including blobs, tables, and queues, differ from traditional environments and create some new attack surfaces. You can handle these by introducing gatekeeper patterns (as demonstrated in *Chapter 8, Windows Azure Patterns*) and add additional borders to your roles.

You need to pay attention to general concepts, such as auditing, authentication, authorization, cryptography, sensitive data, and more, on how these map to the cloud world. You need to decide what storage concepts to use and how these can affect your attack surfaces.

Implementation

In the implementation phase of the SDL for your Windows Azure project, there are a few things that differ from traditional projects. As in the SDL process described in the previous section, there is the process of using proper tools, deprecating unsafe functions and libraries, and performing static code analysis.

More specifically, using the /unsafe check in the C# compiler will cause your code not to run in partial trust. Always treat warnings from the compilers as errors, since the compiler is trying to tell you something that might cause problems, including security-related problems. A good example of a possible security breach is the use of the Reflection.Emit namespace, which allows you to create code during runtime and execute it. You can imagine what might happen when a hacker manages to break into your code and adds his own nifty piece of code to your Reflection.Emit logic.

Using static code analysis such as FxCop or Cat.NET is always a good practice, and adding them to your check-in gates would force developers to take care of all issues that are raised by the tools.

Verification

Typical for the verification phase is black box testing, both in the Windows Azure world as in the traditional one. What is important for your Windows Azure projects is that you need to make sure that you test every kind of input your service(s) receives. This can be a file, input forms, HTTP requests, and so on. Every type of input can be malicious and can be a potential security threat. Use fuzzing, and automate your testing to be able to keep that black box testing running over long periods of time.

Release

The release process of Windows Azure applications is typically easier than that of standard ones. No papers to fill out, no dependencies on other administration personnel, and the team itself can deploy the application to Windows Azure. Part of the IRP is rolling back a version of an application. On Windows Azure, this is quite easy, since you can undeploy a hosted service with just one click, and redeploy a *healthy* service also with one click.

An important part in the release phase is to check if the deployment went well and if all components actually were deployed. Are all required permissions set for those who need to administer the application? Are all the certificates properly uploaded? Is there a process that periodically regenerates certificates?

There are two types of certificates that are involved in the security of cloud services:

- **Management Certificate**: These certificates are stored at the highest level of your account, the subscription level. They are used to enable any service management operation from Visual Studio, Powershell CmdLets, or other tooling. These are stored at the subscription level to enable operations on any cloud services or storage account inside the subscription, by only using one certificate.
- **Service Certificate**: These are certificates that are used by cloud services and therefore, stored on the level of cloud services. These types of certificates enable HTTPS endpoints, but the certificates can be used in other ways.

Microsoft Global Foundation Services

So far, you have seen best practices and a standardized approach to embedding the magical word *security* in your development process. This section outlines some of the details on the specific security and organizational measures to uphold a high standard of security on the floor.

Windows Azure runs in datacenters owned by Microsoft. They are managed by Microsoft **Global Foundation Services (GFS)**. The datacenters are scattered around the globe and their number is still growing.

GFS is part of Microsoft and is responsible for Microsoft's cloud offerings from Windows Azure to Bing.com, XBox Live, Office365, and more. The main focus of GFS is reliability, operational excellence, sustainability, and trustworthy computing. GFS delivers all infrastructure services, such as datacenters, content delivery networks, fibre optic networks, and so on, to fully support, on a 24 x 7 x 365 basis, all these online offerings.

Certifications

The datacenters comply with several industry standards, but it is up to the customer to verify whether their services run with the right compliance and do not conflict with laws or regulations. The following list describes the existing standards Windows Azure complies with:

- **ISO 27001**: At the end of 2011, Windows Azure gained the ISO 27001 certifications for the core features of the platform. The British Standards Institution (BSI) conducted a successful audit on the components of cloud services (worker and web roles), storage (tables, blobs, and queues), networking (traffic manager, connect, and virtual network), and virtual machines (the persistent IaaS feature). Also the supporting features such as the Windows Azure management portal and the service management API were part of the audit as well as the complete management and monitoring lifecycle on all the services.

  This ISO security standard emphasizes that Microsoft complies with the strict rules of this standard and confirms the dedication of Microsoft to deliver internationally recognized, *secure* services and platforms. You can find detailed reports on the Internet. Please go to `https://www.windowsazure.com/en-us/support/trust-center/` for detailed information on the subject.

- **SSAE 16/ISAE 3402**: The audit to get certified with this high level of security standards was conducted to comply with the International Standard on Assurance Engagements and involves standards defined by the International Federation of Accounts. The audit was performed in 2012 and covers cloud services (worker and web roles), storage services (tables, blobs, and queues), and networking (traffic manager and Windows Azure Connect).

- **HIPAA BAA**: HIPAA is a US law that applies to the healthcare domain and specifically to those parts inside the healthcare domain that access personally-identifiable patient information. A healthcare company or ISV delivering to healthcare companies will only use cloud services that comply with this standard. Also on this topic, there is much more detailed information available for those who are concerned with and responsible for security inside the enterprise domain.

- Cloud services (web and worker roles), storage service (tables, blobs, and queues), persistent virtual machines, and networking (traffic manager, Windows Azure Connect, and virtual network) are all compliant with HIPAA.

Privacy

Similar to *security*, privacy is also a standard part of the product and development lifecycle of Microsoft. In 2002, Bill Gates sent an e-mail to all Microsoft staff to emphasize that from then on trustworthy computing and offering true security and privacy had to be part of the genes of the company. The Windows Azure Privacy Statement contains the privacy policy and some best practices on how to deal with *privacy*.

Microsoft defined some policies on how customer data is accessed and where it is located. Customer data is all data that is provided to Microsoft by a customer through the use of the Windows Azure platform. This customer data can contain images, packages, media files, and so on. The following list contains information on how and where it is stored:

- Clients specify the datacenter where the customer data is stored.

- Microsoft can transfer customer data inside a region, such as within Europe, for redundancy reasons. The geo-replication feature replicates data from the storage service between datacenters in a region (for example, Dublin and Amsterdam), although this feature is optional.

- Customer data will not be transferred outside the region except in the following scenarios:

  ° When CDN is enabled on a storage account

  ° For troubleshooting purposes

  ° During deployments of web and worker roles, backup copies of the package might be stored in the US.

Platform security

Windows Azure consists of both hardware and software and is managed by staff inside the datacenters. This section describes some measures that were taken to reduce comprised hardware, software, or data.

The platform is designed to offer defence in depth, which means that the failure of one of the security mechanisms on the platform may not result in the compromising of the security of the complete datacenter (or parts of it). This is achieved by using filtering routers

The filtering routers block attempts to communicate with addresses and ports that are not configured to do so. We can also implement defence in depth, ourselves by using inter-role communication. Setting up inter-role communication only allows instances of these roles to communicate with each other, having the platform block other attempts of communication.

Since being on the cloud means that the management and operation burden is automatically reduced and that patch management with respect to security patches is an activity that is performed by the platform itself, although the user is still in control of this automatic patching process. All the devices inside the datacenter are monitored constantly.

Only a few people are granted access to the datacenter, and they need to change passwords very often. In the Windows Azure platform Privacy Statement, you can find a paragraph telling you that a limited number of staff may access customer data. A complete audit trail of all the administrative actions inside the datacenter is kept and can be viewed.

Adding more security

As you know, building for the cloud allows you to focus on the application level. This is also applicable for *security*. The hardware infrastructure is not yours; you cannot set up firewalls, proxies, or other hardware security peripherals, so there is no way to configure hardware security (or personnel).

Microsoft already takes care of some security threats that target network infrastructure. The following table shows what typical threats to network infrastructure exist and what can be done to mitigate those risks.

Threat	Mitigation
Port scanning	Only ports that are explicitly defined by developers in the definition file of a service are open and reachable from outside.
Denial of Service (DoS)	The load balancers of Windows Azure discover DoS attacks that are initiated from inside a datacenter or the Internet and will partially mitigate them. Windows Azure virtual machines are accessible by using a Virtual IP, and this means that traffic is always routed through the load balancer of the platform. Windows Azure detects DoS attacks from inside the datacenter and removes the virtual machines and accounts involved in the attack.

Threat	Mitigation
Spoofing	Broadcasting and multicasting traffic is blocked, and by the use of VLANs it is impossible to pretend to be the fabric controller; for example, traffic between the FC and root OS inside Windows Azure is encrypted and HTTPS is used.
Packet sniffing	Breaking into a VM and then finding a way into the hypervisor would only allow attackers to see inbound traffic to the VMs that are controlled by the designated hypervisor.

The following table highlights best practices from the whitepaper from Microsoft:

Best practice	Explanation
Cross-site scripting mitigation	Use the Microsoft Anti-Cross-Site-Scripting library.
Usage of custom domain name	Avoid using the default `*.cloudapp.net` domain name, since users might not want to trust that top level domain. It is also not possible to get an SSL certificate for the `toplevelcloudapp.net` domain.
Data protection	Use Shared Access Signatures (SAS) with the lowest privileges possible and with the shortest lifetime. Always use HTTPS, and keep in mind that Shared Access Signatures are only for temporary access to storage, so regenerate them frequently if necessary.
SQL Injection	SQL injection is still a threat, even if you use Windows Azure SQL Database, so you still need to take actions to prevent injection. Use URL encoding to avoid injection attacks on your storage resources.
Fuzz test	Make sure you do throttling at the application level and that every input is validated. You can use free fuzzing parsers that are made available by Microsoft on the SDL portal.
Use Partial Trust	Secure your services as much as possible by using Partial Trust, which prevents most access to the local filesystem, registry settings, sockets, and web connections.
Use the Gatekeeper design pattern	See *Chapter 8, Windows Azure Patterns.*
Multiple storage keys	If the Gatekeeper patterns cannot be used (if you use PHP, for example, which needs to run in Full Trust), you can use multiple storage keys to restrict access.

Summary

In this chapter, you saw how the Security Development Lifecycle is applicable for Windows Azure projects. It describes what activities need to be deployed and what additional efforts need to be put in your project to ensure you think of all possible security and privacy breaches. It describes typical activities in all the phases of projects — requirements, design, implementation, verification, and release. Also privacy regulations and industry standards that Microsoft complies with were described along with some measures that were taken to mitigate risks in general. Finally, it also showed some typical security features around SQL Database.

Besides the SDL story, the chapter also showed you some general best practices on security topics in the Windows Azure world. This chapter does not tell you anything new but merely points out some slight but important differences from traditional development.

The next chapter provides an overview of the new features released on June 7, 2012. Microsoft released some previews of new services and upgraded existing features.

11
What's New in Windows Azure

This chapter contains a brief overview of new features released on June 7, 2012. Microsoft released some previews of new services offered by Windows Azure and upgraded existing features. Scott Guthrie hosted the *Meet Windows Azure* session, in which he announced these new and updated services. This release contains some major services but also presents the renaming of current services and features.

Overview

On June 7, Microsoft announced a new set of features and lifted the platform to a new level of maturity. The following list shows a high-level description of the new features:

- **Windows Azure virtual machines**: Windows Azure now offers a long-desired true infrastructure as a service capability by providing persistent virtual machines for Windows and Linux applications in the cloud. This is not comparable with the VM roles offered earlier, because these were non-persistent and part of the platform as a service offering.

- **Windows Azure virtual network**: This feature allows the provisioning and management of virtual private networks on the platform. It enables the linking of role instances with on-premises applications and peripherals. The virtual network allows administrators to extend on-premises topology with cloud components and to configure IP addresses, routing tables, and different security policies.

- **Windows Azure websites**: This feature enables developers to build and deploy websites more easily and supports different frameworks, including ASP.NET, PHP, and Node.js. It offers 10 free websites when signing up and allows easy scaling of these websites. Open source software such as Umbraco, Drupal, Joomla, WordPress, and DotNetNuke are supported, and SQL Database and MySQL are included in the offering.

- **Windows Azure management portal**: Microsoft introduced a new management portal (the old one is still there) that is not a Silverlight client anymore, allowing a user to access it from more platforms and devices than before. It is fully written in HTML5, but keep in mind that not all services can be accessed from the new portal, and switching back to the old portal is still needed to manage (for example) caching and service bus. The new portal offers a more integrated experience, including monitoring information and diagnostics data, and offers a simpler way to deploy, configure, monitor, and diagnose your cloud applications.

- **Java and Python support**: Microsoft provides new libraries for Java and Python.

- **Interoperability updates**: Microsoft offers an Eclipse plugin for Java, MongoDB integration, Memcached using non .NET languages, and configuration for hosting Solr/Lucene.

- **Updated application services**: Windows Azure media services is available for preview and helps with building large-scale media solutions.

- **Caching is available in two different flavors**: A managed, multitenant cache and a new preview caching service that delivers caching capability on a web or worker role. It offers compliancy with **Memcached**. This new feature is described in *Chapter 6, Key Features Explained*.

- The storage service is enhanced and it offers a more fine-grained manner of redundancy. Besides the already available geo-redundant storage, Microsoft also offers locally redundant storage at a lower rate.

- **Windows Azure SQL reporting**: SQL reporting is now generally available and provides reporting functionality from the cloud.

- **Improved developer productivity and experience**: Built-in support for continuous deployment with websites was announced. The Windows Azure SDK is enhanced with new command-line tooling that runs on Mac and Linux, as well as on Windows.

In the following sections, we will see a little bit more on virtual machines, virtual networks, the new portal, and Windows Azure media services.

Virtual machines

Virtual machines offer an easy way to create a virtual machine inside Windows Azure that you control and manage yourself—a true IaaS capability. This feature contains Windows Server 2008 R2 and some Linux distributions that you can choose from. It allows us to completely build a **VHD** that is similar to the one running in our own datacenter, giving us the opportunity to fully migrate it to Azure. Load balancing between virtual machines and connecting to web and worker roles is possible.

Creating a virtual machine

A virtual machine can be created on the new Windows Azure portal preview (`http://manage.windowsazure.com`). Select the **VIRTUAL MACHINE** node in the preview portal and click on **Create a Virtual Machine**. This will take you to a wizard that guides you through the process of creating a virtual machine. For the purpose of this chapter, we will look at the **QUICK CREATE** option.

By clicking on the **CREATE VIRTUAL MACHINE** option, we start a provisioning process that will finally result in a running VM with the Windows Server 2008 R2 SP1 operating system. We can manage, control, and administer this VM as if it were running inside our own domain. The Windows virtual machine offering includes the OS license fee. The preview offers a 33 percent-reduced rate compared with the fees for cloud services (web and worker roles). Every single VM hour is converted to a number of small instance hours in the same way as cloud services.

The amount of storage needed for the disk(s) is not included and will result in extra GBs on your storage bill.

Connecting to the VM

After the provisioning process is finished, you can connect to the provisioned VM by clicking on **Connect** in the preview portal. Connecting to a VM will open a remote desktop protocol file that is created during the provisioning process, and requires the same procedure as starting an ordinary RDP file.

Setting up a VHD

Select the VM in the preview portal you want to add a data disk into and click on the **Attach** option. This will bring up a screen that allows you to enter the desired size of the disk (between 1 and 1,023 GB). When we have already created some data disks, we will be able to connect to existing ones as well.

After the creation of the empty disk, we will be able to see the newly created disk in the preview portal. To see it, click on the **Disks** tab in the virtual machine's overview screen. We will see two disks, one containing the OS and the one that we just created. The new disk that was created can be used to get additional disk space available, for the VM to install new programs on it for example.

If we select the virtual machine you just created, the following dashboard screen will appear:

It provides an overview of some diagnostics information, such as CPU utilization, data transfers, and disk throughput. You can also see the disks here and the number of cores used.

On the **Endpoints** tab, you will initially see only one endpoint configured, the one that is needed for a remote desktop session. The **CONFIGURE** tab allows you to create an availability set and to change the virtual machine size. An availability set is comparable to a fault domain. Adding at least two VMs in an availability set will offer an SLA of over 99.95 percent instead of an SLA of 99 percent for a single VM configuration. Announced is the new availability of 99.9 percent for single instances, but this is not available yet at the time of this writing.

Virtual network

Windows Azure virtual network allows us to not only create site-to-site connectivity, but also protected private virtual networks. We can connect your on-premise datacenter to the public Windows Azure cloud. To summarize, we can say that you can extend your infrastructure in a safe and reliable way, where virtual private networks are the glue that sticks these together. Virtual network uses IPsec to secure the connection between your datacenter, through its VPN gateway and Windows Azure. We can control the network topology, configure IP addresses and ranges, and security policies.

Upon creation of a VM, as shown in the previous section, you can immediately add it to configured subnets.

Creating a virtual network

Carry out the following steps to create a virtual network:

1. Open the new Windows Azure portal, select **New**, and click on **Network**. Next, click on **Custom Create**, and the following screen will appear:

2. Fill out an appropriate name and select an affinity group (if you already have one), or else create a new affinity group. Click on **Next** to go to the screen where you can configure IP addresses and subnets:

3. In this example, we have configured the address space and one subnet. The creation of subnets is optional but can give you more detailed control of addresses assigned to cloud services or virtual machines; on this screen, click on **Next**.

4. You will now see the DNS Servers and local network screen. Anything on this screen is optional and you can leave the DNS name resolution to Windows Azure, but you can also specify your own DNS servers or other public servers. The connectivity option allows you to create cross-premises connections, but for the purpose of this demo, we will leave this screen as default. Click on **Next**, and the virtual network will be created and will show up in the networks tab.

Upon creation of new virtual machines, you can create it in the virtual network and subnet space you have just set up.

Management portal

The new preview of the Windows Azure portal is completely built in HTML5 (and no longer Silverlight), making it accessible from multiple platforms and mobile devices. It offers an integrated view of all the Windows Azure resources and an intuitive and compelling user interface that makes managing our cloud assets more easy.

Besides the new look and feel, the preview portal offers monitoring charts and diagnostic information and the ability to scale easily while keeping an eye on the number of cores you use. The deployment and configuration of your cloud services has been simplified.

The preview portal supports all the new features from Azure, such as **CLOUD SERVICES, VIRTUAL MACHINES, WEB SITES, NETWORK, SQL DATABASE,** and **STORAGE**, as shown in the following screenshot:

Selecting the cloud service where the Geotopia prototype is deployed and running offers the following features options in the portal:

- **DASHBOARD**: It offers a quick and comprehensive overview of the whereabouts of the cloud service.

- **MONITOR**: It offers the ability to watch metrics up to seven days from now. Also, new metrics can be added (and current ones can be deleted). Metrics are either aggregated (taking all instances of a role) or per instance.

- **CONFIGURE**: On this tab, you set some monitoring options and, you can also edit and save the configuration settings of the roles in this cloud service.

- **SCALE**: This tab offers a slider per role that enables you to slide the number of instances per role. It also offers insight into the number of cores used per role, total used cores, and available cores (default is a maximum of 20).

- **INSTANCES**: The **INSTANCES** tab provides insight into the number of instances (of each role) that are running in your cloud service. You can also see if the update and upgrade domains are correctly configured.

- **LINKED RESOURCES**: This tab provides an overview of your linked resources and allows you to create some linked resources. This is very useful since you can link a SQL Azure database to your cloud service. If you add an SQL Azure database and go back to the **SCALE** tab, you will see something similar to figure 10.

You can see that the linked resource is also displayed on the **SCALE** tab (Windows Azure storage will follow soon). It is now very easy to scale both roles and the databases that you linked with them.

- **CERTIFICATES**: A plain overview of all the certificates you uploaded for this cloud service

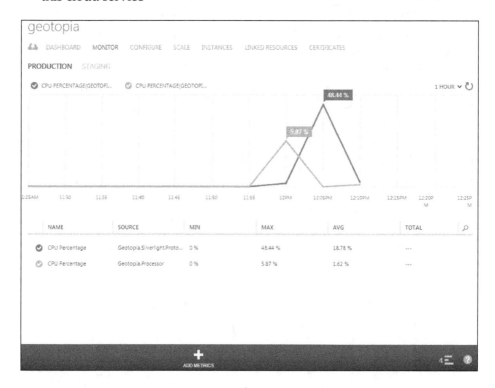

Media services

With Windows Azure media services, you can build workflows for the creation, management, and distribution of media. It offers the built-in flexibility, scalability, and reliability of Windows Azure that we are already used to. You can bring quality media experience for a global audience and build your own YouTube. Features of media services include encoding, conversion, and protection of content and also streaming of media.

Setting it up

Preparing to use media services takes quite a few steps to complete, as follows:

1. Install Windows Azure media services SDK 1.0 from http://go.microsoft. com/fwlink/?LinkID=245171.

2. Start PowerShell and change the directory to the v1.0 folder of Windows Azure media services.

3. Run the `GetMediaServicesEnv.ps1` script, which creates a certificate and downloads a file containing settings. A new browser window appears, where you have to sign in with your Windows Live ID. You need to install Windows Azure SDK 1.6.

4. If you receive the `GetMediaServicesEnv.ps1 cannot be loaded` error, you need to run the `set-executionpolicy remotesigned` command.

5. Download the offered file in a location where you easily find it.

6. Run `SetMediaServices.ps1 –path <location of downloaded file>` and save the displayed management service endpoint, thumbprint, and subscription ID, because you need them for the following steps.

```
PS C:\Program Files (x86)\Microsoft SDKs\Windows Azure Media Services\Services\v1.0> .\SetM
riccardobecker.publishsettings

Certificate imported into CurrentUser\My\riccardobecker-6-26-2012-credentials
Publish settings imported

Management service endpoint: https://management.core.windows.net/
Management certificate thumbprint: 1EDF4F6BC5FD0DBB78E40D7D0C181E531D1C03A6
Subscription Id: dbded203-cb18-4e0c-99e3-de3f1129ffee
PS C:\Program Files (x86)\Microsoft SDKs\Windows Azure Media Services\Services\v1.0>
```

7. Run the following commands in PowerShell:

   ```
   $context = Get-MediaServicesManagementContext
   -managementserviceendpoint <management service endpoint>
   -managementcertthumbprint <YOURTHUMBPRINT > -subscriptionid
   <YOURSUBSCRIPTION>
   ```

8. Next, check if the name you want to give your media services is available. You can do this by running the following and see if the result is `True`:

   ```
   Get-MediaServicesAccountAvailability –managementcontext $context –
   AccountName "<NAMETOVERIFY>"
   ```

9. If your name is available, quickly claim it by running the following script. Verify that the status code returned is `Created`.

   ```
   Add-MediaServicesAccount -ManagementContext $context -AccountName
   "riccardobecker" -StorageAccountName "geotopia" -StorageAccountKey
   <YOURACCOUNTKEY> -Region "North Europe" -BlobStorageEndpoint
   https://geotopia.blob.core.windows.net
   ```

10. Now, it is time to get the media service account key. The value of `$account.accountkey` should contain this key, if everything was successful. This account key, together with your account name (created in step 8), are settings that you need, so store them carefully.

    ```
    $account = Get-Mediaservicesaccountdetails $context –AccountName
    "riccardobecker"
    ```

At this point, our media services account is set up and ready for use!

Using media services

This section shows some code snippets on how to use media services. You can run these snippets in a console application, for example.

First of all, you need to add references to the following assemblies:

```
Microsoft.WindowsAzure.StorageClient.dll
Microsoft.Data.Edm.dll
Microsoft.Data.OData.dll
Microsoft.Data.Services.Client.dll
Microsoft.Data.Services.dll
System.Spatial.dll
Microsoft.WindowsAzure.MediaServices.Client.dll located in the folder
where you installed the SDK.
System.Configuration
```

An example displaying the use of media services

The following diagram depicts a possible scenario that demonstrates how to use media services. The example shows how to upload a media file, how to convert it, how to iterate through all your media assets, and finally, how to download the files again.

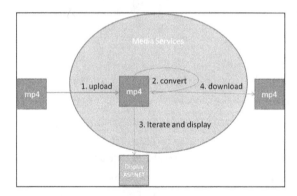

After finishing the preceding *Setting it up* section, we are ready to implement the four steps shown in the preceding diagram. The first step is to offer the ability for users to upload their multimedia files. The second step is to have the uploaded file converted into another format. The third step is to show all the uploaded and converted files on a webpage. The final step is to have users download the converted files.

Uploading

First, you need to add the correct `using` statement, as follows:

```
using Microsoft.WindowsAzure.MediaServices.Client;
```

We are now ready to use media services. The entry to media services is the so-called **context**. You can get a reference to your context by using the account name and account key you generated in the preceding *Setting it up* section.

```
string accountName = "riccardobecker";
string accountKey = "<YOURACCOUNTKEY>";
//get the media context
CloudMediaContext context = new CloudMediaContext(accountName,
accountKey);
```

With `CloudMediaContext`, you can upload some files located on your disk to your context (a context is something logical that encapsulates a storage account and several blob containers in it).

```
var asset = context.Assets.Create(@"D:\Users\Public\Videos\Sample
Videos\Quality Sample.mp4", AssetCreationOptions.None);
```

Converting

After uploading a file, you can decide to convert it to a proper format. In our case, we convert the mp4 file to a streaming format, as follows:

```
// Declare a new job.
IJob job = context.Jobs.Create("Converter");


//convert mp4 to smooth streaming. This is the identifier.
string mediaProcessor = "MP4 to Smooth Streams Task";
//use some Linq to get the proper processor
var theProcessor = from p in context.MediaProcessors
                where p.Name == mediaProcessor
                select p;
// Cast the reference to an IMediaprocessor.
IMediaProcessor processor = theProcessor.First();
// Create a task with the encoding details, using a string preset.
ITask task = job.Tasks.AddNew("My encoding task",
                processor,
                "H.264 256k DSL CBR",
                TaskCreationOptions.None);
```

```
// Specify the input asset to be encoded.
task.InputMediaAssets.Add(asset);
task.OutputMediaAssets.AddNew("Output asset",
                true,
                AssetCreationOptions.None);


// Ok now run the job. You could check the status periodically.
job.Submit();
```

Iterating

To get a list of all your assets inside your context, you need to use the `CloudMediaContext` variable again. Another option would be to iterate through all of the blob containers you have, but that is a pretty awkward job. Besides, Microsoft invented media services to avoid this error-prone job, as the container names are very cryptic and generated by the system.

```
foreach (IAsset asset in context.Assets)
{
// Display the collection of assets.
builder.AppendLine("");
    builder.AppendLine("******ASSET******");
    builder.AppendLine("Asset ID: " + asset.Id);
    builder.AppendLine("Name: " + asset.Name);
    builder.AppendLine("==============");
    builder.AppendLine("******ASSET FILES******");

    // Display the files associated with each asset.
    foreach (IFileInfo fileItem in asset.Files)
    {
      builder.AppendLine("Name: " + fileItem.Name);
      builder.AppendLine("Size: " + fileItem.ContentFileSize);
      builder.AppendLine("==============");
    }
}
```

In the preceding code snippet, we can see it is very easy to iterate through all of the assets located in the proper context. It saves you a lot of work compared to iterating through all of the storage assets yourself, and you get a direct reference of type `IAsset`, which enables you to get all the properties of the designated asset.

Downloading

Downloading files is very easy. Files are part of assets and assets are part of our context. You can use iteration or use LINQ queries to get a hold on your files.

```
foreach (IAsset download in context.Assets)
{
foreach (IFileInfo file in download.Files)
   {
          file.DownloadToFile(@"c:\mediafiles");
   }
}
```

The preceding code snippet iterates through all of your assets and downloads every file that is located in that particular asset.

Summary

This chapter provided a brief overview of the new features of Windows Azure. These features were released by Microsoft in June 2012 and can be regarded as a major release. The Windows Azure management portal is completely rewritten and fully HTML5-compatible, so it can run on any device now. Besides the underlying technology, many features were added to the portal as well.

The release of Windows Azure virtual machines brings infrastructure as a service to Windows Azure, allowing it to compete directly with other IaaS providers, such as Amazon and Rackspace. This new feature enables us to quickly migrate existing, native applications that are part of the cloud or hybrid scenario of our enterprise applications.

Windows Azure media services contains a set of features allowing us not only to expose our media files easily on the Internet (or build another YouTube), but also to convert media assets or even protect them.

The Windows Azure virtual network contains new capabilities with respect to connecting our own datacenter with Windows Azure and manage the single VMs running inside either of the domains in the same way.

Together with these major changes and enhancements, there are also many minor features that you can look up at http://msdn.microsoft.com/en-us/library/windowsazure/gg441573.aspx.

Index

New Hosted Service option 10
New Windows Azure Project screen 44
nslookup command 155

P

PaaS 9
Package button 14
Parallel class 95
partitioning 71
PartitionKey property 71, 74
Platform as a Service. *See* PaaS
platform security 245, 246
PowerShell Cmdlets
  about 191, 213
  list 213
pre-release activity
  Final Security Review 240
  IRP 240
  Release and Archive 241
privacy 245
Production 229
Protected Configuration Provider 191

Q

querying
  about 80
  continuation token 83
  examples 81, 82
queue, operations
  CreateQueue 187
  DeleteMessage 187
  DeleteQueue 187
  GetMessage 187
  GetMessages 187
  GetQueue 187
  GetQueueMetadata 187
  GetQueueServiceProperties 187
  ListQueues 187
  PeekMessage 187
  PeekMessages 187
  PutMessage 187
  SetQueueMetadata 187
  SetQueueServiceProperties 187
  UpdateMessage 187
queues
  about 63, 67, 85

characteristic 67, 85, 86
CloudQueue class, members 91
CloudQueueClient, members 92, 93
creating 86
Idempotency 93
message, inserting 87, 88
message, retrieving 88, 90
operations 90, 91
queues scenario
  cross-domain communication 124, 125
  messages, receiving 124
  messages, sending 123
  overview diagram 122
  project, preparing 122
queues, Service Bus
  about 120
  scenario 121
  working with 120, 121
QUICK CREATE option 251

R

RDBMS 73
Red Dog 7, 8
region 131
relational database management systems.
    See RDBMS
requirements, SDL
  bug tracking tool 238
  quality gates 238
  security and privacy risk assessment 238,
    239
  security requirements 238
right keys, tables
  choosing 73, 74
  for scaling 73
  for transactions 74-76
roles, BizSpark
  Champ 31
  Hosting Partner 31
  Network Partner 31
  Startup 31
RowKey property 77, 87
rules, WASABi
  constraint rules 197-199
  reactive rules 199, 200
Run() method 171

Thank you for buying
Windows Azure Programming Patterns
for Start-ups

About Packt Publishing

Packt, pronounced 'packed', published its first book "Mastering phpMyAdmin for Effective MySQL Management" in April 2004 and subsequently continued to specialize in publishing highly focused books on specific technologies and solutions.

Our books and publications share the experiences of your fellow IT professionals in adapting and customizing today's systems, applications, and frameworks. Our solution based books give you the knowledge and power to customize the software and technologies you're using to get the job done. Packt books are more specific and less general than the IT books you have seen in the past. Our unique business model allows us to bring you more focused information, giving you more of what you need to know, and less of what you don't.

Packt is a modern, yet unique publishing company, which focuses on producing quality, cutting-edge books for communities of developers, administrators, and newbies alike. For more information, please visit our website: www.packtpub.com.

About Packt Enterprise

In 2010, Packt launched two new brands, Packt Enterprise and Packt Open Source, in order to continue its focus on specialization. This book is part of the Packt Enterprise brand, home to books published on enterprise software – software created by major vendors, including (but not limited to) IBM, Microsoft and Oracle, often for use in other corporations. Its titles will offer information relevant to a range of users of this software, including administrators, developers, architects, and end users.

Writing for Packt

We welcome all inquiries from people who are interested in authoring. Book proposals should be sent to author@packtpub.com. If your book idea is still at an early stage and you would like to discuss it first before writing a formal book proposal, contact us; one of our commissioning editors will get in touch with you.

We're not just looking for published authors; if you have strong technical skills but no writing experience, our experienced editors can help you develop a writing career, or simply get some additional reward for your expertise.

Microsoft Windows Azure Development Cookbook

ISBN: 978-1-849682-22-0   Paperback: 392 pages

Over 80 advanced recipes for developing scalable services with the Windows Azure platform

Microsoft Windows Azure Development Cookbook

Neil Mackenzie

1. Packed with practical, hands-on cookbook recipes for building advanced, scalable cloud-based services on the Windows Azure platform explained in detail to maximize your learning

2. Extensive code samples showing how to use advanced features of Windows Azure blobs, tables and queues.

3. Understand remote management of Azure services using the Windows Azure Service Management REST API

Microsoft Azure: Enterprise Application Development

ISBN: 978-1-849680-98-1   Paperback: 248 pages

Straight talking advice on how to design and build enterprise applications for the cloud

Microsoft Azure: Enterprise Application Development

Richard J. Dudley   Nathan A. Duchene

1. Build scalable enterprise applications using Microsoft Azure

2. The perfect fast-paced case study for developers and architects wanting to enhance core business processes

3. Packed with examples to illustrate concepts

4. Written in the context of building an online portal for the case-study application

Please check **www.PacktPub.com** for information on our titles

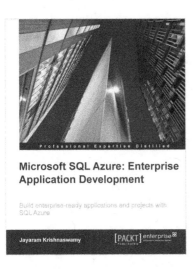

Microsoft SQL Azure: Enterprise Application Development

Build enterprise-ready applications and projects with SQL Azure

Jayaram Krishnaswamy

Microsoft SQL Azure Enterprise Application Development

ISBN: 978-1-849680-80-6   Paperback: 420 pages

Build enterprise-ready applications and projects with SQL Azure

1. Develop large scale enterprise applications using Microsoft SQL Azure

2. Understand how to use the various third party programs such as DB Artisan, RedGate, ToadSoft etc developed for SQL Azure

3. Master the exhaustive Data migration and Data Synchronization aspects of SQL Azure..

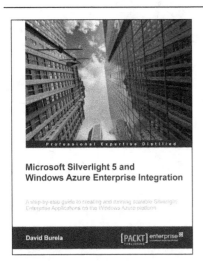

Microsoft Silverlight 5 and Windows Azure Enterprise Integration

A step-by-step guide to creating and running scalable Silverlight Enterprise Applications on the Windows Azure platform

David Burela

Microsoft Silverlight 5 and Windows Azure Enterprise Integration

ISBN: 978-1-849683-12-8   Paperback: 304 pages

A step-by-step guide to creating and running scalable Silverlight Enterprise Applications on the Windows Azure platform

1. This book and e-book details how enterprise Silverlight applications can be written to take advantage of the key features of Windows Azure to create scalable applications

2. Provides an overview of the Windows Azure platform and how the different technologies can be integrated within your enterprise application

3. Examines ways that distributed asynchronous systems can be created to allow scalable processing

Please check **www.PacktPub.com** for information on our titles

www.ingramcontent.com/pod-product-compliance
Lightning Source LLC
LaVergne TN
LVHW062309060326
832902LV00013B/2117